THE GLOBAL SPREAD
OF ISLAMISM AND
THE CONSEQUENCES
FOR TERRORISM

THE GLOBAL SPREAD
OF ISLAMISM AND
THE CONSEQUENCES
FOR TERRORISM

Michael Freeman

with Katherine Ellena and Amina Kator-Mubarez

Potomac Books | An imprint of the University of Nebraska Press

Library of Congress Cataloging-in-Publication Data
Names: Freeman, Michael, 1973– author. | Ellena,
Katherine, author. | Kator-Mubarez, Amina, author.
Title: The global spread of Islamism and the consequences
for terrorism / Michael Freeman; with Katherine Ellena,
Amina Kator-Mubarez.
Description: Lincoln: Potomac Books, an imprint of the
University of Nebraska Press, 2021. | Includes bibliograph-
ical references and index. |
Identifiers: LCCN 2020021093
ISBN 9781640123700 (hardback)
ISBN 9781640124141 (epub)
ISBN 9781640124158 (mobi)
ISBN 9781640124165 (pdf)
Subjects: LCSH: Islamic fundamentalism. | Terrorism—
Religious aspects—Islam. | Middle East—History—1979– |
Islamic countries—History.
Classification: LCC BP166.14.F85 F77 2021 |
DDC 320.55/7—dc23
LC record available at https://lccn.loc.gov/2020021093

Set in Lyon Text by Mikala R. Kolander.

Contents

Figures

THE GLOBAL SPREAD
OF ISLAMISM AND
THE CONSEQUENCES
FOR TERRORISM

CHAPTER 1

The Supply of an Ideology

Terrorism motivated by religious ideology has been on the rise since 1980 and has been called the "fourth wave" of terrorism.[1] Although all major religions have spawned contemporary extremist terrorist groups, the current wave is dominated by Islamic violence and has proven to be "especially dangerous" because of the use of new tactics (suicide terrorism) and its global reach.[2] Generally speaking, previous waves arose from some combination of geopolitical events and local grievances: the anarchist wave was an outgrowth of the Industrial Revolution, democratization, and continued monarchical rule; the anticolonial wave arose from what some perceived to be the too-slow crumbling of European empires after World Wars I and II; and the leftist wave arose from the Cold War and antagonism over U.S. involvement in Vietnam.[3] The fourth (religious, and predominantly Islamist) wave, however, did not seem to arise from any analogous conditions. While there were certainly events that helped catalyze Islamist movements (to be explored later), these events did not seem to create the specific grievances that would lead us to expect the wave of terrorism that followed. In other words, our commonly held notions—of how changes in structural conditions lead to grievances that in turn give rise to terrorism—fail to explain the current Islamist wave of terrorism. Absent a better explanation of this

1

current wave of terrorism, our understanding of it is flawed, as are the policies and actions taken to mitigate and defeat it.

What, then, explains the rise of the current wave of Islamic extremist terrorism, or, more simply, why is it occurring now and not earlier or later? One approach to answering this question would involve examining how the ideologies of the current wave have evolved. For example, al-Qaeda's rise in the 1990s can be attributed to the ideological innovations of Ibn Taymiyyah, Mawdudi, Qutb, bin Laden, and others who transformed notions of jihad from attacking foreign occupiers of Muslim lands to attacking apostate Muslim governments (the "near" enemy) and the external supporters of those apostate governments (the "far" enemy). This ideological evolution approach is useful in describing *how* the ideology evolved but cannot fully explain why particular conceptual innovations gained wider appeal and why other ideologies did not.[4] As Madawi Al-Rasheed argues, "explanations drawing only on theological texts fail to account for the contexts in which this theology is either mobilized [our focus] or suppressed."[5]

Another approach to answering this question would be to examine the causes of terrorism and how potential causal factors, across various levels of analysis, including systemic or "root" causes, might have changed over time.[6] For example, an occupation of foreign territory explains not only *why* resistance would arise but also *when* it would arise (i.e., only after the occupation begins). Western, and primarily American, occupations of Afghanistan and Iraq starting in 2001 and 2003 certainly were significant events in their own right and explain the grievances of various groups in those countries fighting against foreign occupiers (the Taliban and Iraqi secular insurgent groups, as examples). Likewise, Thomas Hegghammer discusses the various conflicts involving Muslims in the 1980s and 1990s (Afghanistan, Bosnia, Chechnya, Lebanon, Palestine, and so on) as drivers of pan-Islamist jihadi movements.[7] These groups are not the subject of the puzzle motivating this book, however, because they are driven by clear grievances that arose in a particular place and time.[8] The focus of this book is instead on the more puzzling examples, such as the places and times where and when grievances did not clearly arise from global or regional events. Ultimately, this "grievances" approach, while useful for many other examples of terrorism, cannot explain the timing issue because the grievances—Western support for Muslim regimes, Western occupation of Islamic lands, the absence of a caliphate, the spread of Western culture, and so on—of al-Qaeda and similar groups *did not drastically* change in the 1980s or 1990s as these groups were forming and growing. The most notable exception to this argument was the Islamist grievance over Western troops in Saudi Arabia before and after the Gulf War in 1991.[9]

What is missing from these approaches is an understanding of what could be called the supply side of ideology. Ideologies are usually driven by demand. As described above, people who have grievances—whether political, economic, social, or religious—seek out (or demand) an ideology that can make sense of their situation. For example, people facing socioeconomic repression might find a Marxist ideology particularly appealing, while people faced with an invasion of their homeland might turn to a nationalist ideology, and so on. According to this approach, the grievances that people face drive the demand for an ideology; the greater the grievance, the greater the demand for the corresponding ideology.[10]

The supply side of ideologies, on the other hand, addresses how ideologies get promulgated and adopted, similar to the discussion of the framing process within social movement theory.[11] Ideologies are not simply present; they must be created (by ideologues and charismatic individuals), and they must be spread so that people with grievances can adopt them. Supplying an ideology is similar to the marketing of a product or proselytizing to gain religious converts. In each case the marketing firm, the missionary, or supplier of the ideology tries to create a demand that otherwise would not exist. In essence the supply side is the outward push of the ideology, while the demand side is the inward pull of the ideology. While much of the scholarly literature focuses on the demand side of ideological extremism by looking at the grievances (globalization, poverty, American imperialism, political repression, etc.) that lead individuals to resort to terrorism, it misses how the supply side of the equation can be, and has been, manipulated.[12]

The argument and cases presented here are explicitly *not generalizable*. To be clear, we acknowledge that most terrorism is demand or grievance driven. There are very few examples of the supply side of terrorism. Modern Islamist terrorism, though, cannot be fully explained without incorporating the supply side. Moreover, misunderstanding the current wave of terrorism as demand driven has led to myriad ineffective policies. Spreading democracy, expanding the economic effects of globalization, or ending occupations of Muslim lands have not, and will not by themselves undermine al-Qaeda or ISIS, because these are not the grievances driving them.[13] Stopping the supply of Islamist ideologies is necessary for this wave and its affiliated groups to be defeated. Stopping the supply is no easy task (we will return to this topic in the conclusion).

Before proceeding, it should be made clear that this book is *not* examining the spread of a *terrorist* ideology per se. Doing so, in terms of Islamic terrorism, would involve tracing the ideological contributions of various individuals (Mawdudi, Ibn Taymiyyah, Qutb, etc.) to what Marc Sageman calls the "global Salafi jihad." Such work has already been excellently done.[14] Instead, this book looks at the broader and more accepted (and not necessarily violent) ideology from which many Islamic terrorists eventually arise.[15]

A few more words about what this book is not are in order. First, although several events in 1979 are integral to the supply story, events in other years (briefly listed below) were also important, and so this book is not arguing that only the events of 1979 were critical. Second, while the supply of Islamism increased dramatically after 1979, this does not mean that its roots do not extend well before 1979; it simply grew much faster after several catalyzing events. Third, as mentioned before, while this book focuses on the supply side of the equation, other issues (like grievances) are always part of the picture for most terrorist movements and waves and even, to some extent, modern Islamist terrorism—they just cannot adequately explain the timing of the current wave. Fourth, this book does not address the roots and spread of Shia extremism.[16] Iranian motivations for exporting the country's ideology, the locations where this has occurred, and the consequences for violence would all follow a different pattern than that presented here.

The ideology considered here is often labeled Islamism but has numerous ideologically overlapping variants in Salafism, Wahhabism, and other strands of political Islam.[17] Regardless of what we call it, and despite differences between the versions, Islamism or political Islam can be defined as "a form of instrumentalization of Islam by individuals, groups and organizations that pursue political objectives. It provides political responses to today's societal challenges by imagining a future, the foundations for which rest on re-appropriated, reinvented concepts borrowed from the Islamic tradition."[18] Jeffrey Bale similarly but more negatively identifies "four essential beliefs that are characteristic" of these Islamist ideologies: "an outright rejection of Western secular values; an intransigent resistance to any and all forms of 'infidel' political, economic, social, and cultural influence over the Muslim world; a pronounced hostility towards less committed and militant Muslims . . . and an insistence on the establishment of an Islamic order or Islamic state governed by a rigid, puritanical application of shari'a."[19] In its most virulent form, the "hostility towards less committed" Muslims leads to violence when it is justified by the concepts of *takfir* (labeling a Muslim as an infidel). This is justification for that Muslim to be killed. At times a *kafir* (the person labeled an infidel) is considered even worse than an actual non-Muslim, and the punishment given is thus far more violent.[20]

For the purposes of this book, the focus is on the various forms of what Thomas Hegghammer calls nonviolent Islamism.[21] Most followers of political Islam are not violent and do not seek to wage physical jihad. However, a small but consequential minority of Islamists have engaged in jihad to achieve their goals.[22] To be clear, though, we should not simply equate Islamism, Salafism, or Wahhabism with terrorist ideologies. Yet, for those who *do* become jihadi terrorists, conversion and adherence to a Salafist or Wahhabi version of Islam is the norm and could at least be considered a generally necessary but not a sufficient condition.[23]

The spread of Islamist ideology has been an important aspect in the rise of Islamic terrorism because it has increased the pool of individuals who could be further radicalized to embrace the use of violence.[24] As revealed after a spate of attacks in Sri Lanka in 2019, influence from Saudi Arabia had gradually grown since the 1980s, with Wahhabis and Salafis taking over mosques and changing how people dressed and behaved. For some "it was a small step from conservatism to the hate-filled ideology of the Islamic State."[25] Similar to many of the other cases and examples described below, Saudi-sponsored Islamism came from the outside in, in the form of "Saudi money for mosques and madrasas, work-abroad contracts and university scholarships," and it displaced a more moderate, tolerant, and inclusive form of Islam.[26]

Understanding this supply side of ideologies is particularly useful in answering the "why now" question of the recent rise of Islamic extremist violence. Put simply, the supply of the ideology from the outside in was a necessary condition for the timing of the current wave of violence. To demonstrate the importance of the supply of Islamism, we first describe in chapter 2 several key events in 1979—the Iranian Revolution, the attack on the Grand Mosque of Mecca, and the Soviet invasion of Afghanistan—that catalyzed Saudi Arabia, the Arab states of the Persian Gulf, Iran, and various nonstate actors to increase their funding and support for various strains of Islamist ideology.[27] Second, the chapters that follow will explain how Islamist institutions (mosques, schools, etc.) were founded, built, and supported by money coming out of the Middle East and elsewhere. The focus of these chapters will be on four cases: Indonesia, Pakistan, the United Kingdom, and the United States. These cases were chosen because they represent multiple regions in the world, each with its own particular dynamics. For instance, Indonesia is the country with the largest Muslim population, but the version of Islam that its citizens practice has historically been moderate. For Pakistan, with the second largest Muslim population in a country, Islam has been more central to its identity and consequently more politically and religiously contested. In contrast, the United States and the United Kingdom have minority Muslim populations, but each has faced different threats from homegrown Islamist terrorists. Additionally, these cases were chosen because of a combination of impact (e.g., Pakistan), data sources, and relevance to Western readers (e.g., the United States and United Kingdom). These four places do not represent every case of this phenomenon; the spread of Islamism is, to varying degrees, a global phenomenon and so similar dynamics are occurring elsewhere. As the Saudis themselves claimed in 2002, they have built mosques, schools, and centers in the United States, Canada, Belgium, Switzerland, Spain, Scotland, Italy, Australia, Croatia, and more.[28] Examples abound, and many of these will be discussed in the conclusion.

Also, we intentionally focus on the spread of Islamism to the geographic periphery of Islam. That should not imply that the supply of Islamism at the core of Islam is not happening or does not matter. We focus on the periphery for three reasons. First, Islamism at the inner core (i.e., Saudi Arabia) is in some ways too easy of a case because of the inextricable connection between the state itself and the religious promulgation of Wahhabism.[29] Second, the supply of Islamism into other Persian Gulf and Middle Eastern states is much more intricately tied up with regional politics and alliances and is often just a piece of the struggle between secular, authoritarian governments and the often suppressed religious opposition movements.[30] Finally, the cases studied here represent some places where Muslims are not the majority (United States and United Kingdom), places that are not Arab (all four), and places where local practices of Islam have different cultural traditions than the Islamist version that arose (Pakistan and Indonesia). For all these reasons, the cases explored here can be thought of as examples of "hard" cases.[31]

Put simply, we connect the dots between several key events of 1979, how these events created incentives for different actors to spread the supply of Islamism, the institutions that they created in various countries, and the terrorists coming out of these institutions. To make these arguments, we synthesize otherwise disparate bodies of knowledge— including the theological foundations of Islamism, the histories of the events of the 1970s, accounts of how the ideology of political Islam has been spread in recent years, as well as scholarly theories on the causes of terrorism—into an argument that explains why Islamism is on the rise and the possible ways in which it can be countered.[32] Each individual piece of this line of connected dots is not by itself new. Taken together, though, they paint an important picture that is not well understood.[33]

CHAPTER 2

Exporting Islamism

Why has the popularity of Islamism been growing for several decades?[1] This chapter will describe how several key events in Iran, Saudi Arabia, and Afghanistan led to a heightened desire by many states, as well as private individuals and organizations, to increase their support for the ideology of political Islam.

EVENTS

The Iranian Revolution: On February 1, 1979, the Ayatollah Khomeini returned to Iran from exile and proclaimed the new Islamic Republic of Iran.[2] This event followed several years of revolutionary churning, during which opposition to the shah and his corrupt and pro-Western policies had grown.[3] Khomeini's regime was avowedly Islamic, and specifically Shia, putting it in opposition to Saudi Arabia and other Sunni states.[4]

The consequences of the Iranian Revolution would be far-reaching. First, it created the concrete reality of an Islamic state, which would prove to be an inspiration to many would-be Islamic extremists around the world, including those in Indonesia.[5] Glenn Robinson refers to the "demonstration effect of Islamist power" as "the Iranian revolution reverberated throughout the Muslim world." The Iranian Revolution,

Noorhaidi Hasan says, "thoroughly transformed the collective Muslim imagination regarding what was politically possible." As David Lesch points out, "the Islamists who survived the secular Arab nationalist era of the 1950s, 1960s, and 1970s could now point with pride to a successful example of religious revolution and Islamic rule in the modern era." This, per Hasan, would further inspire other Islamic extremist movements to believe that their call for stricter Islamic governments in their own country was a truly viable potentiality. Gilles Kepel notes that "after 1979 [i.e., after the Iranian Revolution] there was nobody within the Muslim world or outside it who was unaware of militant Islam."[6]

Second, beyond its inspirational function, the Iranian Revolution also provided a blueprint for how an Islamic state could be created.[7] For example, Mursalin Dahlan, an Indonesian Darul Islam leader, developed a seven-stage plan—modeled directly after the Iranian Revolution—to overthrow the Suharto regime. It included the following stages: "permanent complications" would be created; the nation's leader would be replaced; opposition leaders would appear; the masses would support the opposition; the security forces would be purged; the opposition would take power; and an Islamic state would be proclaimed.[8]

Third, Iran began to set up its own network of Shia-based educational institutions, much as Saudi Arabia did with their Wahhabi education network.[9] In part, this is one of many reasons why Saudi Arabia began to more aggressively promote its own Wahhabi ideology as a counter to the new power of Shia Islam within the region and beyond. The Saudi-Iranian narrative of competition has continued ever since.[10]

The Siege of Mecca: On November 20, 1979, approximately two hundred Saudi citizens stormed the Grand Mosque in Mecca and took control of it.[11] They were led by Juhayman al Utaybi, who claimed that his fellow conspirator, Mohammed Abdullah al Qahtani, was the Mahdi (messianic savior/redeemer). They declared that the Saudi government had "betrayed the faith" and demanded that the country adopt a stricter and purer version of Islam and follow the leadership of the proclaimed

Mahdi. They were Wahhabis who opposed the regime's efforts of modernization and liberalization during the 1970s. By attacking the holiest site in Islam, a place for which the Saudi government, as "Guardian of the Two Holy Places," was responsible, the attackers were challenging the very legitimacy of the Saudi regime.[12] "Saud's authority to govern the kingdom rested on the family's Islamic credentials," Yaroslav Trofimov notes. "With these credentials so dramatically and unexpectedly challenged by Juhayman, the royal family desperately needed its Islamic legitimacy reaffirmed."[13] Although the Saudi regime was vulnerable to these charges, it did not immediately respond. The regime went to the Wahhabi religious leadership and asked for a ruling. After four days the *ulama* (religious leaders) issued a *fatwa* (ruling) allowing the Saudi regime to kill the attackers if they would not surrender, although the ruling did not weigh in on the legitimacy of the attackers' demands. Saudi security forces then stormed the Grand Mosque with ten thousand soldiers as well as thousands of Pakistani troops and allegedly some French commandos. They finally retook control on December 3, when Utaybi and the remaining sixty or so followers surrendered. Saudi Arabia executed all of them on January 9, 1980.[14]

This event was profoundly troubling for the Saudi regime. Its legitimacy and authority rested on its Wahhabi credentials, and the attack in Mecca challenged these very foundations of its rule. Kepel writes, "For the Saudi leaders, the balance they had so carefully constructed over the last decade was under serious threat. Their Islamic legitimacy had been spectacularly called into question."[15] As David Lesch argues, the "blood spilt in Islam's holiest site almost shook the monarchy to the ground."[16]

In response to the attack and to the Iranian Revolution, Saudi Arabia wanted to enhance its own internal legitimacy and counter the appeal of Shia Islam. It accomplished this by increasing its funding for Wahhabi educational institutions both within the kingdom and throughout the world.[17] Internally, the Saudis reintensified their Wahhabi practice, because, although the Wahhabis dominated religious life in the kingdom, their ideology was not universally accepted and had to be supplied and taught within Saudi Arabia.[18] As Sulaiman al-Hattlan put it, "Though the government killed the extremists, it then essentially adopted their ideology." The government gave in to the Wahhabis' demands for a stricter following of sharia within Saudi Arabia.[19] According to Trofimov, "The ulema essentially asked al Saud to adopt Juhayman's agenda in exchange for their help in getting rid of Juhayman himself."[20] Externally, the Saudis engaged in a massive campaign to spread their version of Islam.

The Soviet Invasion of Afghanistan: In late December 1979 the Soviet Union sent its military into Afghanistan to support the communist regime that had come to power in 1978.[21] Before 1973 Afghanistan had been ruled by King Muhammad Zahir Shah, who had been in power since 1933. Shah was ousted by a member of the royal family, Muhammad Daoud, who ruled until 1978, when he was removed in a coup by Afghan communists. While Afghanistan itself had little intrinsic strategic value, it had been the locus of superpower rivalries between the British and Russians for centuries because the British wanted to protect access to India and the Russians wanted access to warm-water ports of the Indian Ocean.[22] The Soviet invasion may have been a modern reflection of these geopolitical imperatives, but it was also part of the ideological Cold War battle between communist and capitalist systems. As a result, this event caused shockwaves that drew the attention of everyone, from neighboring countries like Pakistan and Iran, extraregional Islamic sympathizers from the Persian Gulf countries, and even global actors like the United States.[23] In response to the Soviet invasion, local Afghans began an insurgency campaign that would last until 1989, when the Soviets finally withdrew.[24]

The Soviet invasion of 1979 and subsequent resistance had several important consequences. First, it revived the *possibility and potentiality* of external jihad. Jihad is commonly divided into two kinds—the individual, or spiritual, struggle to live a good Muslim life, and the external, military struggle against infidel invaders of Muslim lands. For centuries prior to the Soviet invasion of Afghanistan, only the first (personal) kind of jihad was possible. After 1979, though, fighting the external jihad became a possibility within the Islamic world (although Islamic scholars disagreed on whether it was actually an obligation to fight in Afghanistan or not). The Saudis exploited this opportunity to channel and refocus desires for jihad externally. By the end of the conflict, jihad had been waged successfully to defeat one superpower (the Soviet Union in Afghanistan), and the belief spread in the decades afterward that jihad could bring down another superpower (the United States).[25]

The second consequence of the Soviet invasion of Afghanistan was that it led to the rise of the mujahedeen (local Afghan fighters). To be clear, the rise of the mujahedeen was very much a demand-driven response to events. Still, the type and level of external support play a critical role in the future "supply" of Islamism. After the Soviet invasion, a massive inflow of funding and organizational expertise came from Saudi Arabia, Pakistan, and indirectly (through Inter-services Intelligence of Pakistan) from the United States. Over the course of the 1980s a total of $6 billion was funneled to the mujahedeen, hundreds of training camps were set up in Afghanistan and Pakistan, and thirty-five thousand Arabs heeded the call of jihad and went to Afghanistan to fight the Soviets.[26] The United States alone spent around $3 billion supporting the mujahedeen, with most of those funds going to the Islamic extremist factions. Saudi funds matched those of the United States.[27] As Jessica Stern argues, "By financing and training the mujahideen, the United States helped to create a multinational jihadi organization, which eventually evolved into the biggest threat to U.S. national security."[28] American support for the mujahedeen also derived from the United States' regional goal of containing the ideological appeal of Shia Islam and the Iranian Revolution. Mahmood Mamdani argues that "whereas the United States saw Islamist social movements as a threat, it was eager to reinforce Islamist—Sunni, not Shia—state projects. This American strategy provided a political opening for the intelligence agencies of

Pakistan and Saudi Arabia to promote exaggeratedly anti-Shia Sunni doctrines, chief among them the Wahhabi doctrine from Saudi Arabia and the Deobandi doctrine from Pakistan."[29] Pakistan also supported the mujahedeen for its own political and military reasons.[30]

This external support, which disproportionately funded Islamist groups, altered what would have been local resistance to an occupying force (a demand-driven explanation) into an Islamist fight against infidels that would become the blueprint for later conflicts, thus demonstrating the power of the so-called supply of Islamism. The third consequence of the Soviet invasion, then, is that in addition to the physical support delivered to the mujahedeen (in the form of people and money), Saudi Arabia in particular also supported the spread of their Wahhabi version of Islam by funding and teaching their ideology in the training camps and madrasas in the region. Mamdani argues that the "result was to flood the region not only with all kinds of weapons but also with the most radical Islamist recruits."[31] In terms of financing and building schools to supply the ideology of Islamism, "in 1879, there were twelve Deobandi medressas. By 1967 there were 9,000 across south Asia, including nearly a thousand in Pakistan. . . . Their growth accelerated during the 1980s, and by 1988 nearly 400,000 boys and young men were being educated by Deobandis in Pakistan. The key to the growth was the huge funds that had flowed into the Deobandi medressas from the Gulf when governments and donors there had decided that the Deobandis were the closest local equivalent to the Wahhabis."[32] According to Bilveer Singh, the number of madrasas in Pakistan had risen from 1,000 in 1979 to nearly 10,000 by 1989, and Gordon Means claims that by 2004 there were 20,000.[33] According to the Muslim World League, with Saudi funds Pakistan had opened 150 Islamic centers and 85 Islamic schools in Peshawar alone.[34]

In Afghanistan most of the Wahhabi money went to two of the Afghan mujahedeen leaders, Abdul Rasul Sayyaf and Gulbuddin Hekmatyar. Sayyaf, who was an Arabic-speaking Pashtun Salafi, had little intrinsic support yet built his mujahedeen group largely through his access to Saudi funds, which he utilized to build training bases, warehouses, mosques, and madrasas near Peshawar.[35] This created an international cadre of Sayyaf-trained and Saudi-financed mujahedeen. According to Greg Barton, "Almost all of the Southeast Asian mujahidin, and certainly all of those later affiliated with JI [Jemaah Islamiyah], trained in [Sayyaf camps]."[36] Some of the Saudi money also went to Abdullah Azzam's Maktab Khadamat al-Mujahideen (the organizational precursor to al-Qaeda), which provided a central base through which to funnel and train Arab volunteers. Even after the war ended and official Saudi funding dried up, private citizens and organizations from the Gulf continued to fund several of the more radicalized mujahedeen groups. Saudi and Gulf funds also led *indirectly* to the rise of the Taliban in the mid-1990s. During the Afghan war, Saudi money supported the largest Islamist party in Pakistan, the Jamaat-e-Islami, as well as its rival, Jamaat Ulama Islami (JUI), and gradually "Wahhabi-fied" them.[37] According to one observer, "In the 1980s, radicalized JUI madrasas and other advanced religious academies sprang up near the Afghan-Pakistani border and became training centers for the Taliban."[38]

Other Events: While the events of 1979 in Mecca, Iran, and Afghanistan are important catalysts to the surge in the supply of Islamism, other events in 1979 and earlier also played some role. The following events, among others, are also important.[39]

First, some of the rise of Islamism can be traced back to the 1967 war between Israel and most of its neighbors. This was seen as a disaster for the secular, pan-Arab regimes of the region in both military and ideological terms.[40] Alternative ideologies to pan-Arab nationalism, like political Islam, began to exploit this weakness and gradually become more popular. The events of 1979 and the subsequent supply of extremist ideology, however, took this simmering ideology of discontent and made it much more resonant.[41]

Second, oil shocks in 1973 raised the revenues from oil production and increased the funding available for the spread of extremist ideologies.[42]

Saudi oil revenue went from $1.2 billion in 1970 to $2.7 billion in 1972, to $4.3 billion in 1973, to $22.6 billion in 1974, and to nearly $100 billion by 1980.[43] This financial windfall was a necessary enabler of the supply of Wahhabism. As Bernard Lewis observes, "the teachers and preachers of Wahhabism had at their disposal immense financial resources, which they used to promote and spread their version of Islam."[44]

Third, in 1977, General Mohammed Zia ul-Haq led a coup that deposed the democratic government of Zulfikar Ali Bhutto in Pakistan. Zia undertook measures to Islamicize Pakistan in 1979; one consequence of this was the "mushrooming in the number of madrasas during the 1980s."[45] Zia also actively supported the mujahedeen in Afghanistan.[46] This will be addressed in chapter 4, in the case study of Pakistan.

Fourth, and also in 1979, Israel and Egypt signed a peace treaty. While this brought peace between the two countries, many in the Islamic world viewed Egypt's actions as a betrayal, especially to the Palestinian cause. They then turned on their own governments (e.g., the assassination of Sadat in Egypt) while also turning to more unconventional means (terrorism) to achieve their aims.[47]

SUPPLIERS

The supply of Islamism comes predominantly from Saudi Arabia and the Gulf states.[48] The organizations providing the supply are a combination of official government entities, private organizations, charities, and individuals. The more prominent organizations and charities are worth mentioning here. However, before describing the various institutions, a brief history of Saudi Arabia is necessary to contextualize the connection between the Saudi regime and Islamism.

The ties between the Saudi regime and the Wahhabi clergy go back to the founding of Saudi Arabia, when Ibn Abd al-Wahhab, in trying to reform Islam, challenged the ruling authority of the Ottoman Empire.[49] When pursued by Ottoman forces, he sought refuge in the settlement of Dariyah, which was ruled by Mohammed ibn Sa'ud, a tribal chieftain.[50] In 1747 these two men settled on a power-sharing agreement, with ibn Sa'ud as the political leader and al-Wahhab as the religious leader. Both sides benefited from this arrangement: "ibn Saud would protect ibn Abdul Wahhab and spread his new creed, while ibn Abdul Wahhab would legitimize Saudi rule."[51] As Stephen Schwartz puts it, al-Wahhab could "imagine himself a new Prophet who would replace the Ottoman caliph as the sole theological authority. . . . For Al Sa'ud, meanwhile, the extremism of the Wahhabis provided a means for the legitimation of political power." Al-Sa'ud needed this legitimation because "the family's religious bona fides were somewhat doubtful," especially after they had backed an earlier "false" prophet.[52] This alliance went on to conquer most of the Arabian Peninsula by 1788. In the meantime, their children intermarried, and the current Saudi royal family can all trace their roots back to both the al-Wahhab and al-Sa'ud patriarchs. The Ottomans defeated this first Saudi state in 1818, but in 1924 the Saudis reconquered Mecca and established the current (and third) Saudi state on the Arabian Peninsula.[53]

When the Wahhabis legitimized the Saudi ruling regime, it came at a price: "A Saudi could openly challenge the king's authority when it appeared that he had failed to adhere to Wahhabi principles. No Saudi king could rule successfully without the backing of the *ulama*."[54] This point was reinforced in March 1964, when the ulama challenged King Saud's authority. In October they called for his abdication, and in November 1964 they deposed him, placing his brother Faisal on the throne.[55] Faisal understood where his power base lay, and "under King Faisal, the Saudi government and the Wahhabi elite developed a close symbiotic relationship. When he ascended to the throne, he knew he had to maintain that relationship in order to remain in power."[56] To do so, King Faisal appointed Wahhabi leaders as the heads of several Saudi ministries, including the ministries for pilgrimage, justice, and (most important in the context of this book) education.[57] Wahhabism had always been taught in Saudi schools; after World War II "almost 80 percent of elementary schooling consisted of instruction in Wahhabi doctrine."[58] After Faisal came to power, though, the "Wahhabification" of the education system intensified. The result was "the entire generation that was born during the 1960s and came of age during the 1980s grew up on Wahhabi doctrines.... In 1992, [it was] estimated that 65 percent of the Saudi population wanted the country to be run along more traditional Islamic lines."[59]

The events of 1979 led the Saudi government to embark on a massive campaign to spread the Wahhabi ideology around the globe. While earlier efforts to export Wahhabism were used to counter communist and nationalist ideologies, Saudi efforts after 1979 were designed to bolster Saudi legitimacy at home and abroad, as well as to counter Shia influences.[60] According to Jason Burke, "Funding a massive campaign to increase the penetration of Saudi-style Sunni Islam overseas would, the house of al-Saud hoped, both roll back the Shia tide while simultaneously bolstering their Islamic credentials at home and abroad. The result was the exporting on an industrial scale of Wahhabi, Salafi, neo-traditionalist or 'hard' Islam."[61] Between 1979 and 2003 Saudi Arabia spent more than $70 billion to spread Wahhabism internationally.[62] According to former George W. Bush administration officials David Frum and Richard Perle, "Since the 1970s [up to 2002], the Saudi government has spent many billions of dollars to support Islamic religious colleges in Pakistan and . . . Islamic day schools in the United States; [and] to convert felons in British and American jails to Islam.... By Saudi estimates, their money has built in the non-Muslim world some 210 Islamic centers, more than 1,500 mosques, and almost 2,000 Islamic schools. In these situations, moderate and tolerant interpretations of Islam are excluded in favor of the Saudis' own extreme creed."[63] Kepel points out that the Saudi proselytization efforts, in which they "printed and distributed millions of Korans free of charge," was the first time in 1,400 years that identical Islamic texts could be found across the Muslim world.[64] The results of this Saudi campaign "to aggressively export the Wahhabi creed to the rest of the Muslim world," according to Abou El Fadl, "was that many Islamic movements across the Muslim world became advocates of Wahhabi theology."[65]

Financial support for spreading Wahhabism came not only from the government but also from private citizens and charities.[66] Frum and Perle claim that Saudi charities have helped build around six thousand madrasas in Pakistan alone. The large-scale construction of madrasas, with funding from official and private Saudi and Gulf sources, also occurred in India, Nepal, and Bangladesh.[67] In terms of higher education, Kepel notes that "by the early 1970s, the Islamist intelligentsia taking shape on the campuses of Egypt, Malaysia, and Pakistan began to spread throughout the Muslim world, courtesy of the networks and financial clout of the Saudi Wahhabites following the 1973 war."[68] Also, in Pakistan, for example, Saudi funds built the International Islamic University, where Abdullah Azzam, the ideological mentor of Osama bin Laden, taught between 1980 and 1984. Saudi and Gulf money also went to Sudan: "huge amounts . . . poured into the training of local preachers in conservative Wahhabi-Salafist strands of Islam."[69] Funds from Islamic charities like the International Islamic Relief Organization also flowed into Iraqi Kurdistan in the 1990s to spread Wahhabi Islam. According to Burke, "the mullahs were paid according to how many converts to Wahhabism they made."[70] In Southeast Asia, Saudi and Gulf funds transformed a tolerant, Sufi-style Islam into an extremist, "hard" style of Salafi Islam. In Kuala Lumpur, for instance, Saudi support helped establish in 1983 the International Islamic University, whose "first allegiance was to the Wahhabi sect of Islamism."[71] Saudi and Gulf funds were also disbursed to "non-Muslim" areas of the world, including, for example, to Montreal to help build the Assuna Annabawiyah mosque, which served the Algerian community and was a locus of Islamism. In the United States, Saudis contributed $10 million for mosque construction over just a two-year period in the 1980s. In Europe, the Saudi-affiliated Muslim World League began "financing the building of mosques . . . [which] they hoped would evolve into ideological support for Wahhabism."[72]

Charities from the Gulf states form the backbone of the supply of Islamism. The most influential charity was, and is, the predominantly Saudi-financed Muslim World League (MWL, or Rabitat al-Alam al-Islami, also shortened to Rabita, Rabitat, or Rabitah). Founded in 1962 by a group of Muslim nations, it was the brainchild of Saudi Arabia's Crown Prince Faisal bin Abdul Aziz (later the king, until his assassination in 1975). It aimed to counter the revolutionary fervor generated in Egypt after the coup d'état by Gamal Abdel Nasser, which Saudi Arabia saw as a threat to its own monarchy and others in the region.[73] King Faisal employed many of the exiled members of Egypt's Muslim Brotherhood, an Islamist party banned by Nasser, and one of the Rabitat's founders was the grandson of Hassan al-Banna, the father of the Muslim Brotherhood.[74]

Following the Iranian Revolution in 1979, the Rabitat became a major source of Saudi funding for the global spread of Wahhabism, directly countering Iranian efforts to disseminate Shia ideology. The primary aim of the Rabitat is listed on its website as "the propagation of Islam" (*da'wa* in Arabic, which translates as "call" but essentially means proselytization).[75] Its activities include the propagation of Salafi thought and practice through the construction of mosques, schools, and social facilities, the sponsorship of foreign students studying in Saudi Arabia, "coordination" of Islamic preachers internationally, and the distribution of the Quran and various Salafi media and literature. The historical connection between the Saudi elite and Egyptian Muslim Brotherhood is key, as the close partnership and symbiotic ideologies continue to reverberate internationally, with global proselytization often taking place with Saudi money and Brotherhood materials and literature. The Rabitat receives much of its money from the Saudi government; some also comes from the royal family and wealthy businessmen. Between 1962 and 2003 the Saudi government gave more than $1.33 billion to the Rabitat.[76] In 1999 the *Muslim World League Journal* reported that the league had spent more than six billion Saudi riyals (roughly $1.6 billion) "in its endeavors to extend services to Islam and Muslims" and that "most, if not all" came from the government of Saudi Arabia.[77]

Another important charity based in Saudi Arabia was the al-Haramain Islamic Foundation. Headquartered in Riyadh, al-Haramain focused on building mosques, constructing schools in poor villages, distributing Islamic texts, sending activists abroad to spread Salafism, and supporting mujahedeen in Afghanistan, the Balkans, the Caucasus region, and elsewhere.[78] The United States went on to unilaterally designate all branches of al-Haramain in 2008, including its headquarters in Saudi Arabia, for providing financial support to al-Qaeda. The United Nations Security Council also listed all branches of al-Haramain pursuant to resolutions 1267 and 1989 as being affiliated with al-Qaeda, and it subjected them to sanctions.[79]

The International Islamic Relief Organization (IIRO), also based in Saudi Arabia and an offshoot of the Rabitat, was established ostensibly to provide disaster relief to Muslim nations but has also financed thousands of social welfare programs around the world and has been identified by the UN as having ties to terrorist groups like al-Qaeda, the Abu Sayyaf Group, and others. In 2006 the U.S. Treasury's Office of Foreign Assets Control designated the IIRO's Indonesian branch for providing logistical assistance to terrorist groups Jemaah Islamiyah and al-Qaeda.[80]

The World Assembly of Muslim Youth (WAMY), also funded by the government of Saudi Arabia, focuses primarily on promoting Islamic solidarity among Muslim teenagers and young adults, organizing regular international sports tournaments, youth camps, and educational exchange and scholarship programs that enable students to study a Wahhabi form of Islam, including in Saudi Arabia. The MWL and WAMY often team up with other internationally recognized Muslim movements—particularly the Muslim Brotherhood—that do not necessarily share their Wahhabi theology but have historical ties and an Islamist foundation.[81] As the Pew Forum has observed, "Between the 1970s and 1990s, the European activities of the Muslim Brotherhood, the Muslim World League and the World Assembly of Muslim Youth became so intertwined that it was often difficult to tell them apart. Indeed, a number of senior Muslim Brotherhood figures—including Kemal el-Helbawy, the Egyptian-born, London-based founder of the

Muslim Association of Britain—have served in leadership positions in the League and the Assembly." Both groups continue to exert substantial influence through outreach and publishing networks. Furthermore, "while the two groups are no longer the sole purveyors of Saudi-style Islam to European audiences, they still represent an important infrastructure for propagating conservative religious views from the Middle East throughout Europe."[82]

These are just a few of the biggest religious charities. Many other smaller ones will be discussed in the case studies that follow this chapter.

LOOKING FORWARD

The connections among the events, incentives, and institutions will be demonstrated in the following chapters, which will pick up the thread at the local level for each case. They show how the money and external suppliers bolstered institutions that promoted Islamism within each country.[83] Each case study begins with a brief history of Islamism in that country and how the events of 1979 increased the supply of the ideology. Subsequent sections within each chapter trace the suppliers of Islamism, the organizations they created, and the specific institutions they funded (mosques, madrasas, *pesantren*, media outlets, political groups, etc.). Again, while the focus is on illuminating the global supply of Islamism (Salafist, Wahhabist, etc.) to local institutions, the connections linking these institutions and organizations to individual terrorists will be noted throughout the chapters. As Saeed Shehabi argues, "The rise of extremism in the form of the Wahhabi-Salafi movement in recent years could not have taken place without the huge investments made by the Saudi government. . . . The seeds that were sown then have now borne fruit in the form of the extensive networks of extremist groups spanning the Muslim world."[84]

CHAPTER 3

Islamism in Indonesia

The situation in Indonesia today is like that of a frog that is slowly but
surely being cooked in a pot of water, whose temperature will eventually
rise to a boil. . . . By the time people begin to realize the danger they pose . . .
extremist ideology has become a popular movement too powerful to halt.
—**Abdurrahman Wahid,** *The Illusion of an Islamic State*

As the most populous Muslim nation in the world and the third largest
democracy, Indonesia has become a key battleground in the war of
ideas—a fight for what many have termed the "soul of Islam."[1] Historically, the version of Islam imported to and practiced in Indonesia has
been moderate, inclusive, and tolerant, although homegrown "purist"
movements have always existed to some extent. There was no robust
demand in Indonesia for the type of exclusivist, Wahhabi-style Islam
practiced in the Gulf region; instead, it needed to "be imported and
supported domestically."[2]

Capitalizing on Islam-based resistance to colonialism, foreign occupation, and authoritarianism in Indonesia, Saudi funding helped sponsor a generation of mujahedeen trained in jihad and Wahhabi thought
during the Afghan resistance to the Soviet invasion. In addition, because
of the funding that began coming to Indonesia in the 1980s to supply

the ideology of Islamism, Indonesia has "been experiencing a rise of religious revivalism and fundamentalism" visible in the growing prevalence of men wearing long robes and beards and of women wearing veils.[3] Sharia law has been adopted by increasing numbers of local districts, and violence against other religions and minorities has increased.[4]

The following section will address the questions of why and how Islamism has spread (or been supplied) to Indonesia in what has been termed a process of "Wahhabi colonialism."[5] The sections of this chapter will describe the historical and political context of the supply of Islamism in Indonesia, external financial suppliers of Islamism who supported the ideology in Indonesia, how they supported various Indonesian organizations, how the support created specific Islamist-focused institutions (schools, universities, media outlets, and mosques), and how Islamist groups have infiltrated mainstream organizations and government. The ties to terrorism will be highlighted throughout.

HISTORICAL AND POLITICAL CONTEXT

Islam arrived peacefully in Indonesia through "trade rather than conquest," beginning with Indian merchants in the twelfth century.[6] Arab traders soon followed, as did waves of immigrants from the Middle East.[7] Islam spread over several centuries into a society also influenced by Hinduism, Buddhism, and traces of animism. The resulting "Indonesian Islam"—often called "Islam with a smiling face"—is a more open religion synthesizing elements from these other faiths and the Malay language underpinning them. There have been efforts throughout Indonesia's history, however, to "purify" Indonesian Islam.[8] The Muslim community organization Muhammadiyah was established in 1912 with a largely urban, well-educated membership encompassing a strand of reformist and modernist Islam that embraced modern science and advocated a rational interpretation of the Quran and Hadith. Muhammadiyah sought the purification of Indonesian Islam from the animist beliefs and spiritual practices that it believed hampered the process of modernization necessary to overcome Dutch colonialism.[9] A competing organization,

Nahdlatul Ulama (NU), was established in 1926 with a predominantly rural following and sought to protect traditional spiritual practices from reformists within Muhammadiyah. NU was also formed to resist the growing puritanical zeal emanating from the Persian Gulf region following the Wahhabis' seizure of Mecca from the Hashemites in 1924.[10]

During the period of Japanese occupation in the mid-1940s and as part of the struggle for independence, reformists and traditionalists from these two main organizations united under a political party, Masyumi, which carried the mantle of "Islam-inspired resistance to foreign rule."[11] A homegrown Islamist movement, Darul Islam (DI), also emerged during this time, and it remains "the fountainhead of many of Indonesia's recent radical groups."[12] Unlike Masyumi, DI remained an insurgent movement that recognized sharia as the sole legitimate system of law or moral values. It did not embrace democratic political engagement but sought to establish itself as an alternative to the secular Indonesian state, with DI leader Soekarmadji Maridjan Kartosuwiryo declaring the "Proclamation of the Islamic State of Indonesia" in 1948.[13] In contrast, Masyumi embraced the democratic political process and was the largest political party in Indonesia after independence in 1945. One of Indonesia's earliest prime ministers, Mohammad Natsir, was a leader of Masyumi and had been part of the 1930s fundamentalist Islamic movement Persatuan Islam (often shortened to Persis), which means "Islamic Union" and mixed the revivalist spirit of the Muslim Brotherhood with a puritanical understanding of Islamic theology similar to that of the Saudi Wahhabis.[14] Masyumi sought to enshrine sharia in a new Indonesian constitution after independence, and the proposed "Jakarta Charter" was to have been a preamble to the Indonesian Constitution, giving the application of Islamic law constitutional status. Masyumi was, however, willing to compromise on constitutional language in the interests of national unity, and it supported the secular Indonesian legal system.[15] The Indonesian Constitution subsequently adopted by the future President Sukarno and the Preparatory Committee for Indonesian Independence established an essentially secular state based on religious and moral principles. It set out five principles governing Indonesian society—the Pancasila—summed up by the phrase "unity in diversity," which was inscribed in Indonesia's official coat of arms and considered by moderate Muslims to encompass the essence of sharia.[16]

Following the 1955 general elections, parties in the new Indonesian Parliament clashed over references to sharia in negotiations over a new, definitive constitution. This led to a constitutional crisis that was quelled by President Sukarno's military-backed assumption of power and restoration of the 1945 constitution. Despite Masyumi's early political prominence, the party repeatedly clashed with Sukarno and was subsequently banned permanently from operating in Indonesia after several of its leaders took part in a regional rebellion against Sukarno's dictatorship in 1958. It was only after this ban that some of Masyumi's former leaders and constituency reoriented themselves toward Islamism, and this was a key trigger for the initial spread of Wahhabi ideology in Indonesia.[17] The former leader of Masyumi, Muhammad Natsir, went on to found the Dewan Dakwah Islamiyah Indonesia (DDII, the Indonesia Council for Islamic Propagation) in 1967 with Saudi support, moving away from his modernist roots and prompting a radical shift toward Islamism during the so-called New Order period.[18]

This thirty-two-year New Order period began after an attempted coup by the Indonesian Communist Party against President Sukarno prompted a heavy-handed military response, led by Major General Suharto. That reaction resulted in the death of an estimated half a million Indonesians. This slaughter was largely carried out by anticommunist killing squads from Muslim organizations, guided by the military under Suharto's command.[19] Suharto then assumed power from the politically castrated Sukarno and embarked on a period of authoritarian rule backed by the military. Muslim groups that had supported Suharto during this transition expected to receive more influence following his ascension to power, but Suharto initially relied on the principles of the Pancasila and the secular constitution, backed by the military, to maintain authority over a geographically, linguistically, and ethnically diverse populace.[20] Liberal Islamic discourse thrived during this time, although resentments simmered, including over the New Order policy of transmigration, which saw millions of mainly Javanese Indonesians forcibly moved to less populated outer islands of the archipelago to encourage economic growth, resulting in ethnic tensions and fears of Islamization.[21] As public discontent over corruption and authoritarian rule weakened Suharto's grip on power, he began to cultivate connections with Islamist groups to boost his legitimacy and to avoid international scrutiny of human rights abuses. He also co-opted Islamist extremist groups to suppress civil society opposition. Inflammatory street protests by radical Muslim groups were tolerated whereas they had previously been suppressed. As Martin van Bruinessen has observed, this shift in New Order policies away from Pancasila and toward Islam "provided the necessary conditions for an increasing orientation of large segments of the Muslim ummah towards the Middle East."[22]

The Asian financial crisis marked the demise of the Suharto regime in 1998, and Islamist groups took full advantage of the political turmoil that followed. Local conflicts erupted in many parts of the country and were co-opted by Islamist groups, which turned them into religious and ethnic battles with devastating communal violence. Calls for jihad against Christians in Indonesia were legitimized by fatwas from Salafi leaders in the Middle East. Public opinion swayed in favor of radical Muslim groups, the idea of an Islamic state, and the implementation of sharia.[23] Much of this turmoil was linked to the transition to democracy and the related redistribution of economic and political resources. The split of the Indonesian National Police (INP) away from the Indonesian National Armed Forces (Tentara Nasional Indonesia, TNI) in 1999 and the decentralization of government in 2001 led to political infighting and violence.[24] This provided fertile ground for Islamist groups—with transnational support and funding—to establish influence throughout Indonesian society, building on a steady supply of Islamist ideology that had been spreading in Indonesia since the late 1960s and with renewed vigor since the early 1980s.

SUPPLIERS

The money to spread Islamism into Indonesia mostly came from charities based in Saudi Arabia, Kuwait, and the Gulf states, although direct
financial support also came from the Saudi government.[25] The most
influential charity was and is the predominantly Saudi-financed Muslim World League (Rabitat). In terms of direct influence, the Rabitat
helped distribute thousands of Wahhabi-inspired books and pamphlets,
authored by Mawdudi, Qutb, and other Salafist ideologues, at dis-
counted prices in bookstores or for free in mosques in Indonesia. The
Rabitat also paid for thousands of mujahedeen, including many from
Indonesia, to go to Afghanistan to fight the Soviets, a key catalyst for
the later creation of Indonesia's highest-profile terrorist group, Jemaah
Islamiyah (JI).[26] This sponsorship saw mujahedeen "alumni" return
to Indonesia schooled in Wahhabi ideology, laying the foundation for
a network of Wahhabi proselytizers motivated to spread the Islamist
message at home. To indirectly spread its influence in Indonesia, the
Rabitat funded Dewan Dakwah Islamiyah Indonesia, an organization
dedicated to Salafist principles.[27] DDII became the representative of
the Rabitat in Indonesia, distributing money from the Rabitat to other
organizations in Indonesia, as well as using the money for its own proselytization activities. (The background and activities of DDII will be
described later.) The Rabitat continues to cultivate close ties with the
Indonesian government, with a high-profile example being its cospon-
sorship of the Second International Conference on Islamic Media with
the Indonesian Ministry of Religion in Jakarta in December 2011. As
participant Mark Woodward has observed, Jakarta was chosen as the
conference venue because it was the site of the first conference in 1980,
and "many observers noted that the timing of the two conferences was
not coincidental. . . . Both were held shortly after social and political
upheavals that presented serious challenges to Saudi Arabia—the Iranian Revolution of 1979 and the Arab Spring of 2011."[28] The Indonesian Ministry of Religious Affairs and the Rabitat went on to launch

an international Islamic news website in 2012 to "increase the public's awareness of Islam."[29]

The al-Haramain Islamic Foundation is another important Saudi charity active in Indonesia. Al-Haramain supported the Yayasan Majelis at-Turots al-Islamy Foundation, led by Abu Nida, which sought to get Muslims to "return to the true path of Islam" by building mosques, *pesantren* (schools), and even a model village where Salafism could be taught and practiced. Al-Haramain also supported the al-Sofwah Foundation, founded by Muhammad Yusuf Harun, which set up courses, trained preachers, and created the "most important Salafi publishing house in Indonesia," which printed and distributed Salafist texts and cassettes.[30] Al-Haramain funded Wahdah Islamiyah, "the driving force behind the *salafi* movement in South Sulawesi," an organization whose members were responsible for some of the Makassar bombings in 2002.[31] Laskar Jundullah, a faction that split from Wahdah Islamiyah and was responsible for the bombings, was led by Agus Dwikarna, who was the local representative of al-Haramain in Makassar.[32] Al-Haramain also funded several schools, including al-Irsyad, which was connected to members of Laskar Jihad (more on these organizations later). The Indonesian branch of al-Haramain was jointly designated by the U.S. and Saudi Arabian governments in 2004 for providing funding for al-Qaeda operatives in Indonesia and funneling money to support the Indonesian terrorist group Jemaah Islamiyah.[33]

Several other charities were funders of DDII, Wahdah Islamiyah, Yayasan Majelis, and other organizations in Indonesia. The International Islamic Relief Organization (IIRO) was one of the sponsors of DDII and funded 575 mosques.[34] In 2006 the U.S. Treasury's Office of Foreign Assets Control designated the IIRO's Indonesian branch for providing logistical assistance to terrorist groups Jemaah Islamiyah and al-Qaeda.[35] The World Assembly of Muslim Youth (WAMY), the Committee of Islamic Charity (CIC), and the World Council of Mosques (WCM) were all sponsors of DDII in Indonesia. The Kuwaiti-based Jam'iyyat Ihya' al-Turath al-Islam (Revival of Islamic Heritage

Society), founded in 1981 and supported by the Saudi religious establishment, also funded Abu Nida's Yayasan Majelis Foundation and the Wahdah Islamiyah.[36] The United States and United Nations designated Jam'iyyat Ihya' al-Turath al-Islam in 2002 for supporting terrorism. The Wahdah Islamiyah also received financial support from the United Arab Emirates–based Jam'iyyat Dar al-Birr (Charity House Society), which built various schools, from kindergartens to colleges, and had a radio station and magazine.[37]

The U.S. and UN designations of some of the charities and funding organizations mentioned above have somewhat stemmed the flow of money from the Gulf to Indonesia. In 2005 construction of DDII's sprawling school and college complex in Jakarta halted due to the sharp drop in Saudi financial support when the building was about 75 percent completed. In 2004 the director of the IIRO Jakarta branch advised that he had not received new funding for a year and that wealthy Saudis otherwise interested in supporting IIRO's humanitarian efforts had been scared off by the crackdown on funding from the Gulf. These new constraints by no means stopped the financial stream altogether, with evidence suggesting that Saudi donors were finding ways to bypass official sanctions and continue supporting groups in Indonesia. Some observers have suggested that international pressure has curbed legitimate funding support for development and humanitarian activities in Indonesia "without preventing more zealously motivated patrons from getting their money through."[38] The Indonesian government noted in 2009 that the involvement of Middle Eastern donors in funding extremist activities in Indonesia had been known since the bomb attacks in Bali in 2002, and the terrorist attacks in Jakarta in 2009 had been funded by sources in Saudi Arabia, with the money sent via courier to avoid the banking system and the threat of detection.[39]

ORGANIZATIONS

Within Indonesia there are numerous organizations that have preached, taught, lived, fought for, and otherwise supplied Islamist ideology, and this section will briefly discuss the most important ones (including some already touched on). The foundation for nearly all of the Islamist groups in Indonesia was the homegrown movement of Darul Islam. As discussed above, DI began as one of several regional rebellions in the late 1940s and early 1950s.[40] It was originally centered in West Java and led by Soekarmadji Maridjan Kartosuwiryo. The various regional rebels all had their own reasons for fighting, but they all opposed giving up control to the newly independent Indonesian government. Religious factors were less important than territorial ones, but Islam became a "common bond" and a way for the different regional rebellions to unify.[41] As a movement, DI sought to be an Islamic alternative to the secular Republic of Indonesia. At its peak in the mid-1950s the larger regional subdivisions of DI had between 12,000 and 15,000 fighters.[42] In 1962, however, Kartosuwiryo was captured and executed. In addition, "the Indonesian army persuaded 32 of his top lieutenants to pledge allegiance to the government in exchange for amnesty."[43] This led to infighting among aspiring DI leaders, effectively leaving the organization leaderless and disorganized. In 1974 leaders from DI factions in Aceh, Java, and South Sulawesi met and decided to recognize Daud Beureueh (from Aceh) as the imam for all DI. Some members of the reenergized DI formed Komando Jihad in 1976 and soon began a campaign of bombings in Sumatra and Lampung.[44] In 1977, however, 185 members of Komando Jihad were arrested and many executed, effectively dismantling the organization. Abdullah Sungkar and Abu Bakar Ba'asyir, who were future leaders of Jemaah Islamiyah and members of DI and Komando Jihad, were also detained from 1978 to 1982.[45] Many other leaders and members of DI sought exile outside Indonesia to avoid the wrath of the state, and many found their way to militant training camps in Afghanistan and Pakistan. Reflecting on the impact of this exile, Indonesia's former chief of counterterrorism, Ansyaad Mbai, observed that "today's terrorists are the progeny of the people we executed."[46]

The period between 1979 and 1987 saw renewed infighting within DI and continued splintering of the group into different organizations.

Leadership crises occurred again in the late 1990s, leading to "the time of many imams," when "groups of DI members had no structural affiliation at all."[47] Over time DI was faced with internal schisms and waves of external pressure from the Indonesian state to such an extent that "the centralized structure of DI was destroyed" and it became more of a "very loose but enduring web of personal contacts" than an organization.[48] Some of the groups emerging from DI include Jemaah Islamiyah and DDII, as well as some networks (called "rings"—Ring Santa, Ring Banten, Ring Condet) operating outside their geographic DI structure and often involved in violent activities.[49] While some of the groups and individuals that originated with DI were linked to transnational Islamist movements, DI itself remained a local, homegrown group. It was critical, however, in seeding a network of Islamist ideologues, many of who went on to embrace Salafi proselytizing efforts and some who went on to commit or support acts of terror.

One of the most influential organizations in Indonesia dedicated to Salafi principles—and directly connected to global Saudi proselytizing efforts—was Dewan Dakwah Islamiyah Indonesia. Muhammad Natsir, a leader of Masyumi who had served as prime minister, founded DDII in 1967.[50] Natsir was a member of the council of founders of the Saudi-funded Rabitat, as well as a board member for various associated bodies. Natsir was inspired by Qutb, Mawdudi, and the Salafi ideology of the Egyptian Muslim Brotherhood. From its beginnings DDII was concerned with the growing Christian influence in Indonesia and hoped to counteract it through the propagation of Islamist ideas through its preachers and mosques.[51] As mentioned earlier, the Rabitat invested heavily in DDII and made the organization the executive agent for all of its activities in Indonesia.[52] Other charities listed earlier also contributed to DDII and its mission. Natsir and the DDII were influential in promoting the spread of Islamism and Salafism from the Arabian Peninsula to Indonesia, and Natsir himself encouraged the Saudi authorities to exert pressure on the Indonesian government to enact policies consistent with Saudi Islamic practices.[53] DDII built mosques, schools, orphanages, and hospitals, distributed copies of the Quran and other books, and published a monthly periodical. DDII also became the main channel in Indonesia for distributing Rabitat scholarships to Indonesian students for study in the Middle East, and the DDII opened an office in Riyadh in the early 1970s to facilitate the close connection with the Rabitat.[54] According to its website, DDII has offices in thirty-two provinces of Indonesia.[55] Abdullah Sungkar, the first leader of JI, was an important member of DDII. In the 1970s he was the leader of the Central Java branch of DDII and one of the more reactionary members of the organization, pushing it from a moderate Islamist group to a potentially violent one. Through all of its activities to promote Islamism, and through all of the members who formed or joined other groups, DDII "provided the embryo for activists" and established "the roots of radicalism in Indonesia."[56]

One of the most important institutions created by DDII—and one of the most influential in spreading Salafism in Indonesia—was the Institute for the Study of Islam and Arabic (LIPIA). LIPIA was established in 1980 as a branch of the Imam Muhammad ibn Saud Islamic University in Riyadh by Sheikh Abdullah bin Azizi Abdullah al-Ammar, a student of the top Salafi scholar in the world, Sheikh Abdullah bin Baz, under cooperative agreement between the Saudi and Indonesian governments.[57] The university followed the curriculum of its Saudi sponsor, and many faculty members were Salafi scholars imported from Saudi Arabia. LIPIA alumni went on to become key figures in the Islamist movement in Indonesia, and they include such notable figures as Chamza Sofwan (Abu Nida), Yazid Jawwas, Ja'far Thalib, and Yusuf Usman Baisa, all of whom will be discussed later.[58] LIPIA created campus study groups, sent students to pursue postgraduate study in Saudi Arabia, and distributed the Quran and books on Wahhabism. The concept of *usroh* (family) communities—small groups established to live by Islamic law and to influence and transform Muslim societies—spread though LIPIA and other campus groups established by DDII. These communities became the basis for political cells, some of which pursued more extreme anti-government activities, including the usroh community established in Central Java by Abdullah Sungkar and Abu Bakar Ba'asyir, who later founded Indonesian terrorist group Jemaah Islamiyah.[59]

These usroh communities formed part of the wider Tarbiyah (which loosely means education or cultivation), an umbrella movement of campus-based Islamic *da'wa* groups for proselytizing. The Tarbiyah movement was highly influential, because other forms of political campus activity were banned by the government at the time. The movement took off, inspired by the fervor of the Iranian Revolution but theologically influenced—and funded—by Saudi Arabia.[60] According to Haedar Nashir, "Within a decade of its birth ca. 1980, the movement had already spread to the most prestigious campuses in Indonesia . . . [and] following the birth of two Tarbiyah magazines at the end of 1986, *Ummi* and *Sabili*, Muslim Brotherhood ideology spread even more quickly."[61] The timing of the Tarbiyah movement is important. As Sadanand Dhume has observed, "Indonesia was rapidly urbanizing in the 1980s. Many college students were the first in their families to acquire a higher education or live in a city. Tarbiyah gave its members a sense of purpose and dignity; simple ideas of right and wrong; a framework for understanding the changes taking place around them."[62] Through the dissemination of literature and the development of Islamist movements on university campuses, DDII, LIPIA, and the Tarbiyah movement helped inspire "the birth of a younger generation of radicalized militants unwilling to compromise with the state authority."[63] According to the International Crisis Group, "no single institution did more to propagate Salafism in Indonesia" than the DDII/Saudi-sponsored LIPIA.[64]

Jemaah Islamiyah, the group best known for high-profile acts of terrorism against foreigners (Bali tourist district, 2002; a South Jakarta Marriott Hotel, 2003; the Australian embassy in Jakarta, 2004; Bali tourist district, 2005; Marriott and Ritz-Carlton Hotels, South Jakarta, 2009), grew out of both DI and DDII. Sungkar and Ba'asyir had been arrested in 1978 as members of DI's Komando Jihad and released in 1982. When they lost an appeal in 1985 and were to be rearrested, they fled to Malaysia. From there they traveled to Saudi Arabia to obtain funding from Rabitat. They soon organized trips for Indonesians to go to Afghanistan to train in the camps of Abdul Rasul Sayyaf and fight with the mujahedeen against the Soviets.[65] Most of the funding for these recruits came from the Rabitat, and almost all of JI's senior leadership subsequently fought in Afghanistan or Pakistan in the 1980s before returning to Indonesia and establishing JI. This included key perpetrators of the devastating 2002 Bali bombings—Dulmatin, Mukhlas, Ali Imron, and Hambali.[66] In 1992 a personal rift between Sungkar and another DI leader, Ajengan Masduki, led to a confrontation in Afghanistan, and Sungkar decided to take those loyal to him and create his own organization.[67] On January 1, 1993, Sungkar and Ba'asyir formally split from DI and established JI. In 1996 they left their bases in Malaysia and Afghanistan and went to a Moro Islamic Liberation Front (MILF) camp in the Philippines. After Sungkar died of natural causes in 1999, Abu Bakar Ba'asyir became emir of JI.[68] JI's goals were similar to those of other Salafist groups—they wanted to establish "religiously pure communities governed by a strict Salafi reading of *sharia* . . . [and desired] the creation of a new theocratic state in Southeast Asia that unites all Muslims and, ultimately, a global theocratic Islamic state."[69] To achieve these goals, JI has engaged in jihad against both near enemy (local) and far enemy (U.S., Western) interests. The attacks against the far enemy differentiate JI from earlier groups like DI, which were much more locally focused. Also, the provocative, high-risk attacks caused fissures within JI, with Sungkar, Noordin Top, Hambali, and others in favor of them and Ba'asyir less so. After Ba'asyir took over in 1999, many of the more extreme members of JI felt he was too moderate and risk averse.[70]

JI has diminished considerably, although splinter groups and individuals remain active, and it continues to exert influence through its schools, discussed further below.[71] It has also spawned other Islamist groups. Ba'asyir and his followers made use of the post-Suharto freedom to establish the Indonesian Mujahedin Council (Majelis Mujahidin

Indonesia, or MMI) with the ostensible purpose of bringing together all Islamist groups in Indonesia working toward the application of sharia.[72] MMI has strong ideological ties and overlapping membership with both DI and JI, and it has a militia, Laskar Mujahidin, which contributed fighters to local ethnic conflicts. Following an ideological split with MMI after his release from prison in 2006, Ba'asyir went on to establish Jemaah Anshorut Tauhid (JAT) in 2008. According to the International Crisis Group, "JAT is rooted in the ideology of Salafi jihadism, with the ultra-puritanism of the Salafi *manhaj* or method combined with the political overlay of an emphasis on jihad."[73] JAT has replaced JI as the country's largest and most active jihadi organization, and it came under the spotlight in 2010 for supporting a militant training camp in Aceh, Indonesia.[74]

Along with Ba'asyir, one of the other central figures in the creation of other Islamist organizations is Chamza Sofwan, alias Abu Nida. His story serves as an example of one person's path and connections to various Islamist institutions. Abu Nida was born in 1954 and, after secondary school, went to a DDII training course to be a preacher. Natsir, the leader of DDII, then sent him to learn Arabic at LIPIA. His next educational step was to study Islamic law at Imam Muhammad ibn Saud Islamic University in Riyadh. While there, he was sponsored by the Rabitat and worked at the local DDII office. After leaving Saudi Arabia, he fought in Afghanistan before returning to Indonesia in the mid-1980s. In Indonesia he briefly taught at the Ngruki pesantren before moving to Yogyakarta, where, supported by DDII, he engaged in da'wa activities at several mosques, pesantren, and universities. Abu Nida's efforts "to spread the Salafi da'wa proved fruitful"; Salafi communities spread throughout Indonesia.[75] With money from Saudi Arabia, Kuwait, and the Gulf states, Abu Nida, along with others, established the As-Sunnah Foundation in 1992. As-Sunnah built a mosque in Yogyakarta, which "became the most important center of Salafi activity in Indonesia," and the organization also published the periodical *As-Sunnah*, which discussed and spread the fatwas coming from Saudi

Arabia's Wahhabi establishment. With more funding from the Saudi charities al-Haramain and IIRO, as well as the Kuwaiti charity Jam'iyyat Ihya' al-Turath al-Islami, Abu Nida also created the Yayasan Majelis at-Turots al-Islamy Foundation in 1994. This organization built a model village, a school called Pesantren at-Turots al-Islamy, and a mosque at a compound where students could live as Salafists.[76] The at-Turots network went on to support the establishment of other schools across Indonesia, with money from the Kuwaiti charity funneled through the at-Turots Southeast Asia office in Jakarta in the mid- to late 1990s. This funding stream was hampered when the United States and United Nations designated the charity Jam'iyyat Ihya' al-Turath al-Islami in 2002 for supporting terrorism.[77]

In 1998 the Forum Komunikasi Ahlus Sunnah Wal Jamaah (Forum for Followers of the Sunna and the Community of the Prophet) was established by a group of approximately sixty Salafi teachers led by Ja'far Umar Thalib, another LIPIA graduate and former mujahedeen, who subsequently was one of Indonesia's best-known Salafi activists.[78] The Forum Komunikasi established Laskar Jihad as its paramilitary wing in 2000, after seeking approval from prominent Saudi and Yemeni sheikhs.[79] The Forum Komunikasi is the largest Salafi organization in recent history in Indonesia and is ideologically aligned with the Saudi religious establishment, in no small part due to Thalib and the other Laskar Jihad leaders of Arab descent. It also forms part of a wider Salafi movement in Indonesia and repeatedly seeks guidance directly from Salafi leaders in the Gulf. Thalib, after studying at LIPIA, went to the Mawdudi Institute in Pakistan to study in the mid-1980s and then spent time from 1987 to 1989 in Afghanistan fighting the Soviets. During this time, he joined the Jama'at al-Quran wa Ahl al-Hadith, a Saudi-supported faction led by Jamil al-Rahman, a fanatical adherent of Wahhabism, and established extensive contacts with the transnational Salafi da'wa movement. After studying in Saudi Arabia and Yemen, he returned to Indonesia.[80] In the 1990s he was involved with Abu Nida's As-Sunnah Foundation and was on the editorial board of its periodical. Laskar Jihad rose to prominence during the post-Suharto turmoil and communal violence, sending several thousand men to the Moluccas to fight against Christians, as well as several hundred to Poso, and engaging in low-level violence across the country, including attacks on cafés, brothels, and gambling sites. Besides these violent activities, Laskar Jihad also conducted door-to-door preaching and built schools and Islamic centers to teach Salafism.[81]

Wahdah Islamiyah and Laskar Jundullah, two other Salafi groups that share a common history, have also been connected to terrorist activity. Wahdah Islamiyah was founded by a DI veteran, Fatul Muin, in 1989 and was originally called Yayasan Fatul Muin. In 1996 Zaitun Rasmin, a Muslim scholar, returned to Makassar in Sulawesi and changed the group's name to Wahdah Islamiyah. The organization soon became "the driving force behind the *salafi* movement in South Sulawesi."[82] Wahdah Islamiyah received funding from al-Haramain, IIRO, and donors, many of whom were alumni of other Islamist institutions. As of 2012, Wahdah Islamiyah maintained seventy branches focused on the dissemination of Salafi teachings, mostly in Sulawesi, and a school modeled after LIPIA, with curricula drawn from Saudi Arabia.[83] Wahdah Islamiyah also had several loose ties to JI. For example, Syawal Yasin, the husband of Abdullah Sungkar's stepdaughter, was "chief of staff of its military department from 1996 to 2000." Also, one of its leaders, Agus Dwikarna, served on the executive committee of Majelis Mujahidin Indonesia (MMI), the umbrella organization for all Islamist groups created by Ba'asyir in 2000.[84] In 1999 Wahdah Islamiyah split into two factions: one led by Rasmin and one led by Dwikarna and backed by Yasin and others. The Dwikarna faction called itself Laskar Jundullah and was responsible for the December 2002 attacks on a McDonalds restaurant and a car dealership in Makassar.[85]

Illustrating the influence of wealthy Saudi individuals, the al-Sofwah Foundation was established in 1992 by Muhammad Yusuf Harun and Abu Bakar Altway, both LIPIA and Imam Muhammad ibn Saud Islamic University graduates, after a direct offer of sponsorship from Saudi citizen Muhammad Khalaf.[86] Funding from Khalaf was directed through the al-Haramain and Jam'iyyat Ihya' al-Turath al-Islami charities. Al-Sofwah was active in spreading Islamism through courses, training programs, and the publication and distribution of Islamist texts through Pustaka Azzam, their publishing house, which "emerged as the most important Salafi publishing house in Indonesia."[87] Al-Sofwah established a distance-learning program whereby students could consult teachers via fax, phone, email, or post, and one of its earliest programs sponsored preachers to travel around Indonesia teaching principles of Salafism. Al-Sofwah also funneled money to other Salafist institutions in Indonesia, such as Nurus Sunnah, As-Sunnah (different from above), and others, which likewise promoted Islamism.[88]

To serve as a final example of the confluence—and reach—of Arabian money and Islamist institutions in Indonesia, it is worth highlighting several other smaller organizations that also received Saudi financial support, including the al-Huda Islamic Foundation, established in 1998 as a network of schools, a teachers' college, and a radio station (Radio al-Iman Swaratama); the al-Ta'ifah Mansoura Foundation in East Java, established in 1994 by Salafi activists from university mosques; the al-Sunnah Foundation (which runs the largest Salafi pesantren in Cirebon, West Java); and the Nda' al-Fatra Foundation in East Java, which also maintains a radio station, as-Salam FM.[89]

The organizations described above are just a few of the most prominent Islamist institutions and are not intended to be an exhaustive list, although those touched on usefully illustrate the significant areas of overlap between many organizations in Indonesia. While some have encountered ideological splits (the International Crisis Group notes a particular split between "Salafis" and "Salafi jihadists"), all have sought to propagate an Islamist ideology throughout Indonesia.[90] Many did not engage in violence, while a few, such as JI, DI, and others, did. All of them, however, spread the ideology of Islamism through organizing classes, building schools, constructing mosques, funding fighters to Afghanistan, printing and distributing Islamic texts, and so on. The following section explores Islamist influence in universities, schools mosques, and media in Indonesia

SCHOOLS, MOSQUES, AND MEDIA

In Indonesia, teaching institutions, mosques, and publishing houses are often established and run by Islamic organizations and are housed together. Some prominent schools, universities, mosques, and publishing groups that have promoted Islamist ideology have already been touched on above, but this section describes a few of the more important schools and universities that have produced or been established by Salafis, as well as the mosques and publishing houses associated with Islamist proselytizing groups.

A few key pesantren (Islamic schools) play a prominent role in the recruitment and radicalization of Indonesians into militant Islamist groups. Pesantren are usually rural-based Islamic schools that teach exclusively religious subjects, in Arabic, and with the goal of producing religious authorities.[91] Out of tens of thousands of pesantren teaching millions of students at any time, only a few dozen are connected to JI and other violent groups.[92] Of the few that are, there are close interconnections among alumni, teachers, and others affiliated with them. By far the most well known and closely tied to terrorism is the Pondok Al-Mukmin Pesantren in Ngruki, Solo. It was established in 1972 by eight founding members, including Sungkar and Ba'asyir, and has been at its current location since 1974. It is controlled and funded by the Yayasan Ngruki Foundation, which also operates several other primary schools and even a university-type school (Mahad Ali, discussed below). The curriculum at all of these schools is dominated by Salafist texts and instruction. At its peak, there were probably about thirty-five hundred students at Ngruki, with about fifteen hundred in 2007 and about three hundred teachers. The vast majority of students graduate and have nothing to do with terrorism or violence of any kind.[93] However, there are numerous alumni and teachers who were active in JI or other groups. Among the students of Ngruki, Fathurrahman al-Ghozi was involved in the 2000 bombings in Manila; Toni Togar, Mohammed Rais, Asmar Latin Sani, and Sardona Siliwangi were involved in the 2003 Marriott Hotel bombing in South Jakarta; and Son Hadi, Jabir, Deni, Ubeid, and al-Anshori were involved in the 2004 Australian embassy bombing. Abu Nida, not a member of JI but involved with other Salafist activity, taught there in the 1980s after returning from Afghanistan.[94] Affiliated with the pesantren in Ngruki is the Universitas an-Nur in Solo, also known as the Mahad Ali al-Ikhlas Islamic University. It is run as a college for the graduates of the pesantren in Ngruki and other pesantren and has ties to JI through one of its directors, Abu Dujanah, who is the secretary of JI's central command.[95] Also, some of JI's 2003 bombers (Sardona Siliwangi) and 2004 bombers were students (Deni, Ubeid, Urwah, Umar) or faculty (Abu Fidah) at an-Nur.

Another important school with ties to JI was Luqmanul Hakiem in Kelantan, Malaysia. It opened in 1992 based on the instructions of Sungkar, was modeled on Ngruki, and had Mukhlas (alias Ali Ghufron) as its director. Noordin Top, responsible for many of the JI-affiliated attacks in Indonesia, took over as director in 1998. At its peak, probably around 350 students attended the school. The government of Malaysia began a crackdown on JI in 2001, and by 2002 Luqmanul Hakiem had been closed down.[96] Its teachers and students were among JI members involved in several attacks: Noordin Top (2003 Marriott bombing, 2004 embassy blast, 2005 Bali attack), Hambali (2003 Marriott bombing and others); Mukhlas, Dulmatin, Amrozi, Ali Imron, and Imam Samudra (2002 Bali attack); Zulkarnaen (JI military strategist); Fathurrahman al-Ghozi (2000 Manila attack); Azhari (the 2000 Christmas bombings, 2002 Bali blasts, 2003 Marriott attack, 2004 embassy blast, 2005 Bali bombings); and Mohammed Rais, Ismail, and Tohir (all involved in the 2003 Marriott attack).[97]

The pesantren in Darusysyahada was another school making up JI's "Ivy League." It taught around 380 students at any time and provided military training to its students during the conflict in Ambon. One of its directors was Mustaqim, a veteran of Afghanistan and one of the

leaders of MMI, the umbrella organization created by Ba'asyir.[98] Two
of the 2004 Australian embassy bombers (Jabir and Ubeid) were students there, and Jabir was a teacher from 1999 to 2004. These are just
a handful of pesantren associated with JI; overall there were probably
around twenty schools affiliated with JI in Indonesia and Malaysia.[99]
Beyond the strict teachings offered at these pesantren, they provided
refuge for radicals and operated as meeting and communication hubs.
The International Crisis Group has suggested that a JI boarding school
can promote radicalization simply by being a place where extremists
periodically show up.[100]

In addition to the JI network, DDII has also been involved in funding
the establishment of pesantren in Indonesia. Pesantren al-Irsyad, for
example, was established by DDII member and LIPIA graduate Yusuf
Usman Baisa. Thalib, the future leader of Laskar Jihad, taught there,
as did fellow LIPIA alum Yazid Abdul Qadir Jawwas. Pesantren Ibn
Qayyim was also established by DDII and was where Abu Nida taught
after teaching at Ngruki.[101] Remnants of the DI movement can also
be found in various networks of pesantren. The Hidayatullah pesantren in East Kalimantan teaches a puritanical form of Islam and was
established in 1973 by Abdullah Said, a former DI activist. Hidayatullah subsequently transformed itself into a network, with branches
in almost two hundred districts all over the country, and gained wide
renown through its Islamist magazine (more on this below). In addition,
Al-Zaytun, a large, extravagant pesantren that opened in West Java in
1999, is rumored to have close links with one particular wing of DI, the
Regional Command IX (KW9).[102]

Besides these pesantren, a network of Salafi madrasas developed that
were associated with some of the key Islamist organizations in Indonesia. Slightly different from pesantren, madrasas are Islamic schools that
usually follow a modern system of education and teach Islamic subjects
alongside general subjects. The main aim of the madrasa is "to produce
graduates like those from modern-style 'secular' schools . . . [but] having
a better understanding of Islam." In reality, however, the distinction is

less obvious. Many Salafi madrasas reject all nonreligious subjects and are reluctant to institute grading systems, while some pesantren teach secular subjects such as mathematics and will allow for grading. Of the tens of thousands of madrasas in Indonesia, most are controlled by the government's Department of Religious Affairs, while some belong to private Islamic organizations and others have been directly established by some of the key Salafi organizations discussed above.[103]

The oldest of the Salafi madrasas is Ihya al-Sunnah, which was established in 1994 in Yogyakarta by LIPIA graduates Ja'far Umar Thalib and Abu Nida. Madrasa al-Turath al-Islami, established by the at-Turots network that was funded by the Kuwaiti charity Jam'iyyat Ihya' al-Turath al-Islami, was founded in the same city in 1995. Between 1995 and 2000 a dozen other madrasas loyal to Thalib were established, and as Noorhaidi Hasan has observed, "the existence of a network of Salafi madrasas closely linked to Ja'far Umar Thalib was of crucial importance to the Laskar Jihad's operations. . . . It was especially through these madrasas that aspiring *mujahidin* from the countryside were recruited."[104] As mentioned earlier, Laskar Jihad went on to wage violence against Christians in the Moluccas, under the "authority" of fatwas issued by Salafi scholars in the Middle East. Abu Nida also established a number of madrasas as part of his own network, among them the lavish madrasa Bin Baz in Bantul and Imam al-Bukhari madrasa in Surakarta, both of which bear inscriptions on the walls identifying their wealthy Middle Eastern donors. According to Noorhaidi Hasan, "the main subject studied in the Salafi madrasas is not *fiqh* [Islamic jurisprudence], which is the main fare in the traditional *pesantren*, but Islamic theology (aaqida), or more precisely Wahhabi doctrine."[105] In addition, teachers and students strictly separate themselves from their physical surroundings, and an atmosphere of exclusivity breeds mutual suspicion, with villagers labeling the madrasas the *pondok orang berjubah* (hostel of men in long robes).[106]

Radicalization and indoctrination also occurred in mosques throughout Indonesia. Many of these mosques were on or near university campuses, examples being the Salman Mosque, the Al-Ghifari Mosque, the Mardiyah Mosque, the Mujahidin Mosque, and the Sholehuddin Mosque. Several of these mosques, as well as the Siswa Graha Mosque and the STM Kentungan Mosque, were funded and supported by DDII and/or by Abu Nida, who organized study groups at several of them.[107] Some of these mosques were also closely tied with JI, including the Al-Ikhsan Mosque, the Al-Mabrur Mosque, the Suprapto-Suparno Mosque, the Solihin Mosque (where JI member Ahmad Sajuli became radicalized), and the Sudirman Mosque, whose preachers (Fikiruddin and Muchliansyah) joined Sungkar and Ba'asyir in Malaysia in the 1980s.[108] The al-Munawwarah Mosque in Pamulang in 2004 came under the control of Muhammad Iqbal (also known as Abu Jibril), a Saudi-educated cleric and former mujahedeen in Afghanistan who lived in Malaysia for a time with JI's founders, Abdullah Sungkar and Abu Bakar Ba'asyir.[109] Iqbal was identified in the U.S. Treasury Department's list of "specially designated nationals," and his son, Muhammad Jibril, was arrested in 2009 for his suspected connections to the July 2009 terror attacks against the Marriott and Ritz-Carlton Hotels in Jakarta. The junior Jibril, a former member of JI's al-Ghuraba cell in Karachi, Pakistan, was accused of traveling to Saudi Arabia to solicit funding for the attacks and in 2010 was jailed for the bombings. He was accused of collaborating with a Saudi national based in Indonesia, Al Khelaiw Ali Abdullah, who allegedly funded the bombings, although Abdullah was later cleared by an Indonesian court.[110]

Along with mosques that are known as centers of support for Islamist networks, Islamist groups in Indonesia have also been accused of co-opting mainstream mosques to preach radical ideologies. Hasyim Muzadi, who has chaired the mainstream Muslim organization Nahdlatul Ulama, observes that countless mosques built by NU members, which had previously observed NU practices, had been "seized" by extremist groups "as a base for constantly delivering radical sermons in order to politicize those who pray there." According to Muzadi, the number of NU mosques seized by extremist groups is in the hundreds.[111]

Funding from the Middle East has also supported the construction of new mosques across the archipelago. It is difficult to establish just how many mosques have been constructed in Indonesia and financed with Saudi money, but researchers have estimated the number is in the thousands. As an indication of the scale of this construction, according to the IIRO's own figures it built 309 mosques in Indonesia in 2003 alone. While some mosques are funded and constructed without specific conditions, in some instances the Saudi funder insisted on appointing the imam for the mosque, usually from Saudi Arabia. Indonesian Salafi organizations have also been effective at training and mobilizing Salafi preachers through mosque and campus networks, and Islamist groups have heavily influenced campus mosques via the Tarbiyah movement.[112] For example, Tarbiyah-linked groups are considered to "occupy" all the main campus mosques in the university town of Yogyakarta, including those at Gadjah Mada University, Sunan Kalijaga Islamic State University, and the Muhammadiyah University of Yogyakarta, leading to conflicts between moderate and Islamist teachers and students.[113]

The supply of Islamism was also accomplished through various media outlets. The first big Islamic publishing houses began appearing in Indonesia in the mid-1980s, after which Salafist and Wahhabi texts were translated and distributed in increasing numbers, including works by al-Banna, Qutb, Mawdudi, Shariat, Azzam, al-Maqdisi, and others.[114] This coincided with a marked increase in the demand for books on Islam. In 2008 the International Crisis Group (ICG) identified more than one hundred Salafi publishing houses, along with many other periodicals or publishing houses linked to Islamist organizations in Indonesia.[115] As the ICG observed, "sales are fuelled by the Indonesian public's thirst for books on Islamic lifestyle, but this in turn opens the door to dissemination of the political material."[116] Among the most popular are the translated writings of Muslim Brotherhood leader Yusuf al-Qaradawi, primarily because they provide guidance on the "correct" or "halal" approach to everyday decisions facing Muslims.[117] Although it is hard to estimate overall sales of Salafi literature, the growing distribution of these books since the 1980s, and now to large, mainstream Indonesian bookstore chains, is evidence of both a surge in production and popularity.

As mentioned earlier, LIPIA translated and distributed copies of the Quran and other Wahhabi texts, while the As-Sunnah Foundation published its eponymous newsletter edited by Abu Nida, Thalib, and Jawwas.[118] Salafist groups also distributed VCDs, DVDs, and video cassettes to spread their ideology. Ar-Rahmah Media is a Jakarta-based company that pioneered the sale of videos from al-Qaeda and other jihadist websites purportedly showing Muslims being killed, but with gory scenes of violence from other conflicts spliced in for effect.[119] Ar-Rahmah Media is owned by Muhammad Jibril, mentioned earlier for his role in the 2009 attacks in Jakarta. *Suara Hidayatullah*, the anti-Jewish, anti-Christian magazine associated with the Hidayatullah pesantren network, achieved a circulation of fifty-two thousand at its peak in the late 1990s and is focused on militant, Islamist messaging, giving information on international jihad and providing interviews and sympathetic articles on radical Islamic groups. Majelis Mujahidin Indonesia also has its own magazine, *Risalah Mujahidin*, and a publishing house, Wihdah Press.[120]

JI built an influential publishing network, including the Arafah Group, al-Alaq, the Al-Qowam Group, and Al Aqwam publishing houses as well as several websites.[121] As the International Crisis Group has observed, JI's publishing arm operates by way of the same complex web of interlinked relationships as the network itself: "like JI's complex relational network, the JI publishing industry would be worth studying if only as an example of Salafi jihadi outreach. But it is also a fascinating example of social networks, because of the way that the school and family ties of the leading publishers bridge factional and organizational divisions."[122] Many of the JI-linked publishing houses are run by alumni of the Pondok Pesantren al-Mukmin in Ngruki. Al-Alaq was established by Ikhsan Miarso, who was in Afghanistan from 1987 to 1990 and set up the company on his return.[123] Al-Alaq is known for printing and reprinting classic jihadi texts. The Arafah Group, run by Ustadz Tri Asmoro Kurniawan, a former member of JI's West Java subdivision, has five imprints, two of which focus on jihadi texts, while others focus on judgment day and Islamic family values. The Al-Qowam Group focuses on family values, the role of women, morality, prayer, and worship, rather than political tracts, and is supported by Hawin Murtadlo, also an alumni of Pondok Pesantren al-Mukmin in Ngruki. Al Aqwam began in mid-2003 and is responsible for publishing Bali bomber Imam Samudra's best-selling justification of his role in the terrorist attack, which he wrote in jail before he was executed. A more recent addition to JI's publishing network is Kafayeh Cipta Media, which was established in 2007 and has ties to LIPIA. Kafayeh Cipta Media focused on translations of downloads from Arabic-language al-Qaeda websites.[124]

Hizbut Tahrir Indonesia (HTI), a self-proclaimed political movement dedicated to uniting all Muslims under a caliphate (discussed in more detail below), expanded the print run of its weekly publication, *A Islam*, from 500 copies in 1995 to 1.2 million copies in 2010 in Indonesia.[125] *A Islam* focuses on contemporary issues facing Muslims in Indonesia. HTI's monthly journal, *Al-Wai'e*, focuses more on international events affecting the Muslim world and is distributed in all Indonesian provinces, selling about 100,000 copies each month. HTI also owns several publishing houses, including Pustaka Thariqul Izzah and Al-Izzah Press, that focus on translating into Indonesian a variety of books written by ideologues from the wider Hizb ut-Tahrir pan-Islamist movement.[126]

Salafi radio stations have also been on the rise, with estimates suggesting that more than a hundred are now operating in Indonesia; they can also be accessed via online streaming. A Salafi radio station on Indonesia's Batam Island made headlines in 2016 when it was accused of being responsible for radicalizing two Singaporean citizens who were detained in Singapore before traveling to Syria.[127]

POLITICAL GROUPS AND MAINSTREAM ORGANIZATIONS

Along with Saudi influence over various Islamist organizations, mosques, schools, and publishing houses in Indonesia, various political groups have emerged with links to foreign or transnational movements. Evidence also points to efforts by Islamist groups, often supported by Saudi funding, to infiltrate mainstream nongovernmental organizations and influence government officials and political leaders in Indonesia, particularly with regard to the implementation of sharia and the establishment of an Islamic state.[128]

The Partai Keadilan Sejahtera (PKS, the Prosperity and Justice Party) "is an Islamist party that emerged following the first post-1999 democratic elections, with roots that extend to the pre-Suharto era.... PKS and Hizbut Tahrir Indonesia are the two most important political forces to emerge from the campus-based Tarbiyah movement."[129] PKS leadership is heavily influenced by Wahhabism and Muslim Brotherhood ideology, and PKS is generally considered to be a local offshoot of the Muslim Brotherhood. Former party chair Nur Wahid "holds a B.A., M.A., and Ph.D. from ... the University of Medina [Madinah] in Saudi Arabia, [while PKS] Secretary-General Anis Matta graduated from the Jakarta branch of Riyadh's Al-Imam Muhammad bin Saud University."[130] The party's founding manifesto quotes a prominent Muslim Brotherhood member, the Egyptian-born cleric Yusuf al-Qaradawi, who believes that democratic means can be used to pursue Islamist ends. The PKS has denied claims that it receives support from donors in the Gulf region, "but allegations made in a lawsuit filed against the party by PKS founder and former head of its sharia commission, Yusup Supendi ... [claim] that 94 percent of funds for its 1999 political campaign came from illegal donations from Middle Eastern benefactors."[131]

Considerable disquiet about the influence of radical Islamist parties, influenced by foreign elements, has been expressed by senior government officials. Indonesia's defense minister in 2006, Juwono Sudarsono, publicly expressed concern that radical movements within Islamic political parties were pushing for the realization of an Islamic state and the imposition of sharia. A former chairperson of the Indonesian Armed Forces has also observed that "before, the extremist threat to the NKRI [unity state of Indonesia] and Pancasila lay outside

of government [in the form of armed rebellions] such as Darul Islam/
NII. But now the extremists have managed to infiltrate the government,
including parliament, and become more dangerous than in the past."[132]

Hizbut Tahrir Indonesia, directly linked to the global Hizb ut-Tahrir
movement, is an organization with growing political prominence in
Indonesia. It somewhat straddles the divide between the Islamist organizations and political parties already discussed in that it considers itself
a political party, but it is not registered as such in Indonesia and does
not recognize the Indonesian democratic electoral system and party
politics. It has also been described as "probably the only Islamic organization in Indonesia that is formally controlled by foreign leadership,
draws its ideology strictly from a Middle Eastern source, and whose
agenda is fundamentally transnational."[133] While Hizb ut-Tahrir was
founded in Palestine, it draws inspiration from Wahhabi and Muslim
Brotherhood ideology and seeks the establishment of a global Islamic
caliphate. As with other Islamist groups, HTI initially utilized student
networks to spread its ideology, beginning at the prestigious Bogor
Agricultural Institute, which was also heavily influenced by the Tarbiyah movement. After the fall of Suharto, HTI launched itself officially in 2000 with an international conference in a soccer stadium in
Jakarta, an event that attracted more than five thousand HTI activists
and considerable media coverage. Since this launch, HTI has continued
to receive a lot of attention in its ongoing campaign for the implementation of sharia and establishment of an Islamic caliphate. This campaign is undertaken via media and publications (already touched on
above), as well as regular public demonstrations, which have protested
a range of things, from proposed fuel hikes to the invasion of Iraq. Like
PKS, HTI has been accused of infiltrating mosques throughout Indonesia for the purpose of dominating their activities, and it has sought
to systematically control the national Mosque Management Committee. HTI has also sought to build a network of influence among leading
public figures and politicians in Indonesia, and it has forged links with
PKS. In 2007 the minister of youth and sports, who was a PKS member,

supported HTI's international "khalifah" conference, and the former army general, Tyasno Sudarto, demonstrated with HTI over the Danish cartoon depiction of Mohammed.[134] While HTI has publicly supported former JI leader Abu Bakar Ba'asyir and asserted that terror attacks in Indonesia were perpetrated by the CIA, the organization ostensibly rejects violence. In many ways it is more radical than local or issue-driven groups, however, in that it seeks a complete overhaul of the Indonesian state and rejects all secular and democratic institutions.

The Front Pembala Islam (FPI, Islamic Defenders Front) is another radical group that has risen to prominence in Indonesia since its founding in 1998 by Habib Muhammad Rizieq Syihab, a religious teacher of Arab descent who was educated in Saudi Arabia. Like Habib Rizieq, many of the FPI's top leadership are of Arab descent. Unlike some of the other radical Islamist organizations in Indonesia, the FPI is not a political party or social organization and is not focused on the establishment of an Islamic state but identifies itself as a "pressure group." FPI calls for the full implementation of Islamic law in Indonesia and takes it upon itself to act as a kind of vigilante enforcement group, or what the International Crisis Group has termed an "urban thug organization."[135] The FPI carries out raids against bars, pool halls, nightclubs, and other venues it suspects of gambling or prostitution and stages violent protests or attacks against other religious institutions, with its protesters and attackers usually dressed in flowing, Arab-style white robes. As an indication of the inspiration drawn from intolerant Wahhabi thought, FPI has targeted minority religious groups, attacking Christian churches and assaulting adherents of Ahmadiyyah, a minority Islamic group, as well as ethnic and sexual minority groups, such as Chinese and transsexuals.[136] Of particular concern regarding the FPI are its close ties with the Indonesian police and military, which have utilized the group for its ability to mobilize supporters and enforce Islamic principles.[137]

With the rise of these groups, concerns have escalated among the two main Muslim organizations in Indonesia, Muhammadiyah and Nahdlatul Ulama (with 30 million and 40 million members, respectively) about Islamist "infiltration" of both organizations. In 2006 Muhammadiyah's Central Board issued a decree emphasizing the importance of the organization being free from "the influence, mission, infiltration and agenda of political parties that seek to achieve their political goals in the name of 'da'wa' [proselytizing activities]."[138] The board decree goes on to identify the "Muslim Brotherhood-affiliated" PKS as responsible for infiltrating and exploiting Muhammadiyah for political ends. This exploitation is alleged to include influence over Muhammadiyah's charitable enterprises, mosques, educational institutions, and mass media activities, specifically for the purposes of proselytization. This board decree followed a tense Muhammadiyah congress in 2005 in which PKS and HTI members allegedly sought to sway deliberations within Muhammadiyah committees toward more radical goals, denounced the establishment of the Young Muhammadiyah Intellectuals network and the participation of women, and sought to influence the election of Muhammadiyah leadership. As the only group specifically identified by the decree, the PKS felt compelled to issue a public response to preserve its political prospects, denying any efforts to gain control of mosques, Friday sermons, hospitals, schools, campuses, or charitable organizations and expressing support for the 1945 Constitution and Pancasila. It continues to tell its constituents, however, that it is a da'wa party committed to the observation of sharia as an obligation of all Muslims. The decree followed a series of opinion pieces in Muhammadiyah's magazine, *Voice of Muhammadiyah*, detailing the "extremist infiltration" of Muhammadiyah schools. Groups tied to the Tarbiyah movements, such as PKS and HTI, have been accused of seeking to introduce Arab-style education in Muhammadiyah universities, with funding by donors in the Middle East. For example, the Muhammadiyah University of Yogyakarta opened an institute of religious education funded by Saudi Arabia and supplied with Saudi teachers, while the Muhammadiyah University of Surakarta provides full scholarships from Saudi Arabia for the study of Islam degree program, and Saudi textbooks constitute obligatory reading. PKS and HTI members are active in both of these programs, and many of the students in Surakarta are alumni of JI's Ngruki pesantren.[139]

Nahdlatul Ulama is concerned with the Islamization of Indonesia. In February 2007 the central leadership council of NU's Proselytism Institute (LDNU) called on all NU members to "tenaciously uphold the teachings and practices of *ahlussunnah wal-jamâ'ah* (Sunni Islam)."[140] Research published by the LibForAll Foundation found that "extremist groups have already succeeded in infiltrating the NU via mosques, Islamic study group councils and *pesantren* . . . the foundation of the NU and its membership."[141] NU manages around fourteen thousand pesantren across Indonesia, and in May 2007 NU leadership gathered the heads of these schools from around the country to discuss the threat of transnational Islamist ideology to the educational and spiritual traditions of the schools. The NU vice chair for the pesantren association, Abdul Adhim, subsequently told the press that "Indonesian Islam . . . is imbued with the spirit of tolerance and courtesy [while t]ransnational Islamist ideology . . . arrives uninvited and without the least bit of courtesy, screaming 'Allahu Akbar' while shattering glass." NU leadership has acknowledged that many of the hard-line groups that have emerged in Indonesia adhere to a Wahhabi worldview, a clear indication of the success of Saudi efforts to export its national ideology to an international market.[142]

Also worth mentioning is the Islamist presence within the influential Indonesian Ulama Council, or Majelis Ulama Indonesia (MUI), established in 1975 in the midst of the New Order period as an adviser to the government on Islamic issues and as a channel of communication between the government and the Muslim population. After the fall of Suharto the role of MUI became more complex, with the organization receiving government funding but acting independently, taking on an influential role in Indonesian civil society, and issuing fatwas on a variety of issues. MUI now has representatives across Indonesia at the provincial level and is a powerful body with regard to Indonesia's trade relations, as it is the sole certifier of halal products and practices. Any Islamic organization can join MUI if MUI considers the organization to be legitimate—a label it extends to extremist groups such as MMI, HTI, and FPI but not to Shiite or Ahmadiyyah groups, though MUI does draw the line at admitting terrorist groups, such as JI. Crucially, MUI does not practice proportional representation, so extremist groups have disproportional influence in the body compared to representatives of the thirty- and forty-million strong Muhammadiyah and NU, and the council has therefore been described as a "bunker" for fundamentalist and subversive groups seeking to influence the direction of Indonesia. As an example, MUI established the Congress for Solidarity of the Muslim Community of Indonesia in 2001, which HTI subsequently dominated. HTI orchestrated the signing of a "Jakarta Declaration" calling for the implementation of sharia in Indonesia. Through the Congress for Solidarity, HTI also secured the establishment of the Muslim Community Forum (FUI), which has been influential in pushing for stricter Islamic norms to be implemented in Indonesian life, including sweeping antipornography measures and the banning of the Ahmadiyyah group.[143]

As a coda to the information presented above regarding the supply of Islamist ideologies into Indonesia, it is worth highlighting an effort by prominent moderate Muslim leaders in Indonesia to expose and ultimately stem the tide of extremist ideologies. Former Indonesian president Abdurrahman Wahid, NU chair Mustofa Bisri, and former Muhammadiyah chair Syafii Maarif (collectively seen as spiritual leaders for around seventy million Indonesian Muslims) undertook a two-year research project in 2007 into the activities of Islamist groups in Indonesia, presenting their findings in a 2009 book, soon published in English under the title *The Illusion of an Islamic State: Expansion of Transnational Islamic Movements in Indonesia*. The book, made available to download on the internet, quickly went viral and is credited with disrupting the PKS' bid for the Indonesian vice presidency in the 2009 elections. A public effort by such influential Indonesian leaders to discredit the PKS and HTI specifically, and Islamist groups more generally, is evidence

of genuine concern about the potential for the supply of Islamist ideologies into Indonesia to threaten the state itself. As the *Jakarta Globe*
reported at the time of the book's release, "Throwing the gauntlet down
at the feet of radical Islam, a group of mainstream Muslim leaders led
by former President Abdurrahman Wahid [released] a book asserting
that Indonesia is being infiltrated by foreign-funded extremists bent
on turning the country into an Islamic state."[144] It remains to be seen,
however, just how much impact this counterattack by moderate Muslims will ultimately have in the battle for the soul of Islam in Indonesia.

CONCLUSION

Indonesia offers a revealing case study of the impact of having a supply of Islamist ideologies directed into a country. It is possible to trace
the emergence of various types of Islamist organizations, movements,
and political groups and their ties to financial suppliers and spiritual
leaders in the Persian Gulf region. The emergence of these groups and
the escalation of their activities coincided with a Saudi proselytizing
effort that took off in the 1980s. Prior to that time, while homegrown
purist movements and Islamist groups existed, their focus was more
local, born out of a struggle for independence from foreign rule. After
independence in 1945, Indonesia retained its pluralist, tolerant version
of Islam and established a secular state based on the principles of the
Pancasila. From the early 1980s, because of the attack on the Grand
Mosque, the Iranian Revolution, and the war in Afghanistan, Islamist
voices gradually grew louder as Indonesian veterans of the Afghan
jihad returned to Indonesia schooled in Islamist thought and backed
by significant financial resources from the Gulf to spread their ideology.[145] The success of this proselytizing effort is evident in the proliferation of foreign-funded Islamist organizations, mosques, schools,
and publishing houses and in efforts to influence mainstream politics
and organizations.

While Saudi charities and individuals have provided legitimate development and relief support to Indonesia, the connections to proselytiz-

ing activities and Islamist groups are evident and widespread, even if some of these funding streams have been curtailed following terrorist designations and the freezing of assets. Along with the spread of Islamism through civil society, Islamist political parties and movements underpinned by money and ideology from the Gulf region threaten the fabric of the Indonesian secular and democratic political system. While many of the groups discussed adhere to slightly different ideologies (primarily that of Wahhabism/Salafism, the Muslim Brotherhood, or Hizb ut-Tahrir), their overall goals are similar and symbiotic, which results in movement between organizations, common funding streams, overlapping networks, cooperative ties, and—sometimes—terrorism.

CHAPTER 4

Islamism in Pakistan

> For three decades, deep tectonic forces have been silently tearing Pakistan away from the Indian subcontinent and driving it towards the Arabian Peninsula. This continental drift is not physical but cultural, driven by a belief that Pakistan must exchange its South Asian identity for an Arab-Muslim one.
>
> —**Pervez Hoodbhoy**, "Pakistan's Westward Drift"

Historically, most Muslims in the Indian subcontinent practiced Sufism, a sect of Islam that involves mysticism and is considered to be relatively inclusive and tolerant compared to Sunni and Shia theologies.[1] Although local Islamist movements have existed since Pakistan's inception, they never gained popular support from the local population. By the late 1970s, however, Pakistan's Sufi culture had come under strain during the rule of General Mohammad Zia ul-Haq, an ardent Sunni Muslim who was sympathetic to Wahhabi Islam and sought to Islamize the country.[2] Zia ul-Haq's Islamist polices enabled him to leverage backing and financing from the Persian Gulf states, particularly Saudi Arabia. The Iranian Revolution and the Soviet invasion of Afghanistan in 1979 further solidified Saudi-Pakistani relations and subsequently changed the trajectory of Islamism in Pakistan.[3] The influx of Saudi financing to Pakistan during the Afghan war—in order to inculcate

Wahhabi Islam and counter Iranian influence in the region—created a generation of Pakistani youth ingrained with jihadi rhetoric and Islamist fervor.[4] Consequently, a "groundswell of Islamist zeal" began to permeate the country, as evidenced by a drastic surge in "the power and prestige of the [Muslim] clerics, attendance in mosques, home prayer meetings, observance of special religious festivals, and fasting during Ramadan," as well as the ubiquitous wearing of abayas (black, full-length cloaks) by women across Pakistan.[5] The implementation of sharia (Islamic law) is also now beginning to gain widespread support among the general population, and sectarian violence continues to percolate between Sunni and Shia groups.[6]

The following sections will describe the historical and political context of Islamism in Pakistan, the establishment of Islamist organizations in Pakistan with the help of Arab funding, and how the support created specific Salafi/Wahhabi institutions (madrasas, mosques, and universities) in the country. The concluding section will talk about the implications of Islamism's deep penetration into Pakistani society.

HISTORICAL AND POLITICAL CONTEXT

Islam arrived in what is now Pakistan in the eighth century through conquest by Muslims from Central Asia, Afghanistan, and Persia.[7] Traveling with them were peaceful Sufi missionaries who proselytized the local population "through their piety and personal example."[8] Sufism's fusion of Islamic, Hindu, and Buddhist philosophies—centered on spirituality, mutual tolerance, and peaceful coexistence—would lead many Hindu and Buddhist disciples to convert to Islam. The resulting "Pakistani Islam" was relatively moderate and tolerant, with the majority of Pakistani Muslims adhering to the Barelvi/Sufi strand of Islam.[9] It has only been since 1980 that Islamist ideologies have permeated the country and gradually been accepted by many Pakistani Muslims.

Islamists have historically tried to subvert Sufi influence in the region by implicating Sufism's deeply rooted traditions as *bid'ah* (heterodox innovations of Islam).[10] The two principal Islamist movements in Pakistan, Deobandism and Salafism, existed prior to Pakistan's inception in 1947.[11] Both groups—which have now come to be "associated with Sunni militancy"—stem from sectarian traditions and adhere to an unyielding and literalist interpretation of Islam that disparages Sufi worship at shrines and overt *dhikr* (Islamic devotional act of chanting the names of God and verses from the Quran and the Hadith).[12] Additionally, both Islamist groups vehemently reject Shia rituals, particularly the Shia public display of mourning during the month of Muharram.[13] The primary difference between these two movements is that Deobandism is uniquely South Asian and did not start out as a militant movement; rather, it was transformed into one due in part to the influence of Salafism.[14] Salafism, on the other hand, originated on the Arabian Peninsula and was first imported into the Indian subcontinent by Indian Muslims who traveled to Arabia (either to study Islam or perform the hajj pilgrimage to Mecca and Medina) in the 1700s.[15] During their stay in Arabia, Indian Muslim pilgrims were indoctrinated with Wahhabi ideology and would return to their home country with their newfound version of Islam. Shah Waliullah, an Indian Islamic scholar from Delhi and a contemporary of Ibn Abdul Wahhab (founder of Wahhabism), was heavily influenced during his stay in Medina in the early eighteenth century. While studying under Sheikh Ahmed Sirhandi, a hardline Salafist, both Waliullah and Wahhab were indoctrinated with the idea of *ijtihad* (an individual's effort to reexamine sharia independent of any Islamic school of jurisprudence).[16] Waliullah later returned to India on a mission to proselytize Indian Muslims to take up the Salafist doctrine, and he urged his disciples "to adopt the Arab dress and mannerisms."[17] His emphasis on Islamic orthodoxy would eventually spawn the Deobandi movement. Syed Ahmed, a *talib* (student) from Waliullah's madrasa in Delhi, also traveled to Mecca and Medina. He returned two years later to India determined to convert the locals of Khyber Pakhtunkhwa (formerly known as the North-West Frontier Province in Pakistan) to Salafism.[18] The Pashtuns of Khyber Pakhtunkhwa never fully embraced the Salafi groups (formerly known as

Hindustani Fanatics) and their Muwahiddun (unitarian) and puritanical version of Islam.[19] The Salafists' devotion to militant "jihad to expand the din (faith) into Dar al Harb (the Indian plains)" especially alienated the traditionally tribal-based and Sufi-adhering locals.[20] The few Muslim groups in South Asia that had practiced Salafism at that time would later be referred to as Ahle Hadith (People of the Prophets Tradition).[21] One prominent Ahle Hadith scholar was Sheikh Abdul Ghaffar Hassan. Born in Umarpur, near Delhi, in 1913, he migrated to Pakistan after Partition. Initially associated with Jamaat-e-Islami (an Islamist political party) from 1941 to 1957, he eventually severed ties with the group due to differences on how to establish an Islamic caliphate. He then taught at the Islamic University of Madinah for sixteen years and subsequently returned to Pakistan to engage in *da'wa* (proselytization) of Muslims to the Salafi/Wahhabi sect till his death in 2007.[22] By the late 1970s Ahle Hadith members in Pakistan would wield significant power, due primarily to Saudi support.

In 1930, when Dr. Muhammad Iqbal, a prominent philosopher, poet, and devotee of Waliullah, introduced the idea of Pakistan as a Muslim state independent from India, Islamist parties fervidly opposed the idea of partition because of concerns that demarcation would divide the Muslim *ummah* (community).[23] In the end Mohammad Jinnah's moderate All-India Muslim League faction, which championed partition, prevailed.[24] Pakistan was officially established in 1947 as a separate homeland for the Muslims of India. It comprised two noncontiguous regions, East Pakistan and West Pakistan, which were separated by more than one thousand miles of Indian territory. Jinnah was appointed Pakistan's first governor-general, and Liaquat Ali Khan was the first prime minister. Jinnah himself was a liberal, Western-educated Muslim but propagated the slogan of an Islamic national identity "as a way of giving semblance of unity and solidity to his divided Muslim constituents."[25] His vision of Pakistan was therefore much more secular and identity based than religiously grounded. Indeed, Jinnah wanted the country to be the "beacon of enlightenment for other Muslims," and he abhorred the very notion of Islamist parties injecting orthodox beliefs into Pakistani politics.[26] Jinnah especially despised Mawlana Sayed Mawdudi's Jamaat-e-Islami (JI, Party of Islam), which was set up as a "counter-League" and a staunch critic of Jinnah's version of a secular, nationalist Pakistan.[27]

Jinnah's death shortly after Partition dealt a major blow to his party and the prospects of a moderate political system. His failure to provide an "Islamic blueprint" left a vacuum that enabled Islamist parties to demand an "Islamic state with an Islamic Constitution."[28] Liaquat's assassination five years later further degraded the fledgling government's ability to promote secular ideals. As political instability intensified in the country, General (later Field Marshal) Ayub Khan seized control of the government and paved the way for military intervention in civilian affairs.[29] Khan was a progressive Muslim who considered Islamists a "dangerous nuisance."[30] He refused to align with the Islamist parties and had much antipathy for them, particularly Mawdudi's JI faction.[31] Mawdudi subscribed to Deobandi Islam, but his quest for Islamism in Pakistan was heavily influenced by the writings of Ibn Wahhab and by his extensive travels to Arab countries, where he wanted to "earn legitimacy by association with the central lands of Islam and the Arabic literary canon."[32] Mawdudi was well received by the Saudi kingdom and served as a trustee for Medina University, and he was later awarded the King Faisal Prize in 1979 for his contributions to Islam. The Saudi kingdom was instrumental in publishing and disseminating Mawdudi's literary work in various languages throughout the Muslim world. His speeches and writings were heard throughout Cairo and Jeddah. The Muslim Brotherhood also incorporated his teachings within their own Islamist propaganda. Sayyid Qutb, a leading Muslim Brotherhood member, openly acknowledged his gratitude to Mawdudi. By the 1950s an "Islamic triangulation" of Wahhabism, Mawdudi's JI, and the Muslim Brotherhood had emerged and come to dominate Islamist discourse.[33] More important, Mawdudi's intimate relationship with both Kings Saud and with King Faisal of Saudi Arabia essentially propelled JI's political influence in Pakistan. With Pakistan's adoption of its first constitution in 1956, Mawdudi's JI won several concessions, which included changing Pakistan's name to the Islamic Republic of Pakistan and inserting the "repugnancy clause," which stipulated that "no laws could henceforth be passed that were repugnant to the teachings of the Quran and the Hadith, and all previous laws were also able to be vetted to ensure that they so conformed."[34] JI and many of the other Islamist groups wanted to abolish the remnants of the British-influenced criminal and civil laws and replace them with an Islamist state based on sharia. Mawdudi was also a proponent of militant Islam and emphasized that jihad had primacy over all other Islamic injunctions.[35]

The secession of Bangladesh in 1971 led to a national identity crisis within Pakistan. In an attempt to recoup from its humiliating defeat by India, Zulfikar Bhutto propagated a "national ethos on anti-Indian and pan-Islamic slogans."[36] Bhutto was not an Islamist in his personal beliefs but publicly portrayed himself as such in order to prevent Islamist parties from seizing power. More important, Bhutto needed to display his support for Islamism as he looked to the Middle East for financial assistance and a strategic partnership.[37] When the Islamist parties united under the Pakistan National Alliance (PNA), a faction spearheaded by Mawdudi, their primary demand was for installation of a completely Islamic state under sharia. Bhutto responded by implementing his own stringent Islamist policies. By 1973 he had drafted a new constitution that declared Islam to be the state religion. Previous laws were expected to "be brought in conformity with the injunctions of Islam as laid down in the Holy Qur'an and Sunnah."[38] Bhutto further pushed his Islamic rhetoric in both domestic and foreign affairs by banning alcohol, gambling, and nightclubs and by making Friday the official rest day instead of Sunday (which was later reversed by Nawaz Sharif). Moreover, not only did he help create the Organization of the Islamic Conference (OIC), the second-largest intergovernmental organization, one comprising fifty-seven Muslim states and spread over four continents, but he also hosted a major OIC conference in 1974. Bhutto also declared the Ahmadiyya sect in Pakistan to be non-Muslim. In 1977 Bhutto's reign came to an abrupt end after he was overthrown in a coup d'état led by General Zia ul-Haq, the army chief of staff, who later authorized Bhutto's execution on March 18, 1978.[39]

Islamization in Pakistan reached unprecedented levels under the military dictatorship of Zia ul-Haq. As a fervent sectarian Islamist, he entrenched orthodox Sunni Islam within the military, political, and social fabric of Pakistani life. Islamist teachings were also engrained in the military curricula as the Pakistani army's motto went from that of his predecessors' "Unity, Faith, Discipline" to "Iman, Taqwa, Jihad fi Sabeelilah (Faith, Obedience to God, Struggle in the path of Allah)."[40] Zia ul-Haq further enacted the draconian Hudood Ordinances, which "prescribed physical punishments (whipping, stoning, and amputation) for a variety of transgressions."[41] While the Ahmadi were already vilified under Bhutto, Zia ul-Haq further attacked other minority sects, including Shias and Barelvis, who were also banned from practicing their rituals.

The Soviet invasion of Afghanistan was especially significant for Pakistan because Zia ul-Haq was able to establish relations with the United States, solidify a steady influx of petrodollars, and declare Pakistan "the regional vanguard of Sunni Islam."[42] Unlike his predecessors, Zia ul-Haq was an admirer of Mawdudi, and shortly after the onset of the Afghan war he forged a "military-mullah nexus" with JI by appointing many of its members to key ministerial positions.[43] JI acted as the leading conduit for ideological, financial, and weapons support for the most notorious and traditionalist Afghan mujahedeen groups fighting the Soviet-backed regime in Afghanistan.[44] After the war JI maintained close relations with the Pakistani military and thus was able to yield significant power even during civilian rule. While there were many moderate Muslims who opposed the Islamist parties and Zia ul-Haq's Islamization of Pakistan, the burgeoning religious middle class exerted greater influence and leverage under Zia ul-Haq's policies. Islamist parties also received tremendous financial assistance from the newly affluent Pakistani émigrés who had capitalized on the Saudi oil boom of 1973. The majority of migrants who returned from Saudi Arabia were not only wealthy but also more religiously conservative, and they brought their newfound religiosity back with them. In 1983 alone Pakistani Gulf migrants sent $3 billion back home, and a significant portion of these remittances went to Islamist groups.[45]

Saudi Arabia's role in financing and supporting Islamism in Pakistan increased after the Iranian Revolution and the anti-Soviet jihad in Afghanistan. Zia ul-Haq had crafted Pakistan into a Sunni Muslim state, but the Iranian Revolution had altered the degree of sectarian politics in the country. Consequently, Pakistan became "the site of a protracted shia-sunni proxy war" between Saudi Arabia and Iran.[46] Pakistan's state patronage to Deobandi and Wahhabi militant groups, including Sipah-e-Sahaba (SSP, later known as Ahle Sunnat Wal Jamaat, or ASWJ) and Lashkar-e-Jhangvi (LeJ), served as a counterweight to Iranian influence. Pakistan's support for the terrorist groups also stemmed from its fear of the Indian threat. Under Zia ul-Haq, Pakistan welcomed Saudi financing and promulgation of Islamism with open arms.[47] Saudi funding for Islamist militant groups was often routed directly through the Pakistani military and the Inter-services Intelligence (ISI).[48]

The Soviet withdrawal from Afghanistan in 1989 and Pakistan's ambitions of becoming a nuclear armed state resulted in the souring of relations between the United States and Pakistan.[49] Isolated and economically wounded, Pakistan pivoted even further to the Middle East to compensate for the perceived "abandonment" by the United States.[50] Thus, the relationship between Pakistan's military, the Islamist parties, and Saudi Arabia continued; after Zia ul-Haq's death in a mysterious 1988 plane crash, his successors as president, General Aslam Beg and the ISI head, Lieutenant General Hamid Gul, were both fervent Islamists. Also, Iranian influence in the region diminished, consequently enabling Sunni militant groups and Islamist parties to overpower many of the militant groups and Islamist parties formerly backed by Iran.[51] When democracy returned to Pakistan with the 1988 election of Benazir

Bhutto, the eldest daughter of Zulfikar Bhutto, Islamist parties vehemently opposed Bhutto's position as prime minister on the grounds
that Islam prohibited women from governing. The Saudi kingdom also
opposed a woman heading an Islamic state and had misgivings about
the Bhuttos' ties to Iran.[52] Following in her father's footsteps, Bhutto
responded by fully endorsing the Afghan Taliban and making repeated
trips to Saudi Arabia to meet with King Abdullah to rectify relations.[53]
Her attempts at appeasement with the Saudi kingdom and the Islamist
parties proved futile, however, and Bhutto was ousted by Nawaz Sharif
in 1988.[54] Sharif and his family were bitter rivals of the Bhuttos and
the ISI considered Sharif the ideal protégé of Zia ul-Haq and one who
would be willing to align with the Islamist parties.[55] This proved true
as Sharif agreed to their demands and pledged to incorporate sharia
into Pakistan's constitution. In 2000, as the bill for integrating sharia
was about to be passed, Sharif was ousted and exiled (he stayed in
Saudi Arabia for eight years as a guest of the king) in a coup d'état led
by General Pervez Musharraf.

Relations between Saudi Arabia and Pakistan improved even more
during Musharraf's presidency from 2001 to 2008.[56] In 2006 Musharraf
honored King Abdullah with the Nishan-e-Pakistan, the most prestigious
civil award given to an individual by the Pakistani government. The
following year Musharraf received the King Abdulaziz Medal, which is
an award presented to an individual who has made significant contributions to the Saudi kingdom. More important, Musharraf's alignment
with the Islamist parties—in an effort to undermine his rivals' chances
of winning a sizable number of votes from the electorate—inadvertently
created "a bigger presence for the extremist Islamist groups in Pakistan's polity."[57] Musharraf's later fallout with the Islamist parties and
eventual abdication from power came after his mishandling of the Lal
Masjid (Red Mosque) incident, a bloody clash between the Pakistani
government and Islamist militants at the mosque. In the aftermath
there were more than ninety-two civilians dead plus eleven from the
armed forces.[58] Islamist parties, including JI and Jamaat-ud-Dawa

(JuD), condemned Musharraf's harsh response and organized massive protests shortly thereafter. Although the majority of Pakistan agreed with Musharraf's handling of the situation, there were many others who sided with the Islamist parties. The Lal Masjid clash served as a rallying point for Pakistani hard-liners, who would retaliate against the Pakistani establishment. The incident resulted in the nullification of a ten-year peace agreement between pro-Taliban groups and the Pakistani government along the Afghan border.[59]

ORGANIZATIONS

The Islamist parties' growth under Zia ul-Haq accelerated with the financial assistance of Saudi Arabia. The majority of Saudi funds were allocated to the Ahle Hadith factions, which are the most "radicalized elements within the Sunni fundamentalist factions in Pakistan."[60] Although members of the Ahle Hadith sect constitute less than 6 percent of the population, this group has nonetheless exerted disproportionate influence and has committed acts of violence against other Muslim sects.[61] The ties between Ahle Hadith organizations (which adhere to Salafi/Wahhabi Islam) and terrorism are particularly evident in Pakistan. The number of Ahle Hadith organizations is difficult to discern, given there is no formal directory of Islamic-based organizations in Pakistan. The majority of Ahle Hadith organizations partake in politics and da'wa, but many, described below, have been accused of engaging in and promoting jihadi activities, including suicide operations and attacks against non-Muslims, *kafir*s (Muslim apostates), and the Pakistani government.[62]

One prominent Ahle Hadith organization in Pakistan that is closely linked to Saudi Arabia is Markazi Jamiat Ahle Hadith (MJAH), founded by Ehsan Elahi Zaheer.[63] Zaheer was first trained in Salafi madrasas in Gujranwala and Faisalabad and subsequently left to study at the Islamic University of Medina from 1963 to 1965. While there, he was taught by Sheikh Abdul bin Baz, the Grand Mufti (highest-ranking Sunni Islamic scholar who can interpret or expound Islamic law) of Saudi Arabia, who also taught Osama bin Laden. By the 1980s Zaheer had written extensively against Shia Islam, denounced Shias as heretics, and accused them of "being Zionist agents in Islamic countries."[64] Since MJAH's inception, it has campaigned for sectarian violence against Muslims from other sects, as well as other Sunni denominations. Also, MJAH claims to be the only "genuine" Ahle Hadith movement, which strictly emulates the Saudi ulama with regard to an orthodox interpretation of sharia. MJAH's subsidiary organization, Ahle Hadith Youth Force, has mobilized impoverished youth to engage in sectarian violence against Shias and Barelvis. Tehrik-e Mujahidin (TM) is the jihadi subset of MJAH that emerged in 1989 and forcefully converted Shia and Barelvi mosques to Ahle Hadith mosques.[65] Zaheer's sectarian campaign against non-Wahhabi Muslims had earned him financial support from Saudi Arabian charities, including the al-Haramain Islamic Foundation, which allegedly provided direct financial assistance to TM and all of the MJAH madrasas.[66] After Zaheer's assassination in 1987 as the result of a bomb inside a Lahore mosque, King Fahd ordered his body flown to Saudi Arabia, where Sheikh Abdul bin Baz led the funeral prayers.[67] The group continues to grow in strength and in 2019 was led by Sajid Mir, an Islamic professor and Salafist.

Another prominent Ahle Hadith political organization in Pakistan is Jamaat-ud-Dawa, based in Muridke, Punjab.[68] It was established in 1986 by Hafiz Mohammad Saeed, Dr. Zafar Iqbal, and Hafiz Abdul Rehman Makki, all of whom were linked to Medina Islamic University and influenced by Salafism while studying under Sheikh Abdul bin Baz. JuD's primary goal was, and continues to be, to cultivate a jihadi culture that emphasizes martyrdom and intolerance of kafirs (apostates or in this case non-Salafi/Wahhabi/Deobandi). The indoctrination often takes place through madrasas.[69] JuD also provides military training to its members and has been incredibly successful in converting Muslims to the Ahle Hadith sect. It has established more than 2,000 recruitment centers throughout Pakistan and since 1994 has developed a network of JuD model schools, led by Dr. Zafar Iqbal, in which children are provided Islamic and modern education with an emphasis on English and computer science. Although there is abhorrence for Western modernity, JuD schools have nonetheless capitalized on technology through their website, social media, and online publications to spread messages on jihad and encourage children to become martyrs.[70] Many of the textbooks emphasize the importance of jihad and the concept of *qurbani* (sacrifice). An advertisement for JuD schools appeared in *Ghazwa*, a Pakistan-based monthly magazine: "Do you want your children to grow up to be a doctor, engineer, economist, officer, businessman, or leader? But do you also want that they should not become 'slaves' of the English people? Then you should put your children in the Al Da'wa System of Schools (ADSS). At ADSS, they will become guardians of Islam and Qur'an. . . . At Da'wa's school, we also prepare your children for jihad. We offer classes of martial arts."[71] JuD's annual gatherings reportedly attract more than 100,000 attendees and include Lashkar-e-Taiba (LeT, the military wing of JuD) recruits, their families, and other foreign delegates. Although JuD was banned by Pakistan in 2002, it continues publishing its monthly religious magazine, *Al-Dawat*. More than 80,000 copies of a single issue were printed and distributed throughout the country, mainly in urban areas of Punjab, Lahore, and Karachi. The issue centered on the moral decadence of society and the erosion of Islamic behavior among Pakistani youth. Additionally, the magazine decried television, music, and movies and perpetuated anti-Shia and anti-Jewish conspiracy theories.[72] In March 2019 Pakistan moved against JuD, taking over their headquarters, mosques, and other buildings and arresting more than 120 activists.[73]

As the militant wing of JuD, LeT has been active in the Jammu and Kashmir border area.[74] Half of LeT recruits are Pakistani youth from lower socioeconomic backgrounds in Punjab. LeT also recruits educated youth from high schools and universities so as to conduct complex military operations, and it targets families from rural areas who "have often converted to the [Wahhabi] school of thought after the head of the household has spent a period working in Saudi Arabia."[75] LeT boasts a membership of more than fifty thousand, and its foot soldiers are trained by the Pakistani army at eight special camps in Pakistani-controlled Azad Kashmir. Its primary source of funding comes from Saudi Arabia and the Pakistani government, with 50,000 rupees ($810) given to a recruit for "each corpse returned" and 15,000 rupees ($245) given to the recruit's family.[76] LeT indoctrinates prospective insurgents into the Ahle Hadith sect through two training sessions: Dora A'ama, a twenty-one-day course in which students are introduced to the Ahle Hadith school of thought; and Dora Khasa, a three-month course in which students are inured to violence and conditioned to believe that the Ahle Hadith sect is the only pure Islamic sect and that individuals who belong or adhere to other sects are *kafir*.[77] Upon completion of the program, recruits often grow long beards and wear traditional Arab clothing. Moreover, they take a surname of the Prophet's companions or a prominent figure in Islam's triumphant days such as Abu Hamza, Abu Hureira, or Abu Osman.[78]

LeT was the first jihadi militant group to introduce *fedayeen* (commando) missions in Kashmir. Fedayeen missions are not primarily for recruits to attempt suicide; rather, the objective is to inflict as much damage to the opposing forces as possible. Typically, women and children are slaughtered, and victims are decapitated or dismembered.[79] LeT is believed to "represent a threat to regional and global security second only to al-Qaeda."[80] They orchestrated the July 2006 bombings of commuter trains in India that killed more than 209 people and injured more than 700 others. LeT later conducted attacks in Mumbai on November 26, 2008, that killed 166 people and left nearly 200 wounded.[81]

Although LeT received backing from the ISI, Saudi charity-based organizations, including the International Islamic Relief Organization and World Assembly of Muslim Youth, also heavily funded LeT.[82] Leaked U.S. embassy cables revealed that LeT successfully carried out its operations by using a "Saudi-based front company to fund its activities."[83] Additionally, LeT's main headquarters in Muridke has been funded "through local collections complemented by money from Saudi charities and Pakistani expatriates in Europe and the Middle East."[84] JuD has also been known to travel to Saudi Arabia under the guise of fundraising for the construction of new schools at exorbitant prices and siphoning off a huge portion of the money to fund insurgent groups, namely LeT. Militants also seek donations during the *hajj* pilgrimage because of "a major security loophole since pilgrims often travel with large amounts of cash and the Saudis cannot refuse them entry into Saudi Arabia."[85] LeT's financial stockpile has enabled the militant group to disseminate jihadi propaganda across the country via billboards, posters, and graffiti, which contain exhortations such as "A martyr assures salvation for the entire family" and "Jihad is the shortest route to Paradise."[86]

Iran also asserted its influence in Pakistan by financing Shia militias such as Tehrik-i-Nifaz-i-Fiqh-i-Jafaria (TNFJ, or Movement for the Implementation of Jafaria Religious Law) and providing scholarships for Pakistani students to study in Iranian religious seminaries. Iran also funded Sipah-e-Mohamadi Pakistan (SMP), which was created in 1993 to safeguard Shias from Sunni militant groups. SMP was accused of killing prominent Sunni doctors and in 2011 was responsible for the bombing attack on the Saudi Arabian consulate in Karachi.[87]

Saudi Arabia followed suit by "subsidizing countervailing Sunni militias" (through the ISI), including Sipah-e-Sahaba, which demanded that Shias—who make up 15 to 20 percent of Pakistan's population—be declared apostates through a constitutional amendment, as was done with the Ahmadiyya community.[88] SSP was also strongly anti-Barelvi and anti-Iranian and demanded that the death penalty be given to individuals who slurred or mocked the *sahaba* (the Prophet's companions) or his wife, Aisha. By 1992 SSP had registered as a political party, and one year later it established an alliance with the Peoples Party of Pakistan (PPP). The party boasted more than three hundred thousand members, many of whom were recruited from Deobandi madrasas in Punjab. In 1995 SSP aligned with the Taliban against mujahedeen commander Ahmad Shah Massoud's Jamiat-i-Islami and the Afghan Shia Hazaras. SSP was accused of perpetrating mass human rights abuses and partaking in the massacre of Hazaras and Iranian diplomats in August 1998.[89] It maintained its offices in Pakistan and Saudi Arabia until it was officially banned in 2002 and placed on a terrorist watch list by the United States in May 2003. SSP's leader, Azzam Tariq, was placed under house arrest; however, he was released shortly thereafter. That same year Azzam ran for a seat in Pakistan's National Assembly and won.[90]

Lashkar-e-Jhangvi, an offshoot of SSP, was another prominent anti-Shia militant group supported by the Pakistani military and covertly funded by Saudi Arabia. Both SSP and LeJ operated in "the same sectarian circles and appeal to the same constituency." In addition, LeJ "proclaim[ed] fidelity to the founder of the SSP, and there is little that distinguishes between the ideological positions of the two organizations."[91] LeJ's founder, Malik Ishaq, has been incarcerated since 1997 on terrorism-related charges. He was suspected of being the mastermind behind the 2009 attack on the Sri Lankan cricket team, in which six members of the national team were injured and two Pakistani police officers were killed.[92] LeJ recruited several prominent terrorists into its organization, including Ramzi Yousef, Khalid Sheikh Mohammad, and Abu Musab al-Zarqawi. Yousef, who had trained at a LeJ camp, was responsible for the World Trade Center (WTC) bombing of 1993. He built the vehicle bomb that damaged the North Tower of the WTC and killed six New Yorkers.[93] Qari Abdul Hayee was a LeJ militant accused of involvement in the abduction and murder journalist of Daniel Pearl.[94]

By 2001 LeJ had successfully conducted more than 350 terrorist operations.[95] One notorious terrorist attack perpetrated by LeJ against Shias in Pakistan was in July 2003 in Quetta. While 2,000 and Shia worshippers were commemorating Muharram, three LeJ suicide bombers opened fire with automatic weapons and shortly thereafter detonated themselves. More than 55 people were killed and hundreds of others injured. Several months later LeJ suicide bombers targeted another Shia mosque in Quetta, leaving more than 200 dead.[96] LeJ remains active in Pakistan and has publicly denounced Shias as "American agents" and enemies of the Muslim ummah, or community. LeJ's recent targets have been Shia Hazaras in Balochistan.[97]

Jaish-e-Mohammad (JeM, or Army of Mohammad) is another anti-Shia terrorist organization, established in 2000 by Maulana Masood Azhar.[98] Azhar was the former leader of Harat-ul-Mujahideen (HuM), a Pakistani-based militant group created during the Afghan war. JeM's primary source of funding was Saudi Arabia, as well as the ISI, which funneled money through the Pakistani-based charity Al-Rashid Trust.[99] After 9/11, relations between the Pakistani military and JeM were severed when President Musharraf allied with the United States in its Global War on Terror (GWOT). Prior to 2001 the majority of JeM operations focused on the Jammu and Kashmir border and Shia shrines throughout the country. In October 2001 JeM officially expanded its attacks by raiding a Kashmir state assembly in Srinagar and killing thirty-five people. JeM, along with LeJ, was also responsible for the kidnapping and beheading of journalist Daniel Pearl in January 2002.[100] Shortly after Pearl's death, Musharraf responded to international pressure and banned JeM, labeling it a terrorist organization. JeM retaliated by targeting the Pakistani civilian government, Shias, Christians, and Western nationals.[101] In 2003 JeM split into Khuddam-ul-Islam (KuI) and Jamaat ul-Furqan, but international designations still treat it as a single terrorist entity.[102]

MADRASAS AND MOSQUES

Since the 1980s there has been a dramatic surge in the construction of and attendance at madrasas.[103] The influx of Ahle Hadith madrasas, particularly in Pakistan, has stemmed mainly from Saudi financial support.[104] One report estimates that Saudi and UAE charities send $100 million per year to support Ahle Hadith and Deobandi clerics just in the southern Punjab province. In 2005 alone the House of Saud approved a $35 billion plan to build mosques and madrasas in South Asia, where "Wahhabi groups across Jammu and Kashmir were [the predominant] beneficiaries of this largess."[105] The growth of madrasas was due to "the convergence of the Iranian revolution, Soviet intervention in Afghanistan, the CIA-ISI nexus to create a band of militant Islamist [sic], the Islamisation program of the military regime of Ziaul Huq (1977–1988) and the unremitting flow of external funding for ideology-based religious education."[106]

Students in these madrasas are often youth from lower socioeconomic strata who do not have access to public schools. In addition to offering religious training, many of these madrasas provide free tuition, board, and meals.[107] Although Ahle Hadith madrasas have combined Islamic education with a modern curriculum, many of these madrasas have nonetheless been accused of promoting Islamic radicalization and propping up jihadi elements within Islamist organizations.[108] Despite such allegations, Ahle Hadith madrasas continue to recruit prospective students. One reported tactic is exploiting underprivileged families. *Maulana*s (clerics) of Islamist organizations, including JuD and JI, approach these families and persuade them that the family's poor living conditions are a "direct result of [the] family's deviation from 'the true path of Islam' through 'idolatrous' worship at local Sufi shrines."[109] The family is then advised that to be forgiven for their transgression, they must "sacrifice" one of their sons to Islam. The son is then sent to a madrasa for jihadi training, and the family typically receives a cash stipend of $6,500 per child as compensation for their "sacrifice to Islam." Once the child arrives at the madrasa, he is secluded from the wider community and inculcated with "sectarian extremism, hatred for non-Muslims, and anti-Western/anti-Pakistan government philosophy."[110]

One prominent Ahle Hadith madrasa in Pakistan is Jama Salafiya (JS) in Faisalabad. Directed by Sajid Mir, JS serves as the hub of all MJAH religious activities and has strong links to Medina University and Umm al-Qura University. Its primary objectives are *tablighi* (preaching) of Islamism and jihadi operations. The madrasa is also the main center for the Ahle Hadith Youth Force, which is heavily involved in sectarian activities. Two prominent madrasas connected to LeT are Jamia Abu

Bakr and Jamaa Dirasat ul Islamia, which both follow the same curriculum as the Islamic University of Medina. All the courses in these madrasas are taught exclusively in Arabic, and dozens of students from both madrasas are granted scholarships and admission to Medina annually.[111] More than two dozen students from the Jamaa Dirasat ul Islamia madrasa were arrested in 2007 amid investigations into the 2005 Bali bombings that killed twenty and injured a hundred others.[112]

Markazi Jamiat Ahle Hadith (MJAH, mentioned earlier) receives financial and material support from its umbrella institution, Wifaq ul Madaris Salafiya, which has complete control of Salafi madrasas throughout Pakistan. From 1988 to 2000 there was a 131 percent increase in the number of Ahle Hadith–based madrasas across Pakistan, and the numbers continue to rise. According to Pakistani government estimates, there were more than thirty-six thousand students studying in Ahle Hadith madrasas in 2006, and of the five hundred Ahle Hadith schools, three hundred are affiliated with the Wifaq ul Madaris Salafiya and the Islamic University of Medina.[113]

For centuries Islamism was unable to penetrate Khyber Pakhtunkhwa Province in Pakistan; however, the Afghan jihad eroded the Pashtun tribal system and made the region vulnerable to Islamist recruitment. Consequently, madrasas sprang up all over Khyber Pakhtunkhwa, starting during the Afghan war and increasing in number from 13 in 1980 to 150 in 2013.[114] One of the madrasas was JI's Ahle Hadith Rabita madrasa, which produced and disseminated jihadi literature and mobilized public support for Islamism.[115] The influx of thousands of Salafi/Wahhabi Arab men who settled in the region also altered the ideological landscape in Khyber Pakhtunkhwa. Support for the Ahle Hadith madrasas continued after the war, and with Zia ul-Haq's Islamization fully rooted in Pakistan, locals in Khyber Pakhtunkhwa eventually "cast aside their aversion to Wahhabi groups" and "embraced Wahhabi political and jihadi ideas."[116] One well-known Saudi-financed madrasa in Khyber Pakhtunkhwa is the Jamia Asaria, which is regarded as the most sophisticated and organized madrasa in all of Pakistan. Built in

2007, the madrasa accommodates up to 1,200 students, and tuition is 90 percent subsidized by Saudi Arabia.[117] Saudi financing for the Jamia Asaria madrasa is often sent through illegal *hawala* (informal financial transfer systems) channels under the guise of *zakat* (charity) money.[118] The Ahle Hadith madrasa of Quetta (Baluchistan), founded in 1978, also has close ties to the Islamic University of Medina. All the teachers graduated in Saudi Arabia, and courses are taught only in Arabic. It controls 25 madrasas in the province.[119]

While Saudi funding helped propagate Ahle Hadith madrasas, it is important to recognize that the Pakistani government—especially under Zia ul-Haq—also contributed to the mushrooming of Ahle Hadith madrasas in the country. In fact, the Pakistani state apparatus was complicit in the Salafi/Wahhabi proselytization efforts, given the "generous financial incentives" Saudi Arabia provided Pakistan.[120] Consequently, the curriculum of Deobandi madrasas, which taught poetry, mathematics, mysticism, and alchemy alongside religious teachings in the 1940s, were replaced by the more rigid Salafi/Wahhabi curriculum, which emphasized memorization of the Quran and focused chiefly on religious matters. Deobandis were initially revivalists of Hanafi Sunni Islam, which was a more moderate form of Islam in response to British colonialism. With increased funding from the Middle East, however, it later became more rigid in its interpretation of Islam.[121]

Saudi charities, including the Muslim World League, the al-Haramain Foundation, the World Assembly of Muslim Youth, and the International Islamic Relief Organization, financed many Deobandi madrasas that promulgated Salafi and Wahhabi tenets. The MWL purportedly provided more than $200 million to these madrasas.[122] The Darul Uloom Haqqaniya madrasa in particular had gained notoriety as a "jihad factory" during the Afghan war because of the plethora of senior Afghan Taliban members who had graduated from the madrasa. A plaque that announced the Darul Uloom Haqqaniya madrasa as "a gift of the Kingdom of Saudi Arabia" illustrates the Saudi kingdom's financial assistance.[123] Another Deobandi madrasa known for its extremist rhetoric was Jamaat-Farida (for boys) and Jamaat-Hafsa (for girls) in Islamabad. The founder of both madrasas was Maulana Abdullah Ghazi, who studied at Jamia Ulum-e-Islamia, which was also a beneficiary of Saudi funding. Ghazi was indoctrinated with the Salafi ideology and thus promulgated Salafi and Wahhabi teachings in his own madrasas. Many of his students would later become notorious for kidnapping prostitutes, destroying "un-Islamic" CDs and videos, and distributing across Islamabad leaflets that demanded the imposition of sharia in the city.[124]

In 2006 Musharraf tried to clamp down on madrasas; however, his attempts proved futile. According to a 2009 survey conducted by Pakistan's Ministry of Education, there were "1.5 million students in 13,000 madrasas acquiring a parallel religious education."[125] Studies conducted by the International Center for Religion and Diplomacy (ICRD) in 2010 reveal that textbooks used in madrasas throughout the country continued to portray non-Muslims as (1) *kafir* (infidels) or *mushrikeen* (People of the Book), (2) *dhimmi*s (non-Muslims living under Islamic rule), or (3) *murtid*s (apostates). Significantly, non-Muslims are not depicted as Pakistani citizens whose rights should be protected. Ahle Hadith madrasas frequently use *Riaz-ul-Saleheen* (The guardian of pious people), a textbook loosely interpreting the Hadith (teachings and actions of the Prophet) written nine hundred years ago, which disparages mingling with non-Muslims and Shias. Additionally, greeting Christians, Jews, Hindus, and Shias with the Islamic phrase "Salam" (peace be on you) is highly discouraged.[126]

Perhaps the most visible example of Saudi influence in Pakistan is the Shah Faisal Masjid, the national mosque of Pakistan. Named after Saudi Arabia's King Faisal bin Abdul Aziz, Faisal Masjid is one of the largest mosques in the world and has a capacity of 300,000 people.[127] Located inside the mosque is the International Islamic University of Pakistan, which was established in 1980 by Zia ul-Haq. The university has more than 120 religious academic programs and more than 17,000 students. It also collaborates with various Saudi educational institutions, including Umm al-Qura University, Islamic University of Medina, Imam Muhammad ibn Saud Islamic University, and King Abdul Aziz University. Many of the prominent Salafi/Wahhabi teachers from these Saudi institutions are visiting scholars at the International Islamic University and other college campuses throughout Pakistan.[128] The promotion of Islamism in many Pakistani universities has had a profound impact, as evidenced by the pervasiveness of jihadi rhetoric among male students and the wearing of abayas by female students, which was a rarity three decades ago.[129]

INSTITUTIONS

It is important to note that the decade-long rule of Zia ul-Haq is often referred to as "the turning point for Pakistan's educational system . . . the bedrock on which militant extremism was founded."[130] Zia ul-Haq sought to imbue public school curriculums with Islamist rhetoric: "The highest priority would be given to the revision of the curricula with a view to reorganizing the entire content around Islamic thought and giving education an ideological orientation so that Islamic ideology permeates the thinking of the younger generation and helps them with the necessary conviction and ability to refashion society according to Islamic tenets."[131] Because part of the National Education Policy and Implementation Program of 1979 was heavily subsidized by Middle Eastern countries, curricula in state-run schools were completely revised and subsequently became saturated with Islamic content.[132] Emulating Saudi curricula, Pakistani national schoolbooks from grades one through twelve promoted intolerance against nonbelievers, including Hindus, Christians, Jews, and non-Muslims, as well as Ahmadi, Shias, and Sufis. Such biased references were not limited to Islamic studies textbooks. Rather, social studies textbooks for both elementary and primary grades contained similar disapproval of religious minorities, especially of Hindus. Non-Muslims were frequently portrayed in either derogatory terms or were completely omitted.[133] The primary goal was to instill a distinction between a "true Muslim" and the "others."

An Islamic alphabet chart for public curricula gives revealing examples: shown with the Urdu equivalent of the letter *A* is the word *Allah*, with *B* is *bandook* (guns), with *H* is *hejab* (although the accompanying image is of a woman wearing an abaya, which is not traditionally worn in Pakistan), and with *J* is *jihad*. Jihad in particular had its own comprehensive chapter, which laid out different kinds of jihad, including *jihad bin nafs*: "A Jihad by sacrificing one's own life and self. It means that every kind of physical effort may be put in for the service of Islam, so much so that one may sacrifice even one's life for the propagation and cause of Islam."[134] Although the chart was not approved by the government, it continues to be used by many public schools, as well as madrasas. There were attempts in 2006 by the government to reform the national curricula; however, financial constraints and pressure from Islamist parties to keep the status quo have hindered any prospects for reform.[135]

In terms of higher education in Pakistan, the Abu Bakr Islamic University (ABIU) in Karachi was founded by Zafarullah Choudhrey in 1977 with Saudi funds. Choudhrey was a hard-line Salafist and a member of the Salafist faction, Jamaat-e-Mujahideen, which formed during the Afghan war. Choudhrey went to Saudi Arabia to study at Imam Muhammad ibn Saud Islamic University in Riyadh from 1980 to 1985 with the objective of receiving guidance from Saudi ulama on creating a truly Islamic curriculum that he could incorporate at ABIU. Choudhrey managed to secure hefty financial support from the Saudi ulama. ABIU therefore strictly adheres to the same curricula as the Islamic University of Medina and Imam Muhammad ibn Saud Islamic University in Riyadh. Teachers are recruited primarily from Saudi Arabia and students are taught only in Arabic. ABIU offers free board and lodging for admitted students. ABIU also has a subsidiary institute for women, Jamia Aisha Siddiqa.[136] ABIU has been accused of receiving funds from LeT and serving as a recruitment center for prospective recruits to the Ghuraba cell of Jemaah Islamiyah (JI) of Indonesia. The Ghuraba cell was a combined effort by al-Qaeda, JI, and LeT to recruit and train a "new generation" of highly intelligent terrorists who could launch sophisticated attacks against the United States. LeT was instrumental in training Ghuraba's members and future JI leaders, and these training sessions often occurred on ABIU grounds.[137] According to leaked reports written by Joint Task Force Guantanamo (JTF-GTMO), when a JI commander, Hambali, was captured in 2003, he revealed that his brother, Abdul al-Hadi, would likely be his successor. Shortly thereafter, Abdul al-Hadi and a prominent LeT member, Mustafa Ibrahim Mustafa al Hassan, were captured at ABIU.[138]

CONCLUSION

Multiple events steered Pakistan toward the Arabian Peninsula. Migrant workers capitalizing on the oil boom in Saudi Arabia returned to Pakistan wealthier and more conservative. As they returned, they gained political power and aligned with conservative Islamist groups. At the same juncture, the poorest strata of Pakistani society were being indoctrinated in many Saudi-funded Ahle Hadith madrasas. Although not all Ahle Hadith–based Islamist parties and madrasas spawn terrorism, the reality is that the hard-line interpretation of Islam espoused by these groups condones and promotes extremism and sectarianism in the country. Saudi Arabia continues to fund many Ahle Hadith–based madrasas and Islamist groups that align with the Salafi/Wahhabi school of thought. The Pakistani state has tolerated and even welcomed the influence of Wahhabi and Salafi thought into Pakistan.

Pakistan's ISI, with the silent consent of the Pakistani civilian government, has knowingly promoted the supply of the Islamist ideology. Choosing to cooperate with Islamic extremists has led to Islamist violence in Afghanistan, India, and within Pakistan in the form of sectarian violence between Sunnis and Shias.[139] Targeted attacks, assassinations, and suicide bombing attempts perpetrated by LeJ, SSP, and the Pakistani Taliban against non-Deobandi/Wahhabi/Salafi groups continue to plague Pakistan.[140] It remains to be seen to what degree Pakistan will be capable of stopping or willing to reverse this tide of Islamism.[141]

CHAPTER 5

Islamism in Britain

Maybe in the West the dream is to become a great footballer. For us it is to become a great martyr. —**Muslim activist** quoted in Quintan Wiktorowicz, *Radical Islam Rising*

The influence of Saudi proselytizing since the 1970s has not only been felt in traditionally Muslim countries; secular, Western nations have also been the target of efforts from the Gulf region to spread Islamist ideologies. The countries of Europe have been no exception. As Alison Pargeter has observed, "during the 1980s and 1990s Europe became a melting pot of Islamist ideologies, partly as a result of the Saudi money that was sloshing around the continent."[1]

While these Islamist movements in the West are not necessarily connected to terrorism (although some are), they can pose a political threat, inspired as they are by resistance to Western democratic values and by an "us-versus-them" ideology. This ideology sees non-Muslims and Muslims who do not share Islamist beliefs as *kafir* (nonbelievers), a term that carries negative connotations, particularly in Islamist literature, and discourages interaction with Western society in general. As Eric Brown has observed, "although some mainstream Islamists pepper their politics with salutary declarations about the benefits of

democracy, equality and human rights, it's clear that many do not juris-
tically or ideologically accept the sovereignty of Western liberal government."[2] The purpose of Saudi-backed *da'wa* in the West, according
to Sheikh Yusuf al-Qaradawi—an "intellectual leader" of the Muslim
Brotherhood, is the conquest of the West not by "the sword or armies,
but by preaching and ideology."[3]

This chapter analyzes the spread of Islamism in Britain, where the
threat of homegrown Islamic terrorism placed a spotlight on the spread
of Islamist ideologies among Britain's immigrant communities. After
decades of British preoccupation with Irish Republican Army (IRA)
terrorism in Northern Ireland, the attacks of 9/11 and the London suicide bombings of July 2005, undertaken by British-born Muslims and
resulting in the deaths of fifty-two civilians, drove an urgent shift of
focus toward minority Muslim communities in Britain and the ideologies and connections that led to this act of terror on British soil.

While it is difficult to present an exhaustive picture of Islamist proselytization in Britain, the following section will address the questions of
why and how Islamist ideologies have taken root in Britain. Subsequent
sections will describe the historical and political context of the supply
of Islamism in Britain, external financial suppliers who supported the
ideology in the United Kingdom, how they supported the establishment
and activities of various organizations, and how the support promoted
Islamist ideologies throughout religious, educational, and media institutions. Again, the ties to terrorism will be highlighted throughout.

HISTORICAL AND POLITICAL CONTEXT

The history of Islam in Britain is mainly one of modern immigration,
with the majority of the contemporary Muslim population comprising
people who immigrated to Britain between 1950 and 1970 and their
descendants. During the first part of the twentieth century it was estimated that there were around ten thousand Muslims in Britain. By
2009 there were one million to two million, or around 2 to 4 percent
of the population.[4]

The first significant group of Muslims to immigrate to the United Kingdom were sailors who arrived from India in the 1700s to work for the British East India Company. The next wave of Muslim immigration to Britain came mostly from Yemen following the opening of the Suez Canal in 1869, as Aden was a key refueling stop for ships traveling between Britain and East Asia via the canal. Yemeni immigrants and their descendants are now one of the longest-established Muslim communities in Britain, with an estimated eighty thousand Yemenis living in Britain by 2009.[5]

Most immigrants to the United Kingdom have come from former British colonies, and by far the largest influx of Muslims into Britain occurred from the 1950s to 1970s as former colonies gained their independence. These immigrants came mostly from the Indian subcontinent—India, Pakistan, and what is now Bangladesh. Turkish Cypriots came between 1950 and 1970, fleeing the civil unrest that was taking place toward the end of British rule. After two generations, there are now around 300,000 Turkish Cypriots in the United Kingdom.[6] The next wave of immigration came from Africa, particularly Kenya and Uganda, although Muslim students also came from the West Indies, Trinidad and Tobago, and Guyana, with many choosing to stay in Britain after their studies were completed.[7] Political disruption in East and North Africa in the 1980s and 1990s led to another wave of Muslim migrants and refugees, including a substantial number from Somalia.

The Arab Muslim communities in Britain are smaller than and not as established as those from Asia and Africa. The majority are students and businesspersons who do not relocate permanently to Britain but spend several months at a time in the country. As an illustration, the Home Office estimated in 2000 that around sixty-three thousand Saudis visited Britain temporarily each year.[8] The high oil prices of the 1970s did facilitate the arrival of more wealthy Arabs, from countries such as Saudi Arabia, Syria, Lebanon, Egypt, Palestine, Jordan, and the Gulf states, who saw their investments as more secure in Britain. Therefore, in comparison to earlier waves of migrants, those coming from the Middle East in the latter part of the twentieth century were often skilled migrants from middle- or high-income families.[9] Violence across the Middle East also spurred many media outlets to move their offices to London (as discussed later in this chapter).[10]

According to the 2011 census in the United Kingdom, Muslims constitute the second-largest religious group in Britain.[11] Almost 50 percent of the Muslim population resides in or around London, with Muslims totaling 12.4 percent of city inhabitants. The London suburb of Tower Hamlets boasts the highest population of Muslims, at 34.5 percent (more than seven times the total UK percentage), and also the highest population growth, at 26 percent. Muslim immigrants have been concentrated within urban communities since the 1960s, as male migrant workers shared dwellings and established local communities before their wives and families arrived, swelling populations within those communities. There is also some evidence of discrimination by public housing authorities that persisted for decades and further contributed to the segregation of Muslim communities in Britain.[12]

As well as being the second-largest religious group in the United Kingdom, Muslims are also the fastest growing (aside from those identifying with no religion), moving from 3 percent to 4.8 percent of the population in the decade between 2001 and 2011.[13] The 2001 census showed Britain's Muslims to be a very young group, with one-third of Muslims being under sixteen years of age and 50 percent under twenty-five. The majority of these are second- and third-generation British Muslims, while another significant portion are refugees and asylum seekers.[14] The United Kingdom is also seeing an increasing number of Muslim converts. A 2011 survey by Kevin Brice from Swansea University in Wales found that the number of British converts to Islam had recently passed the one hundred thousand mark—twice as many as there were in 2001—with as many as five thousand new conversions annually.[15]

In terms of health, education, and socioeconomic status, the 2001 census revealed that 20 percent of sixteen-to-twenty-four-year-old Muslims were unemployed; 16 percent of Muslim women and 13 percent of Muslim men reported poor health (more than any other religious group); and 31 percent of Muslims left school with no qualifications (compared to 15 percent of the total population). Politically, after the elections in 2010 the number of Muslim members of Parliament doubled from four to eight, although in proportion to their population Muslims remain underrepresented.

While it is easy to speak of the Muslim community in Britain as if it were a monolithic entity, the history of immigration reveals wide variations in nationality, ethnicity, language, and culture that preclude easy characterizations. As Innes Bowen reports, Muslims in Britain subscribe to all manner of interpretations of Islam, from Deobandi to Salafi, and from Barelvi to Shia.[16] Despite these differences, suggests Humayun Ansari, Minority Rights Group International believes that Islam in Britain "has played a cohesive role among many Muslim workers since it transcended ethnic, linguistic and political frontiers, and stimulated a sense of identity that ignored doctrinal and other differences." This was particularly true in the early 1960s as Muslim immigration to Britain swelled. Twenty years later, at the end of the immigration bubble, various Islamic communities had emerged, and each had established mosques and "organizations that bore their own particular national, ethnic, linguistic and doctrinal imprint." As Ansari has observed, these bodies were concerned primarily with "the promotion of religious life, the provision of assistance and moral support, and the improvement of social, cultural and educational conditions," and from the mid-1980s British Muslims "became more effectively organized in their dealings with local government and other areas of public life."[17]

By the mid-1990s, although Muslims in Britain were still geographically segregated and economically disadvantaged, there had been a significant increase in participation and visibility in public and political life. New umbrella organizations had been established that were centered on Islam, rather than ethnicity, as a unifier. Despite embracing different ideological strands and interests, these umbrella organizations sought to function as national representatives of Britain's Muslim communities.[18] One of these umbrella organizations is the Muslim Council of Britain, which now boasts more than five hundred affiliate bodies (national, regional, and local organizations, mosques, charities, and schools).[19] Many of these umbrella organizations, however, are linked to influential ideological movements; for example, the Muslim Council of Britain is linked to Jamaat-e-Islami (discussed later).

As with other Muslim-majority countries and those with large Muslim minorities, Britain was impacted by both the 1979 Iranian Revolution and the war against Soviet occupation in Afghanistan. During this time Saudi Arabia and Britain shared the common goal of ousting the Soviet Union from Afghanistan, utilizing local militias supplemented with foreign fighters, including from Britain. According to Madawi Al-Rasheed, "Common political goals between Britain and Saudi Arabia meant that Saudi emissaries to British Muslims were tolerated. They were given clearance to enter the UK and an almost free hand to preach the call for *jihad*, in the process recruiting young British Muslims for the war in Afghanistan."[20] At the same time, the Islamic revolution in Iran provided an inspirational political ideology for Muslim minorities in Britain who, according to the author of *Londonistan*, Melanie Phillips, "felt estranged from British secular society and were looking for a cause that would cement their identity."[21]

Toward the end of the war in Afghanistan, the publication of Salman Rushdie's *The Satanic Verses* in Britain revealed fissures between the Muslim and mainstream communities, highlighting Britain as a front in the struggle between Iran and Saudi Arabia for supremacy over the global *ummah* (community of Muslims). Certain elements of the book were considered blasphemous by many Muslims, and the book's 1988 release sparked violent protests in the United Kingdom.[22] These were centered in the town of Bradford, where crowds of Muslims burned copies of the book on international television. Multiple bookstores were bombed in London, and unexploded devices were found in several more across the United Kingdom. The secretary of the Bradford

Council of Mosques, Sayed Abdul Quddus, claimed that Rushdie had "tortured Islam" and should be hanged.[23]

The book's release served as a lightning rod for wider discontent among Muslims regarding Western values in Britain (or a perceived lack thereof). Analyzing the response by British Muslims, Gilles Kepel suggested that the political, cultural, and economic context for immigrants in Britain had led to a distinct Islamic identity not seen elsewhere in Europe, and it was an assertion of this identity that was on display in the public reactions to *The Satanic Verses*.[24] According to Kepel, "The roots of the Rushdie affair go right back to the first time in history when Islam had to face both the situation of being in a minority and a loss of power: in the British Empire of the Indies. It was then that, in the face of this unprecedented challenge, Islamic modes of resistance against the onslaught of foreign modernity were developed; decades later, they were transposed almost intact onto the situation in the Muslim districts of British industrial cities."[25]

Capitalizing on Muslim reactions to the book, the Supreme Leader of Iran, Ayatollah Khomeini, issued a fatwa in 1989 calling for the death of Rushdie and his publishers, sending the author into hiding. Khomeini's fatwa was issued—some would say deliberately—only one day before the official announcement of the Soviet withdrawal from Afghanistan. Thus, the success of Saudi Arabia and other allies in Afghanistan was lost in the coverage of the fatwa, particularly in Britain. The fatwa furthered the Iranian-Saudi rivalry because Khomeini "became the unchallenged champion of all those Muslims disgusted by what they perceived as Riyadh's spinelessness."[26]

Hot on the heels of the Rushdie affair, the 1990–91 invasion of Kuwait and Gulf War further affected the Saudi reputation among British Muslims after the Saudi kingdom allowed foreign troops into the country for the purpose of liberating Kuwait. Then the Bosnian war between 1992 and 1995 provided images of European Muslims being massacred, further inflaming British Muslims and sparking a wave of fundraising and recruitment for jihad.[27] In an obituary for Kalim Siddiqui, founder of the Muslim Parliament of Britain and a vocal supporter of the Rushdie fatwa, Jorgen Nielsen has suggested that the ideologue "sailed close to the legal wind" when he began collecting money to buy weapons for the struggle in Bosnia.[28]

As Madawi Al-Rasheed notes, Saudi Arabia's alignment with the United States during the Gulf War led to "the crystallization of a Saudi Islamist opposition whose outspoken members took refuge in London after being subjected to interrogation, harassment and imprisonment in Saudi Arabia."[29] Some of these opposition leaders have played a prominent role in spreading Islamist thought in Britain. For example, Mohamed al-Masari, who was granted asylum in the United Kingdom in 1994, went on to run the Committee for the Defense of Legitimate Rights (CDLR) in Britain, claiming in 2004 that it was the "ideological voice" of al-Qaeda.[30]

Around the same time, Islamist asylum seekers from North Africa were arriving in Britain, many having fought the Soviets in Afghanistan. They joined an existing pool of Saudi dissidents and opposition figures from other Arab countries. Reda Hussaine, recruited by French and British intelligence services to provide information on Algerian radicals in London, has alleged that "thousands and thousands" of Algerian Islamists were granted asylum in Britain beginning in the mid-1990s, and then "dozens of jihadis started to arrive every week, to raise money, make propaganda."[31] Even the founder of Islamist groups Hizb ut-Tahrir and al-Muhajiroun in Britain, Omar Bakri Muhammed, observed in 2005 that "Britain is harbouring most of the Islamic opposition leaders of the Muslim world."[32]

SUPPLIERS

The supply of Islamism is a complicated picture in Britain. Along with the Saudi (and to a lesser extent the Iranian) government, exiled dissidents and opposition leaders, former mujahedeen, and wealthy individuals from the Gulf region have all been part of the patchwork of interested parties who have supported the spread of Islamist thought in the country. Getting an accurate picture of the flow of funding to support Islamist ideologies in Britain is a difficult task, as most of this information is not made public or is deliberately masked. Indications of the scale of funding from the Gulf region can be pieced together, however, by examining the main suppliers in Britain and the influence they have in the country.

As with other countries examined here, one of the main vehicles for disseminating Saudi funding support in Britain is the Muslim World League (MWL). The website of the London office of the Muslim World League outlines its vision there as "integrating efforts in education and introducing Islam" by organizing "conferences, symposia and various cultural events open to faith and non-faith groups and to the British society at large."[33]

A reporter for the Channel 4 program *Dispatches*, for an episode called "Undercover Mosque," visited the office of the MWL in London, where an imam confirmed the literature they disseminated was from the Muslim World League and the World Assembly of Muslim Youth (WAMY) in Saudi Arabia, as well as the Saudi Ministry of Islamic Affairs. This included works by Sheikh Abdul Aziz bin Abdullah bin Baz, the Grand Mufti in Saudi Arabia until his death in 1999, that advocated for jihad and the strict implementation of sharia, including the killing of Muslims who support homosexuality. The London office of the MWL also disseminated copies of the Quran from Saudi Arabia that contain explanatory footnotes indicating that certain verses that encourage peace and tolerance are no longer applicable, as well as other notes explicitly advocating segregation from non-Muslims.[34]

A 2007 investigation into "extremist literature" in British mosques by the Policy Exchange think tank found that the MWL branch in London was "one of the major providers" of Islamist material encountered during its investigation of almost one hundred mosques and Islamic centers across the United Kingdom. The report emphasized the fact that much of the material recovered from mosques, schools, and Islamic centers—ranging from radical to simply conservative—was connected in some way with Saudi Arabia, "whether by virtue of being written by members of the Wahhabite religious establishment; being published and distributed by official, or semi-official Saudi institutions; or being found in Saudi-funded, or linked, mosques and schools."[35]

Saudi funding does not simply support literature within mosques, cultural centers, and schools. It also extends to the provision of personnel for these institutions. As Madawi Al-Rasheed has noted, "Since the 1980s more Saudis are occupying key posts in mosques and other religious centres due to the lack of indigenous specialists. They work as directors, mosque imams, Arabic languages instructors and religious educators in the various Saudi-sponsored schools, colleges and organizations in the British capital, and tend to be seconded from Saudi institutions and universities. Many hold 'diplomatic status' which makes them invisible in British labour force surveys."[36]

Saudi Arabia has relied on other members of the Muslim community in Britain, particularly those aligned with the Muslim Brotherhood but also other groups that adhere to similar—if not identical—ideologies. Thus, Saudi influence in Britain is rendered even more opaque by the fact that it is often other members of the Muslim community who serve as mediators of the Saudi supply chain. As Al-Rasheed also observes, "While Iraq, Palestinian and Lebanese immigrants negotiate Saudi economic and media interests, Egyptians and Pakistanis promote Saudi religious transnationalism in the British capital. Saudi-funded religious institutions employ Egyptian and Pakistani directors, preachers, teachers and Arabic language instructors."[37]

Beyond literature and personnel, Saudi funding has provided critical support to the establishment of new mosques, Islamic centers, and schools. The Center for Religious Freedom has estimated that worldwide, between 1982 and 2002, 1,500 mosques, 210 Islamic centers, 202 colleges, and 2,000 schools were built with Saudi money in non-Muslim countries alone.[38] In Britain this investment can be seen through the registration of new mosques, the number of which began skyrocketing in the mid-1970s. In 1967 there were only four purpose-built (new construction) mosques in Britain. As of 2012 there were around 200 purpose-built mosques out of an estimated 1,500 mosques in Britain, with the remainder being converted houses or other nonresidential conversions.[39] As Madawi Al-Rasheed has noted, "notwithstanding the difficulty in estimating Saudi funding, it is clear that in Britain the number of annual mosque registrations grew suddenly between three and fourfold after 1974. While the extent of Saudi funding remains a matter of speculation, the rise in the number of mosques in Britain was related to the Saudi oil boom of the early 1970s."[40]

The supply of Islamism also comes from individuals and nongovernmental organizations in Saudi Arabia and the Gulf region, which can be even harder to track. Individual donations from princes, business leaders, and charities are channeled to British Muslims as gifts or grants to mosques, schools, and cultural centers. According to Al-Rasheed, some of those donations for "prestigious and highly visible projects" are highlighted in official Saudi publications, but donations for less prestigious organizations "tend to be covert, as they pass through personal networks and connections, which people are reluctant to disclose." Al-Rasheed suggests that British Muslims are more likely to disclose Saudi funding of programs "when things go wrong," citing the example of Sheikh Zaki Badawi, principal of the Islamic College, who was willing to discuss "Saudi control over British Islam and the funds dedicated to the purpose" only after he became independent of their patronage. Compounding this code of silence, the literature and research available on Muslims in Britain tends to avoid the issue of Saudi funding support, or, when it does touch on the subject, there is in many cases a tendency to either exaggerate or minimize its magnitude.[41]

ORGANIZATIONS

Organizations focused on political Islam or Islamism began proliferating in the United Kingdom in the 1980s and 1990s, particularly following the Rushdie affair in the late 1980s. The roots of most of these organizations can be traced to several key Islamist movements emanating from Saudi Arabia and South Asia.

One of the key pan-Islamic movements that has given rise to Islamist organizations in the United Kingdom is the Muslim Brotherhood (MB), whose leaders are closely tied to Saudi Arabia (both ideologically and financially) as a result of being exiled there from Egypt in the 1950s. According to the Pew Research Center, "About 400 mosques and prayer spaces in Europe were said to be at least indirectly associated with the Muslim Brotherhood as of 2008."[42] The key MB-affiliated organization in Britain is the Muslim Association of Britain (MAB), established in 1997 by Kemal el-Helbawy, a former member of the Central Guidance Bureau of Egypt's Muslim Brotherhood and the first executive director of the Saudi-sponsored World Assembly of Muslim Youth (WAMY).[43] Pew reported that "Rachid Ghannouchi, the exiled leader of Tunisia's Islamist party and a major intellectual figure in global Brotherhood circles, also lives in London and is associated with the MAB."[44] The Muslim Association of Britain gained public attention during Britain's anti–Iraq War movement, which allowed it to capitalize on broad public opposition to the Iraq War to increase its own profile, condemn Western governments, and push for other Muslim causes: "MAB's involvement with anti–Iraq war campaigning, defense of the right to wear the *hijab* (veil), Palestine, and its close association with the revolutionary leftist Respect political party founded by former Labour MP George Galloway, provide it with opportunities to influence discourse within the Muslim community, particularly among the young. It has used this influence to exert a malign influence on what had been growing Muslim-Jewish contacts in Britain prior to 9/11."[45]

MAB has eleven branches in the United Kingdom and works closely with the Muslim Council of Britain and other Muslim Brotherhood–linked organizations in Europe through the Federation of Islamic Organizations of Europe.[46] In 2005 an offshoot of MAB was established—the British Muslim Initiative (BMI), a political activism group that in 2006 and 2008 ran an "Islam Expo" funded by the government of Qatar.

BMI is led by Muhammad Kazem Rashid Maruf Sawalha, a former senior Hamas activist and former leader of MAB. Sawalha, along with Tunisian Islamist Rachid Ghannouchi and Daud Abdullah, a graduate of King Saud University in Saudi Arabia and deputy director-general of the Muslim Council of Britain (MCB), came under scrutiny in 2009 after advocating attacks on the British navy if it tried to stop arms for Hamas from being smuggled into Gaza. This prompted the director of the Center for Islamic Pluralism to suggest that "the British government should stop funding organisations such as the MCB and supporting events such as Islam Expo, which hosts scholars from Saudi Arabia and Pakistan who hold extremist views."[47]

A movement that has had a trajectory similar to that of the Muslim Brotherhood in Britain is Jamaat-e-Islami (JI), with both groups squarely adhering to an Islamist ideology that calls for the establishment of a distinctly Islamic system of government following sharia law. The establishment of the first formal Jamaat-e-Islami–affiliated organizations in Britain, the UK Islamic Mission and its affiliate, Dawatul Islam, took place in the 1960s. These groups are still active, "promoting Islamic education with a particular emphasis on Jamaat-e-Islami thinkers and perspectives."[48] In addition, Jamaat-e-Islami established the Islamic Foundation as a research body in Leicester in 1990, the associated Markfield Institute as a seat of higher learning in 2000, and Kube Publishing as a media arm in 2007.[49] Other bodies in the United Kingdom affiliated with—or arising out of—Jamaat-e-Islami include the Islamic Forum Europe (IFE), the Islamic Society of Britain (ISB), the Islamic Foundation, Young Muslims UK, the Young Muslim Organization UK (YMO), the UK Islamic Mission (UKIM), Muslim Aid, and the Muslim Council of Britain (MCB).[50] The MCB was formed as an umbrella organization in 1997 at the request of Tory home secretary Michael Howard and is designed to represent all British Muslims, despite the presence of a number of Islamists in its ranks.[51] These groups are not always in agreement and can operate with varying degrees of activism, but all follow an Islamist ideology based on the writings of Abdul A'la Mawdudi, founder of JI.

Author and former self-identified British Islamist Ed Husain claimed in his personal account of involvement with the Islamist groups YMO, Hizb ut-Tahrir, and ISB that the East London Mosque was controlled by the Bangladeshi wing of Jamaat-e-Islami and that the mosque served as a gateway to extremism.[52] The now-defunct British organization Awaaz noted in a 2006 South Asia Watch report that the ideology taught at the East London Mosque revealed a "noticeable convergence of JI political ideology and authoritarian forms of salafi theology."[53] Elaborating on this "convergence," the Awaaz report noted the considerable overlap and cooperation between Jamaat-e-Islami and Muslim Brotherhood personnel and other "Salafi-Wahhabi organizations and networks" in Britain supported by Saudi Arabia:

> The JI and MB, under independent and official Saudi and gulf patronage, effectively operate under a division of labour globally regarding their respective spheres of influence. Usually, the JI and MB act in concert with each other and in a complementary way. Individuals from both also work together under a single group, as in the case of several UK organizations. It is not at all unusual to find, for example, a JI-controlled "centre," with strong MB representation in its management (as well as some Deobandi representation). The centre may have extensive Saudi funding, employs a Wahhabi-Salafi (inevitably Saudi approved) cleric for mosque or religious functions, runs Salafi study circles for young people (a key inculcation strategy), houses a fundraising charity run by the JI or MB, has a youth branch, receives local authority funding and support, and is considered "moderate" and "representative" by the public sector.[54]

As an example, Awaaz noted that individuals involved in the World Assembly of Muslim Youth (WAMY) in Britain may also be involved in the Muslim Brotherhood, the Muslim Council of Britain, and the

Muslim Association of Britain and could also work with other Jamaat-e-Islami organizations.

Beyond JI and MB, Sadek Hamid has identified the Jamiyyat Ihya Minhaj as Sunnah organization (JIMAS, or Society for the Revival of the Prophetic Way), led by Manwar Ali, as "instrumental" to "the spread of Salafism in the UK." This spread, he claims, was "underwritten by the financial investment into religious institutions and distribution of literature from Saudi Arabia and the return of religious studies graduates from Saudi Arabia's two main universities."[55] JIMAS adheres to a strict Salafist ideology and seeks to engage Muslims in Britain at the grassroots level, connecting local grievances with pan-Islamic issues. A former member of JIMAS, Usama Hassan, recalls the organization promoting a "sense of being under siege. It was all a conspiracy against Islam, and we were the guardians of Islam. That's how we saw ourselves."[56] Hassan came to Britain in the mid-1970s after his Pakistani father was sent there by the Saudi Ministry of Religious Affairs to lead a Saudi-funded Wahhabi mosque in Leyton. Hassan spent time in a training camp in Afghanistan in 1990 and later recruited mujahedeen to fight in Afghanistan and Bosnia; one of his recruits was Omar Sheikh (later convicted of beheading journalist Daniel Pearl), whom Hassan met at a JIMAS study circle. After the Gulf War brought American troops to Saudi Arabia, JIMAS split along ideological lines, with Abdul Wahid leading a breakaway faction called the Organization of Ahl al Sunnah Islamic Societies (OASIS), which retained a pro-Saudi stance and became known for its "intolerant and polemical attitude to former colleagues and other Muslim groups."[57] OASIS also established the Salafi Institute in Birmingham.[58]

Markazi Jamiat Ahle-Hadith (or simply Ahle Hadith) is another key Salafi organization in Britain, centered at the Green Lane Mosque in Birmingham, with more than forty Ahle Hadith branches throughout England, as well as two based in Scotland.[59] The movement is allegedly funded by Saudi Arabia and linked to various madrasas and training camps in Pakistan and Kashmir.[60] The Green Lane Mosque was highlighted by Channel 4's *Dispatches* exposé "Undercover Mosque," which revealed sermons encouraging the beating of women and capital punishment for homosexuals. The 2007 Policy Exchange investigation also found at the Green Lane Mosque examples of Saudi literature that outlined "Wahhabite belief."[61]

The UK branch of the global Islamist organization Hizb ut-Tahrir (HT, Liberation Party) was established in 1986. As discussed earlier, HT operates as a pan-Islamic political party that seeks the establishment of a Muslim caliphate governed by sharia law, and it has spread to almost forty countries, though it has been banned from operating in many of these, including some in the Middle East, North Africa, Central and South Asia, and a number of Western countries. Then-UK prime minister Tony Blair sought to ban the organization in Britain following the 7/7 bombings in London in 2005, but this effort was later dropped, apparently for lack of evidence to proscribe the group and because of fears the move would serve as a recruiting tool for HT.[62] Britain's National Union of Students has banned the organization, although there is little evidence to suggest that this has prevented HT activities on university campuses. Other countries have criticized Britain's failure to ban the activities of the organization. The lack of such a ban has allowed HT to grow to the point that the UK is now considered the global operating headquarters of Hizb ut-Tahrir. Even the *Daily Times* in Pakistan has reported that "the most lethal British export to Pakistan and elsewhere in the region is Hizb-al-Tahrir, an organisation banned in Pakistan for seeking to overthrow democracy and replace it with khilafat. Al Tahrir is an example of the 'zone of contact' that exists in the UK between Pakistanis and the Salafi Arab ideologues."[63]

The British wing of HT was co-founded by Omar Bakri Muhammed when he came to the United Kingdom in 1986 after having been expelled from Saudi Arabia. Bakri studied at the Islamic School of al-Saltiyah in Mecca and is committed to an Islamist ideology inspired by Salafism.[64] In a 2005 interview Bakri asserted that "when I first came to Britain, half of me was Ikhwani-Jihadi and the other half was Salafi-Tahriri[;]

in short, I was a combination of different modes of knowledge and I channeled all this energy into developing networks here in the UK."[65] Bakri founded the Saudi wing of HT in Mecca on March 3, 1983, the fifty-ninth anniversary of the destruction of the Ottoman Caliphate.[66] Bakri had previously been associated with the Muslim Brotherhood, having joined that organization at a young age in Syria and studying with them for several years prior to joining Hizb ut-Tahrir in Lebanon. Bakri has also previously presented himself as the spokesperson of the International Islamic Front, which he has described as the "political wing" of al-Qaeda.[67] Despite having been expelled from Saudi Arabia, Bakri remained influenced by Salafi-Wahhabi thought and retained close ties to the country after his expulsion: "I contacted my brothers in Saudi Arabia and instructed them to pursue their underground activities as part of the global HT network."[68]

A former prominent HT member in Britain, Maajid Nawaz, recalls being recruited to HT by its promises of an alternative identity. He quickly became involved in HT's "extensive" recruitment activities in Britain. Nawaz was sent by the organization to Newham College in London to recruit young people to the HT cause. He became president of the college's student union: "I knew exactly how to manipulate their grievances. And I did it. We took over that college."[69] Another British former HT member, Usman Raja, who "begged to become a suicide bomber" in the mid-1990s, revealed that many of HT's activities are underpinned by Wahhabi teaching: "Saudi literature is everywhere in Britain, and it's free. When I started exploring my Muslim identity ... all the books were Saudi. In the bookshops, in the libraries, all of them. . . . I could go and get a car, open the boot up, and get it filled up with free literature from the Saudis, saying exactly what I believed. Who can compete with that?"[70] Estimates of active HT membership in Britain vary widely, from five hundred to eight thousand members at different times. An estimated six thousand to seven thousand people attended the HT-hosted Are You British or Are You Muslim? conference in London in 2003.[71]

Al-Muhajiroun (The Emigrants) is an organization with goals very similar to those of HT, having been founded by Omar Bakri Muhammed after his falling out with HT in Britain. When asked about his motivations for establishing al-Muhajiroun, Bakri Muhammed said, "I had worked hard for three years to build a platform for HT in Saudi Arabia, and the upper echelons of [HT] did not appreciate these efforts. From an Islamic perspective, I had no choice but to organize the dedicated cadres I had built up under the aegis of Jamaat al-Muhajiroun." Speaking about the membership of al-Muhajiroun, Bakri has asserted that "anybody who does not follow the path of the Salaf cannot join al-Muhajiroun." The organization relies heavily on funding from Muslim businessmen "here and abroad," according to Bakri.[72] Al-Muhajiroun has both a proselytization and a jihadi network and, like HT, is banned from university campuses in the United Kingdom but uses a variety of names and front groups to gain access.[73] This includes Al Ghurabaa (The Strangers), al-Firqat un-Naajiyah (the Savior Sect or Saved Sect), and Ahlus Sunna wal Jama'aah (ASWJ).[74] Al-Muhajiroun was dissolved in 2004 by Bakri, who left the country shortly thereafter for Lebanon. Successor groups, including the Savior Sect, Al Ghurabaa, ASWJ, Islam4UK, and Muslims against Crusades, have continued Bakri's work under the leadership of Bakri's protégé, the radical cleric Anjem Choudary, who is active in Britain.[75]

Al-Muhajiroun re-formed in 2009 after leading ASWJ members were released from prison, but it was subsequently proscribed in January 2010 under the Terrorism Act 2000, as was Islam4UK. This followed on from the proscription of Al Ghurabaa and the Savior Sect in 2006, although evidence suggests al-Muhajiroun–linked members and groups are still active.[76] A 2005 study of the group found that al-Muhajiroun had more than fifty fronts or platforms under which it operated, with Choudary himself acknowledging "we use different platforms depending on what we are dealing with" and that "the important thing is not the name, the important thing is that you plant the seeds in the hearts of the people." These platforms continue to proliferate; a 2010 study identified a number of them, including the Salafi Youth Movement, Salafi Media,

London School of Shari'ah, the Global Issues Society, Islamic Da'wah Foundation, London Da'wah, Submit2Allah, Tayfatul Mansoorah, Mansoor Media, London Da'wah, and the Path to Tawheed.[77] Bakri claimed that he still has "influence" in Britain, providing teaching and advice via Choudary and through online Skype classes. Michael Olumide Adebolajo, a suspect in the murder of British military officer Lee Rigby in May 2013, is alleged to have attended events by al-Muhajiroun and successor groups.[78] A study by the Henry Jackson Society, a counterextremism think tank, found that in the twelve years leading up to the proscription of al-Muhajiroun, one in five people convicted of Islamist-related terrorism offenses in the United Kingdom had links to al-Muhajiroun or its offshoots.[79]

The Tablighi Jamaat (Society for Spreading Faith) is another large Islamist organization active in Britain. The movement was founded in India in the 1920s as a response to Hindu proselytizing and gained a large following in the Indian subcontinent, continuing to expand in both India and Pakistan after Partition. Theologically, the Tablighi movement is closely related to Deobandism, a conservative school of Sunni Islam that emphasizes religious orthodoxy and personal piety and exclusion. While the Tablighi and Deobandi movements originated in India, they are closely aligned with the Wahhabi and Salafi schools of thought emanating from Saudi Arabia. They have also been closely linked to the Pakistani Taliban, and some "Tablighi Jamaat leaders from South Asia have been linked to some of the same networks as Taliban scholars."[80] A former member of the movement, Farad Esack, has observed that Tablighi Jamaat members in Pakistan were drawn to the Taliban because Tablighi Jamaat "attracts angry people—people who need absolutes, who can't stand the grayness of life," which in turn "lends itself to being recruited by a Taliban-type project."[81] As Khaled Abou El Fadl has observed, "militants exploit the alienated and withdrawn social attitude created by the Tablighis by fishing in the Tablighi pond."[82]

Given the geographical roots of the movement in the Indian subcontinent and the large South Asian diaspora in the United Kingdom,

Tablighi Jamaat has significant influence across Britain. As evidence of this, a large Tablighi complex was established in Dewsbury and functions as a regional European headquarters, coordinating Tablighi activities throughout northern Europe. The headquarters, directed by Maulana Hafiz Patel, was built in 1978 with funds from the Saudi-backed Muslim World League. The leader of the 2005 London bombing plot, Mohammed Siddique Khan, has been linked to the Dewsbury mosque.[83] In addition, according to the Pew Research Center, the British shoe bomber Richard Reid and the American Taliban member John Walker Lindh, captured by U.S. forces with Taliban soldiers in Afghanistan in 2001, had both "spent time in Tablighi circles."[84] In 2012 the organization developed plans "to build a mosque on a site in West Ham, close to the Olympic Park, to accommodate more than 9,000 worshippers, which *The Independent* estimated to be about four times the capacity of St Paul's [Cathedral in London]. If the plans were approved, the building would place the site on a par with Morden's Baitul Futuh [London], the largest mosque in Western Europe." Furthermore, while the plans indicate the significant following Tablighi Jamaat has in Britain, the Newham Council rejected the mosque proposal on the grounds that it was "too big."[85]

Ansar al-Sharia (Supporters of Sharia) is an Islamist organization that was closely aligned with the Finsbury Park Mosque in London before being banned from that mosque. The group was led by the infamous hook-handed imam of Finsbury Park, Abu Hamza al-Masri. In the 1990s Hamza, along with his teacher, the radical cleric Abu Qatada, were considered propagandists for the Algerian terrorist group Groupe Islamique Armé (GIA, or Armed Islamic Group). Qatada arrived in Britain in 1993 and was granted asylum. He has been described as Osama bin Laden's "spiritual ambassador in Europe" and has been detained for almost nine years in the United Kingdom but never prosecuted, despite the Jordanian government having convicted him in absentia in 2009 for terrorism offenses.[86] Along with his association with the Finsbury Park Mosque, Qatada operated from the Four Feathers Social

Club on Baker Street in London and focused on teaching "a handpicked few . . . an elite hardcore of activists."[87] Britain worked for several years to deport Qatada to Jordan and in June 2013 approved a treaty with Jordan that paved the way for his expulsion from the United Kingdom in July 2013.[88] Hamza came to Britain from Egypt in 1979 on a student visa and became acquainted with Islamism after meeting radical Palestinian cleric Sheikh Abdullah Azzam during his pilgrimage to Mecca in 1987. He was among a group of "hard-liners" at the Regents Park Mosque in the 1990s, before he left to spend time in Afghanistan and Bosnia in the mid-1990s. He returned in 1995 and "launched himself like a hurricane on the Islamic circuit," beginning at a small mosque in Luton where a group of "jihad veterans" gathered and then moving on to the Finsbury Park Mosque.[89] Hamza was eventually convicted in the United Kingdom in 2006 of offenses under the Terrorism Act 2000 and other statutes, and he was extradited to the United States in 2012 to face a number of terror charges. Along with Bakri, Qatada and Hamza formed what foreign security agencies have dubbed "Londonistan's unholy trinity."[90] While being aligned to groups such as al-Muhajiroun and Ansar al-Sharia, all three traveled and spoke widely at mosques, conferences, and universities across the United Kingdom and were influential in spreading an Islamist ideology through Muslim communities in Britain.

Islamist organizations have also been established by Saudi dissidents in Britain. Mohamed al-Masari and Saad al-Faqih were granted asylum in the United Kingdom in 1994 after claiming they had been subjected to persecution by the Saudi government. The two dissidents went on to establish the Committee for the Defense of Legitimate Rights (CDLR) in Britain. Al-Masari and al-Faqih parted ways in 1996, which al-Faqih claims was due to al-Masari shifting CDLR from its previous basic principles of renouncing violence and avoiding pan-Islamic issues. Al-Masari went on to claim in 2004 that the CDLR was the "ideological voice" of al-Qaeda. Al-Faqih, meanwhile, established the Movement for Islamic Reform in Arabia (MIRA), which is focused on replacing the

House of Saud with a popularly elected government.[91] In December 2004 the U.S. government accused al-Faqih of being affiliated with al-Qaeda, and both al-Faqih and MIRA were designated by the UN 1267 Committee. Both al-Masari and al-Faqih have been linked to the purchase of a satellite phone that was utilized by al-Qaeda bombers prior to an attack in Nairobi in 1998.[92] While the United Kingdom sought to deport al-Masari in 1996, both remain active in Britain, and al-Masari returned to the headlines in 2016 in connection with an alleged plot to assassinate the Saudi king.[93]

MOSQUES

The wave of Muslim immigration to Britain from the 1950s to 1970s was followed by a wave of new mosque construction or repurposing, particularly in London, where the greatest number of Muslims settled. Religious organizations can be established without any form of registration in the United Kingdom unless they are seeking a not-for-profit status, in which case they must register as a charity, which provides significant tax benefits. "As a consequence," notes one scholar, "virtually all mosques and Muslim organizations in Britain are registered charities, and this provides a measure of their growth. In 1963, 13 mosques were registered in Britain; from 1966 they began to register at an annual rate of nearly 7%; this increased to 18[%] from the mid-1970s. The last published list, for 1999, gives a total of 584 mosques in England and Wales."[94]

Architect Shahed Saleem touched on the importance of the mosque to migrant communities in Britain: "Muslim communities . . . emerged in the inner-cities of towns and cities and it is here that Muslim social and religious institutions were subsequently established. As industry declined, these Muslim communities suffered spirals of unemployment, deprivation and discrimination. As grassroots community projects within this context, mosques, apart from serving a primary religious function, have come to represent a certain empowerment of marginalised working class communities who have bypassed the establishment to fashion part of the city in their image." Thus, Saleem suggests that mosques in Britain are "intimately connected to social and cultural identities."[95] Mosques play a critical role in the day-to-day life of Muslims, much more so than Christian churches, as they provide education and welfare services and—importantly—serve as a venue for different groups who wish to use the facilities for their own activities.[96] Mosques in Britain are generally governed by a hierarchical structure comprising a board of trustees, chairman, management committee, imam(s), and members. While mosques have formal programs run by the imam and other teachers, they also host study circles, which can be run by anyone.[97] This is important to note with regard to some of the Islamist organizations identified above, some of which at different times have utilized or even infiltrated mosques to conduct their own activities but have not necessarily managed or been endorsed by the mosque in question.

The Quilliam Foundation, a counterextremism think tank established by former Islamists Ed Husain and Maajid Nawaz, undertook a survey of more than 500 mosques in Britain in 2008, with questions focused on whether they had women's facilities and classes for children and where imams were from and were trained. Among these mosques 44 percent did not include English in any aspect of their Friday sermons, and only about 10 percent had facilities for women. Out of 254 mosques that responded to polling questions regarding their imams, the survey found that 97 percent of imams came from outside Britain.[98] Religion scholar Ron Geaves suggests that foreign Islamic seminaries are not designed "for a 21st Century secular democracy like Britain, where Islam is a minority religion. . . . Imams educating in them tend to see Islam as good, and everything else as bad."[99] The Quilliam Foundation reported in 2008 that only two institutions in the United Kingdom offered graduate and postgraduate Islamic studies programs for imams: the Muslim College in London, funded by the Libya-based World Islamic Call Society; and the Markfield Institute for Higher Education in Leicestershire, funded by the Islamic Foundation, whose chairman is also the vice president of the Islamist group Jamaat-e-Islami.[100]

As indicated above, while many mosques in Britain are not "Islamist" in nature, some have been connected with the spread of Islamist ideologies. A comprehensive survey of these mosques is difficult, but it is possible to highlight some of the more prominent ones. One of the most renowned of these is the Regents Park Mosque (also known as the London Central Mosque and the Islamic Cultural Center), which was primarily funded by Saudi Arabia and run by a Saudi diplomat, Dr. Ahmed Al Dubayan. The mosque was established in 1944, and most of its funding was provided by the Egyptian government initially. This changed in the 1970s with the Saudi oil boom, after which the mosque and cultural center became, according to Madawi Al-Rasheed, "Saudi institutions in all but name." Furthermore, in 1977 Saudi Arabia rebuilt the mosque at a cost of £6 million, adding an education and cultural activities wing, and provided an additional £3.2 million for maintenance and administration.[101] Then in 1978 Dr. Zaki Badawi, seconded from the King Abd Al-Aziz University in Saudi Arabia, became the new director of the mosque, and he was succeeded in 2000 by another Saudi, Hamad al-Majid. According to Al-Rasheed, Regents Park is a repository for boxes of Qurans from the King Fahd Holy Quran Printing Complex in Medina, and "visitors to the London mosque and centre have no doubt that they are in a religious institution with close financial ties to Saudi Arabia."[102]

The Regents Park Mosque's official bookstore sells copies of fatwas delivered by religious figures from Saudi Arabia, including Bin Baz. During visits to the Regents Park Mosque in 2008, an undercover reporter found that many of the theological works being promoted came directly from the Saudi religious establishment and consequently promoted a Wahhabi ideology: "The preachers I heard in the women's section took their theology directly from Saudi Arabia. One of them had recently returned from three years of study in Saudi Arabia, and the other preachers almost exclusively directed me to the works, sermons, fatwas and online sites of the scholars of the Saudi Arabian religious establishment and their adherents." The reporter surreptitiously filmed a female teacher at the mosque conveying messages of intolerance and exclusion, including against homosexuals, for whom punishment must be to "kill them, throw them from the highest place."[103] Dr. Ghayasuddin Siddiqui, himself the leader of the Iranian-inspired Muslim Parliament of Britain and Muslim Institute, has observed that "as long as the Islamic Cultural Center in Regents Park remains in the hands of Saudis, there will never be unity among Muslims in Britain." He goes on to note that "if you are a supporter of Wahhabism, then basically there is no integration . . . no respect for the other side."[104] Siddiqui has further observed that "Saudi Arabia has immense influence in Britain through their support of mosques and imams. When the Muslim community came to this country they were not organized and they did not have enough resources, so they went to Saudi Arabia to collect funds and through that avenue they were able to influence and propagate their ideology all over this country."[105] Former Hizb ut-Tahrir member Ed Husain revealed in 2009 that despite being refused official permission for its activities in the mosque, HT had been holding study sessions at Regents Park "every weekend for over 10 years."[106]

Beyond Regents Park, Saudi Arabia went on to establish al-Muntada al-Islami in Parsons Green, London, in 1986. It consisted of a prayer hall, lecture theater, bookshop, gymnasium, guest rooms, and a school (which in 2000 had around 150 students). Madawi Al-Rasheed has observed that "reading the various publications of the centre, one has the impression of a strong association with Saudi religious associations." He further notes that al-Muntada's magazine has printed fatwas that draw heavily on opinions issued in Saudi Arabia, and the center also distributes fatwas directly from the imam of al-Furqan Mosque in Mecca.[107]

The Green Lane Mosque in Birmingham was also visited by an undercover reporter. The BBC's *Dispatches* investigative program, in a sequel to its first program on the mosque investigation, reported that "the mosque receives guidance from the Saudi religious establishment." The mosque is associated with the Salafi organization Markazi Jamiat Ahle-Hadith, which, as discussed earlier, is funded by Saudi Arabia and is an influential member of the Muslim Council of Britain. The undercover reporter visited the mosque over a period of four months and found that the main English-language preacher, Abu Usama, repeatedly spoke of Christians and Jews—and the Western countries in which they lived—as enemies of Islam and that, while he did not agree with the actions of terrorists, he felt closer to them than to non-Muslim *kafirs* (nonbelievers), whom Muslims should hate. The documentary revealed further that the Green Lane Mosque took part in direct video links with the Saudi religious establishment, including with the Grand Mufti, Abdul Aziz al-Sheikh, from whom mosque members could ask questions and receive fatwas on a variety of issues directly. Dr. Irfan Al Alawi of the Islamic Heritage Society identified Green Lane Mosque as "one of the extreme Wahhabi centers in the UK."[108]

The East London Mosque in Tower Hamlets claims a vision of providing "a range of holistic, culturally sensitive services for the communities of London, drawing on our Islamic values and heritage, with a view to improving quality of life and enhancing community cohesion." At one time it also claimed to address issues of extremism, noting that "our imams and community workers encourage constructive engagement in society and a rejection of extremism in all its forms."[109] However, according to a former member of the mosque, Ed Husain, the mosque was built with money from Saudi Arabia, received donations toward operating costs from the kingdom, and employed Saudi-trained imams. The mosque is under the control of Jamaat-e-Islami and was the site of a power struggle and financial disputes between two JI factions in the 1980s—Dawatul Islam and the Islamic Forum Europe—with leaders attracting funding "by associating themselves with Saudi Arabia's missionary arm, the Muslim World League."[110] Critically, as Husain has observed, the mosque "housed the infrastructure of activist organizations" such as Hizb ut-Tahrir.[111] Despite cooperating in various ways with the British government—to the extent of undertaking a government-subsidized expansion into the London Muslim Center in 2006—the mosque was still being chaired by a life-long devotee of Jamaat-e-Islami. In addition, the expanded center was being run by a Saudi-trained imam who prohibited gatherings of "dissenting Muslims" (those who oppose Salafi or Wahhabi thought), and the mosque bookstore sells publications by leading Wahhabi figures and containing chapter titles such as "The Virtues of Killing a Non-Believer."[112] A Channel 4 documentary in 2010, "Britain's Islamic Republic," broadcast on the *Dispatches* series, found that in the preceding few years the mosque had continued to host Islamists, in person or over video link. Among them was al-Qaeda–linked Yemeni imam Anwar al-Awlaki. Reporters sent undercover into the mosque for the documentary also found that two Islamist groups (the Islamic Forum Europe and the Young Muslims Organization UK) were thriving as part of the mosque community and holding a variety of events, camps, and training programs based on the Islamist teachings of the Jamaat-e-Islami.[113]

The United Kingdom Islamic Mission (UKIM) is another Islamic group that is well known for cooperating with the UK government and promoting tolerance and interfaith dialogue, although the Channel 4 *Dispatches* program's "Undercover Mosque" report found evidence of both Saudi financial support for some of UKIM's Islamic centers and a selection of radical preachers providing teaching at UKIM's Sparkbrook Islamic Center. The leader of the center also acknowledged that the UKIM is ideologically aligned to the Islamist group Jamaat-e-Islami, and the UKIM's website noted that it was established in 1962 by a small group from the JI-linked East London Mosque. As part of its mission, outlined on its website, the UKIM seeks to ensure that British society can be "saved from the pernicious effects of materialism and secularism."[114]

Other mosques have also played host to Islamist ideologues. The Greenwich Islamic Center went as far as seeking a court injunction to remove young extremists from the mosque who were spreading a message of "hate and intolerance" and distributing literature and videos.

Radical Islamist Omar Bakri Muhammed preached for several years at Greenwich—as well as Luton Central Mosque—under the auspices of Hizb ut-Tahrir and al-Muhajiroun. Brixton Mosque has also been identified as having "strong Wahhabi leanings."[115] The imam of Brixton Mosque, Omar Urquhart, a convert to Islam and a graduate of Saudi Arabia's Islamic University of Madinah, estimated in 2005 that 60 percent of the mosque's five hundred members were black and had converted to Islam.[116] Radical Jamaican imam Abdullah el-Faisal preached at Brixton Mosque after being sent there by Saudi religious authorities in 1991, and he later set up his own center in Tower Hamlets. He had spent seven years studying in Saudi Arabia at the Imam Muhammad ibn Saud Islamic University in Riyadh after receiving a scholarship and was found guilty in the United Kingdom in 2003 of soliciting people to murder and inciting racial hatred.[117] The Brixton Mosque adheres to a Salafist ideology and works with converts and prisoners, but its chairman, Abdul Haqq Baker, argued soon after 9/11 that the mosque was targeted by extremist groups that used its premises and surrounding halal restaurants as recruiting grounds. It has been alleged that both Richard Reid, the would-be shoe bomber, and Zacarias Moussaoui, the so-called twentieth hijacker from the 9/11 plot, attended the Brixton Mosque in the mid-1990s.[118]

One of the most infamous mosques in Britain with Islamist ties is the Finsbury Park Mosque, which has been dubbed by some a "suicide factory," given its links with prominent terrorist suspects, including some of the 7/7 bombers. Finsbury Park Mosque was constructed in the late 1980s with funding from Saudi Arabia.[119] During a raid of the mosque in 2003, police found "nuclear, biological and chemical (NBC) protective suits, blank firing weapons, a stun gun and a CS canister, [which they] suspect . . . had been [used] in terror training camps in the UK."[120] According to the authors of *The Suicide Factory*, Abu Hamza's "takeover" of the Finsbury Park Mosque was "greatly assisted by the fact that a large number of Islamist radicals—many of them veterans of the bloody conflict in Algeria—had already infiltrated the mosque."[121]

SCHOOLS AND UNIVERSITIES

The government of Saudi Arabia provides generous funding assistance to educational institutions in Britain, both secular and Muslim. The *Financial Times* reported in September 2012 that over the preceding decade the Saudi Arabian government had been "the largest source of donations from Islamic states and royal families to British universities, much of which is devoted to the study of Islam, the Middle East and Arabic literature."[122] Most of the Saudi funding has gone toward the establishment of Islamic study centers, with Cambridge and Edinburgh Universities establishing such centers after receiving £8 million apiece in 2008 from Prince Alwaleed bin Talal of the Saudi royal family. In a 2011 report titled "Keeping Britain Safe," the All-Party Parliamentary Group on Homeland Security (an unofficial grouping of MPs and peers) highlighted "significant concerns" over "unregulated foreign funding of universities, which in many cases has a political purpose and can have direct effects upon the institutional structure, curriculum and even appointments and events schedule at the recipient university."[123]

Support is also provided to British students for study abroad in Saudi Arabia. The Islamic University of Madinah reserves 85 percent of student slots for international students and attracts more than 5,000 students from 139 countries.[124] This number includes many students from the United Kingdom, and as Paul Vallely from *The Independent* has observed, "despite the fact that British students gained the reputation in Medina of being unreliable, lazy, and prone to dropping-out, there have so far been hundreds of British graduates who have returned to the UK espousing the rigid Saudi worldview."[125] Journalist Malise Ruthven suggests that this alumni network is a powerful tool in furthering Saudi Arabia's global proselytizing mission: "through informal networks of disciples and former students, Wahhabi preachers reach lay audiences that are far larger than the madrasas (seminaries) in which they teach."[126]

Evidence of the propagation of Islamist thought has been found in British schools and universities. In 2010 the BBC's *Panorama* series ran "British Schools, Islamic Rules," showing how a young Saudi researcher went undercover into a network of more than forty Muslim weekend schools and clubs and found they were teaching the official Saudi national curriculum to around five thousand pupils. The curriculum included teachings that encouraged intolerance toward non-Muslims, particularly with regard to Judaism and homosexuality. While "the Saudi government said it had no official ties to the [network] of schools and did not endorse them . . . a building in west London where *Panorama* obtained one of the textbooks is owned by the Saudi government. The director of education for the Saudi Students' Schools and Clubs said the Saudi Cultural Bureau, which is part of the embassy, had authority over the network."[127]

Saudi teaching materials are not limited to this network of schools. The King Fahad Academy in West London is an independent day school, run with the explicit support of the Saudi Arabian government and the supervision of the Saudi embassy in London. A former teacher there, Colin Cook, told Channel 4 that while he was teaching there in 1998 the school was following the same curriculum used by schools in Saudi Arabia, one based on official Saudi textbooks. He described an exercise that required children to describe the repugnant characteristics of Jews, asserting that "these books will poison the minds of anyone who reads them."[128] An investigation by the Policy Exchange think tank in 2007 found at least eight textbooks at the academy issued by the Saudi Ministry of Education with content ranging from the importance of avoiding non-Muslims to the weakness of women.[129] The influence of Islamist ideologies is not limited to the existence of Saudi textbooks in schools; it extends to the ideologies of teachers, some of whom are encouraging segregation and intolerance of non-Muslims. The producers of the second *Dispatches* episode on mosques in Britain recorded the deputy headmaster of the Islamic secondary school Darul Uloom, in Birmingham, preaching against democracy and against associating with non-Muslims.[130]

University campuses have also been highlighted as a key forum for the propagation of Islamist ideologies, and many Islamist organizations have been found to operate there, often as part of official campus Muslim student groups or councils. Tahrir Abbas has noted that "there were a number of Salafi organisations influencing impressionable minds throughout the 1990s in Britain. Organisations such as Al-Muhajiroun[,] . . . Supporters of Shariah, and HT had much success in 'infiltrating' university Islamic societies in Britain before their actions began to be viewed with suspicion."[131] The 2011 report issued by the All-Party Parliamentary Group on Homeland Security stated that "radicalization on UK campuses is a major concern" and that "some universities and colleges have become sites where extremist views and radicalization can flourish beyond the sight of academics."[132] Concern for the extent of these activities was reiterated with the arrest of Omar Farouq Abdul Muttalib, widely dubbed the "underwear bomber" after his attempted bombing of a U.S. airliner. Abdul Muttalib had been a student at the University College of London and was president of its Student Islamic Society.[133]

A 2010 report by the Center for Social Cohesion highlighted the fact that more than 30 percent of individuals involved in Islamist terrorism in the United Kingdom were university educated, and radical individuals tied to terrorist plots had been part of—or even led—their university's Islamic society. These include Yassin Nassari, former president of the University of Westminster Harrow Islamic Society before being arrested at Luton airport with a blueprint for a Hamas rocket in his luggage; Waheed Zaman, former president of the London Metropolitan University Islamic Society before conspiring in a plot to detonate a liquid bomb on a transatlantic flight; and Mohammed Naveed Bhatti, Omar Khyam, and Jawad Akbar, who all took part in prayer meetings at Brunel University and later contributed to "dirty bomb" and "fertilizer bomb" plots in the United Kingdom in 2007.[134]

Islamic societies on university campuses are active in the spread of Islamist ideology. A survey by the Center for Social Cohesion in 2008 found that active members of university Islamic societies were more than twice as likely as Muslim nonmembers to agree that it is justifiable to kill in the name of religion. In addition, active members were almost three times as likely as Muslim nonmembers to believe that apostasy should be punished according to sharia law and were twice as likely to subscribe to Islamist beliefs, support a global caliphate, and consider the wearing of hijab as part of Islam rather than personal choice.[135] Gultasab Khan, the brother of London 7/7 bomber Mohammed Siddique Khan, has observed that the older generation of Muslims—those who had immigrated to Britain—welcomed the increasing piety of their youth, with the common wisdom holding that it was "better them being Wahhabi than on drugs."[136]

The report by the Center for Social Cohesion also highlights the active presence on campuses of Islamist groups such as Hizb ut-Tahrir and al-Muhajiroun and goes on to identify a long list of "radical preachers" invited to speak to university Muslim groups between 2005 and 2010. As Sadek Hamid has observed, "HT's main site for physical recruitment is . . . still in higher education. After being banned by the National Union of Students, it created front names across the UK such as the Millennium Society, Muslim Media Forum and the 1924 Society, among many others."[137] A 2012 study by the group Student Rights found that a total of 214 university events across the United Kingdom featured known extremists; among the evidence were seventeen video clips of the late terrorist Anwar al-Awlaki. Student Rights had previously found that Islamist groups were using social networking sites to radicalize students, with "videos of armed insurgents" and "hate-filled speeches" posted on websites linked to Islamic societies at several UK universities.[138] Home Secretary Theresa May said in 2011 that university campuses in the United Kingdom were not taking the issue of radicalization seriously enough and that extremist groups could easily form groups on campus and conduct recruitment activities "without anyone knowing."[139]

MEDIA AND PUBLISHING HOUSES

Britain hosts a thriving Islamic publishing industry that produces a wide range of publications, including periodicals influenced by or expounding

Islamist ideologies. According to a media guide on Britain's Muslims published by the British Council in 2006, the United Kingdom's relaxed attitudes to censorship and press registration mean that "minority communities, non-Western organisations and non-Christian faith groups that want a global audience for their message tend to choose London as their centre of operations." Ehsan Mahsood, author of the media guide, further suggests that Muslim mass-media institutions influenced by Pakistan emerged in Britain in concert with the migration of Muslims from South Asia in the mid-twentieth century, with the aim being "to provide English speakers with an interpretation of world events (particularly developments in predominantly Muslim countries) through what was—and is—considered an authentically Muslim view."[140]

Muslim News International was one of the first of these Islamic periodicals. It was established by Ahmed Bawany in London in 1963 and was influenced by Mawdudi, the founder of Jamaat-e-Islami. The weekly periodical *Impact International* was established in 1971 by a group of young professionals with direct ties to Mawdudi, and it is still published in London. With a rapidly growing audience in the Pakistani diaspora in Britain, *The Jang* (*jang* means war, conflict, or disagreement), Pakistan's most popular Urdu-language daily newspaper, established a London edition in the 1970s. Reflecting events in South Asia, the *Agency Afghan Press* was set up in 1980, as Mahsood notes, "with a mandate to influence Western media coverage of the Soviet takeover of Afghanistan." Again, the media outlet had close links to Jamaat-e-Islami, as well as the mujahedeen alliance fighting in Afghanistan.[141]

The influence of Saudi Arabia and Iran can also be seen in the publishing industry in Britain. *Arabia: The Islamic World Review* was established in the 1980s, funded from sources in Saudi Arabia, and two magazines, *Africa Events* and *Inquiry*, were established around the same time, funded by sources in Iran. Newer periodicals have focused more on the British Muslim community, including the *Muslim News*, *Muslim Wise*, *Q News*, *Emel*, *Islamica*, and *New Civilisation*—the last a monthly political magazine published by Hizb ut-Tahrir UK. Ehsan Mahsood has observed that while these periodicals work to promote positive role models in the Muslim community, the editorial content in most, with the exception of Q News, is "low on self-criticism—a price perhaps of the close access that their writers and editors have to leading players in British (as well as international) Muslim life."[142]

The Saudi Research and Marketing Group (SRMG) describes itself as "the largest integrated publishing business in the Middle East" and has a subsidiary in the United Kingdom that publishes three Arabic-language newspapers focused on pan-Arab political affairs: *Asharq al-Awsat*, *Arrajol*, and *The Majalla*. As Melanie Phillips has observed, "London has become the most important center for Islamic thought outside the Middle East. It is home to some of the most influential Muslim and Arab research institutions, lobby groups and doctrinal groups—Sunni, Shia, Ismaili and Ahmadi—and is a world center for the Arab press, home to the newspapers *Al-Hayat* and *Al-Quds al-Arabi*, the Middle East Broadcasting Company (MBC) and a long list of specialist Islamic publications."[143] Not all of these are Islamist publications, but many have links to Islamist movements and organizations discussed earlier, particularly the Muslim Brotherhood and Jamaat-e-Islami. Other Islamist groups discussed have also put out various publications at different times, and most will record teachings by their leaders and imams for wide distribution. For example, radical clerics Abu Qatada, Abu Hamza, and Omar Bakri Muhammed all shared "a lucrative sideline" selling audiocassettes and videos of their speeches, and Qatada and Hamza both contributed regularly to *al-Ansar*, the Groupe Islamique Armé's newsletter produced, for a time, out of the Finsbury Park Mosque.[144]

Along with a thriving market of Islamic news outlets, there has been an abundance of Islamist books, CDs, and videos entering the British market and distributed for free, having been funded by the Saudis. Yahya Birt, director of the City Circle, a networking body of young Muslim professionals, suggests that Saudi Arabia has "flooded the Islamic book market with cheap well-produced Wahhabi literature whose print runs can be . . . five to 10 times that of any other British-based sectarian publication, aggressively targeted for a global English-speaking audience. This has had the effect of forcing non-Wahhabi publishers across the Muslim world to close."[145] Smaller bookshops catering to a more mainstream Muslim market have gone out of business, a point reinforced by the Channel 4 *Dispatches* investigative program, which suggested that these stores could not compete with the bigger stores that accepted reams of free Saudi literature.[146]

In addition, the internet has revolutionized the spread of Islamic (and Islamist) theology and ideologies. According to Ehsan Mahsood, "One of the most popular websites for speakers of English is www .islamonline.net. It is published by journalists sympathetic to the modernising wing of Egypt's Muslim Brotherhood. Based in Cairo but with a network of global correspondents, the site contains a mix of daily world news, features, chat, audio and a chance to pose questions on the practice of Islam live to a panel of theologians from different countries."[147] Al-Muhajiroun and its offshoots have been very active online, with at least six YouTube channels broadcasting videos of lectures and other propaganda with titles such as "Martyrs Are Beautiful."[148] Journalist Malise Ruthven has observed that "Wahhabi and Salafist ideas are spread throughout the world through online fatwas (legal rulings) issued by Wahhabi sheikhs, conferences and lectures, television stations or cheap booklets."[149] Salafi Publications is based in Birmingham and was established in 1996, according to its Twitter account, and is active through its Salafi Radio online streaming channel, as well as Facebook and Twitter.[150] Ruthven suggests that this proliferation of online Islamist resources has encouraged new trends of self-radicalization: "in a recent survey of jihadists, the risk consultancy Europe Exclusive Analysis concluded that 'activists invest considerable time and energy in self-study of Wahhabi Islam and subsequently the jihadi strain of Salafism.'"[151] Islamist groups have become more careful, particularly post-7/7, to circumvent laws on hate speech by hosting private blogs and web domains and removing overtly Islamist literature from websites. An HT media spokesperson, Abdul Wahid, explained that "the decision to remove some of our overseas literature from our British website was a considered response to the legitimate proposition that people who read it out of its context might see it as offensive."[152] Sadek Hamid suggests that this shift reflected a new media-savvy leadership seeking to avoid unwanted government attention, while "masking the fact that pamphlets and websites for other countries still retain standard HT propaganda."[153]

Islamist literature has also been found to have a heavy presence in some public libraries in London. For example, James Brandon and Douglas Murray found that eight council-run libraries in the Muslim-dominant suburb of Tower Hamlets "have become saturated with extreme Islamist books," and Salafi and Wahhabi authors, as well as books issued by the Muslim Brotherhood, Jamaat-e-Islami, and Hizb ut-Tahrir, dominate collections on Islam at the expense of works by more moderate Muslim authors.[154]

CONCLUSIONS

According to Jonathan Birt, Wahhabi proselytizing had the greatest impact on British Muslims during the period from 1989 to 1995, when an aggressive recruitment campaign "provoked significant religious reactions from the established South Asian sectarianisms" and moved British Islam toward more "purely scripturalist" ideologies. While Birt suggests this has become a general feature in Muslim societies globally, "it is perhaps underemphasized that petrodollar Wahhabism has been a key agent of this change in recent decades."[155]

A critical point that this chapter highlights is that, while direct Saudi proselytizing efforts have helped to spread Salafi-inspired Islamist ideologies, so too have anti-Saudi movements that adhere to similar ideologies inspired by Saudi education, literature, and jurisprudence. As the Awaaz–South Asia Watch report of 2006 suggests, "salafi-jihadi clerics have arisen from both anti- and pro-Saudi salafi tendencies. Similarly, the Afghan-Arabs who went to fight the Soviets in Afghanistan were strongly supported by the Saudi Government (and the U.S. and

Pakistan), but later became the core of the international salafi-jihadi network and rejected the Saudi state."[156] In the United Kingdom this means that while Saudi Arabia has a direct impact on the spread of Islamist ideologies through proselytizing efforts by the Muslim World League, WAMY, and other groups, it has also had a huge indirect impact through Saudi dissident groups that have found refuge in Britain after being expelled from Saudi Arabia yet who adhere to—and spread— similar ideologies. As Ed Husain has acknowledged, "today's jihadis are Wahhabis who have taken up arms against the Saudi rulers and their backers, Western governments included."[157]

Additionally, the Saudi religious establishment has had an influence through the activities of other movements active in the United Kingdom, such as the Muslim Brotherhood and Jamaat-e-Islami, which are themselves ideologically aligned with Saudi Arabia. In Britain they are often organizationally entwined as well. Alliances or informal cooperation takes place in the United Kingdom between Islamist groups that might otherwise oppose each other on sectarian grounds. Funds, personnel, literature, and meeting spaces are often shared. This also applies to what Awaaz terms "independent salafi exile groups," such as the Committee for the Defense of Legitimate Rights (CDLR) and al-Muhajiroun, that have been known to cooperate with each other and even with groups linked to Iran and Algeria.[158] The British example shows that Saudi Arabia's global proselytizing mission is not reliant on Saudi expatriates but works through a variety of groups and networks. As Madawi Al-Rasheed has observed, "in the Saudi/British case, global reach has been reliant on other diasporas (mainly Muslims and Arabs) for the promotion of religious transnational connections, serving mainly to consolidate Saudi legitimacy in three concentric circles—one domestic, one Arab, and one Islamic."[159]

Thus, a key feature of the spread of Islamist ideologies in Britain is the cooperation among Islamist groups and movements that might otherwise be in opposition. A shared ideology and opposition to Western values and democratic government has allowed for cross-fertilization among Islamist groups. These groups therefore have greater impact in the United Kingdom than they might have in isolation, and their efforts are often fueled by Saudi money. According to the Awaaz report, "It is . . . possible to speak of a broader political 'axis' of organizations comprising JI, MB, Wahabbi-Salafis, Ahl-e Hadith, other right-wing political Deobandi groups, and even the Tablighi Jamaat. On sectarian grounds, Wahhabi-Salafi clerics would oppose each of the other groups as 'deviates' or worse; but on practical grounds, wealthy Saudis and others would fund them."[160]

Some of the most revealing insights regarding the spread of Islamist ideologies in the United Kingdom have come from former self-identified Islamists who have confirmed the extent of Islamist proselytizing in Britain and described in detail the connections between different groups and their international links. Some of these "reformed Islamists" have expressed frustration that although the supply of Islamism into the United Kingdom has been relentless, so too has the UK government's tolerance for it. Ed Husain writes, "If British policy makers and elected officials are content to tolerate intolerance, and give a platform to those who are committed to destroying democracy and advocate religion-based separatism, why should a minority Muslim population turn on its own?"[161] The provision of asylum to key dissident Islamist leaders from a variety of countries, a permissive environment for unfettered free speech and dissemination of ideas, and a close relationship between the governments of Saudi Arabia and Britain has meant that the supply of Islamism in Britain has been a continuously running tap whose source has not yet run dry.

CHAPTER 6

Islamism in the United States

Why would a young American Muslim who is not of Arab descent and has not lived in an Arab country give a khutba [sermon] that is more relevant to certain Arab societies than their suburban mosque or community? . . . "Arabization" of Islamic discourse is what it is! —**Haris Tarin**, Muslim Public Affairs Council, 2013

The spread of Salafism and Wahhabism into the United States differs in many ways from the cases analyzed earlier in this book. While there has been an influx of Islamism into the United States, it has not been as extensive nor has the ideology taken root as deeply as in other regions and countries. Moreover, the extent of the supply of Islamism in the United States is fiercely debated. Some scholars, security analysts, government officials, and activists argue that Saudi influence is pervasive in mosques and Islamic organizations, as well as U.S. prisons.[1] They further contend that even if Saudi Arabia has not directly sponsored terrorist activities in the United States, the form of Islam it preaches has the potential to radicalize impressionable American Muslim youth.[2] However, though there have been terrorism-related accusations and convictions of Saudi-funded individuals, organizations, and mosques, the numbers have been relatively small. There is insufficient evidence to argue that in the United States a significant number of recipients of Saudi financing have promoted extremism or engaged in terrorist activities or that Wahhabi Islam has penetrated the American Muslim community.

To show the precise extent of Islamist influence in the United States, this chapter first describes the historical context of Islam and Islamism in the United States. Subsequent sections look at the degree of external Islamist influence affecting Islamic organizations, mosques, and individuals in the United States. The final section shows why and how the spread of Islamism into the United States has so far been relatively constrained. Together these sections suggest that the economic position, social integration, and ideological pushback of the American Muslim community have limited the influence of Islamism in the United States.

HISTORICAL AND POLITICAL CONTEXT

Muslim immigration into the United States was a gradual process that got under way in the nineteenth century and continued into the mid-twentieth century. By the 1950s more than 1,000 mosques had been established. After World War II the rate of Muslim immigration began to increase. For example, from 1948 to 1965 the number of students from Muslim-majority countries in the United States increased from 2,708 to 13,664.[3] The majority of Muslim students came from Iran, followed by Egypt, Pakistan, and Turkey. Many came to acquire technical knowledge that would benefit their home countries. Others came to escape persecution from postindependence, secular, nationalist regimes that perceived Islamist groups as a political threat.[4] Many of these marginalized students were inspired and actively involved with Islamist movements, namely Jamaat-e-Islami (JI) in Pakistan and the Muslim Brotherhood in Egypt.

The civil rights movement of the 1960s in the United States was pivotal in allowing these new Muslim immigrant students to openly practice their religion, engage in *da'wa* (proselytization), and promote Muslim unity among all Islamic sects.[5] Despite attempts to unify Muslims along religious lines and transcend ethnic, racial, and cultural differences, the majority of Muslim Americans still identified themselves in national, ethnic, or cultural rather than religious terms. By the 1970s and 1980s, however, nationalist movements had waned in popularity. Instead, disillusionment with the failures of nationalist governments in the Muslim world, coupled with the Soviet invasion of Afghanistan and the Iranian Revolution, paved the way for Muslim political engagement with a renewed focus on "Islamic causes."[6] Beginning in the 1990s groups such as JI and the Muslim Brotherhood dramatically increased their missionary campaigns in the United States with financial backing from the Gulf states.[7]

The 1960s and 1970s were also a significant time for many African American Muslims who broke away from black-oriented Islamic organizations such as the Nation of Islam (NOI) and the Moorish Science Temple of America and instead embraced traditional Sunni Islam.[8] As Saudi publications gradually penetrated African American neighborhoods, many black residents were offered scholarships to study in the Middle East. Many of these individuals (discussed in subsequent sections) returned to the United States after having converted to Wahhabi Islam.[9]

The Persian Gulf War of the early 1990s was an important point for the history of Islam in the United States.[10] Although the majority of American Muslims did not approve of Saddam Hussein's Islamic narrative of the war, many did agree with his accusation of Western hypocrisy over the right to self-determination, especially since American Muslims viewed the United States as backing the Israeli occupation of Arab land while condemning Iraq for occupying Kuwait.[11] Many Muslims around the world viewed the war as a U.S. attempt to regulate a rogue ally and assert dominance over the oil supply in the region. Muslim organizations in the United States expressed consternation at the "presence of foreign military forces in the birthplace of Islam. . . . A continuing policy of categorical support for Israeli occupation, ambitions, and oppression of the Palestinian people, coupled with the overriding focus on controlling energy resources, open[ed] a serious credibility gap between American decision-makers and the Muslim and Arab peoples."[12]

ORGANIZATIONS

Of the numerous Saudi-funded organizations in the United States, the most prominent are described below. They have had various connections to violent extremism, some fleeting and some more insidious.

Many Islamist students from South Asia and the Middle East who came to the United States in the 1960s were instrumental in establishing national Muslim institutions throughout the country. The Muslim Students Association (MSA), created in 1963 at the University of Illinois, is a primary example. The MSA received significant financial contributions from the Middle East because the majority of MSA's founders and members were also members of leading Islamist movements, including JI and the Muslim Brotherhood.[13] The primary objective of MSA was promoting Islamic unity that transcended cultural and national identities or divides. For many of these South Asian and Arab Muslim students, Islam was the ideological foundation for their existence and way of life. The hope was to establish a utopian Muslim community under the guidance of Islam.[14] The MSA activities went beyond da'wa and focused on charity drives and educational, athletic, scientific, research, and social activities. Essentially, MSA tried to establish a "divinely guided community that enjoys good, preaches love, and lives in peace."[15]

The MSA's source of funding was primarily the Muslim World League (MWL).[16] MSA heavily distributed fliers, and more recently it has posted publications of the World Assembly of Muslim Youth (WAMY) on its website. The website featured English translations of works by prominent Islamist scholars, including Ibn Taymiyyah, Sayyid Qutb, Mawdudi, and Abdul Wahhab. The *Wahhabi Book of Tawhid* was also featured on the website of the University of Southern California's MSA chapter.[17] MSA members were linked to terrorism on several occasions; one prime example is Rutgers MSA co-founder Ramzi Yusuf, a conspirator involved in the 1993 World Trade Center bombing who is currently serving a life sentence. In recent years more than a dozen other MSA members have been arrested or convicted on terrorism charges.[18]

Beginning in the late 1990s, many of the Islamic organizations and mosques that were initially funded by Saudi Arabia began to generate their own funds from local Muslims. Consequently, they stopped receiving Saudi financial support. The majority of these organizations, including MSA, also started to steer away from Wahhabi Islam and practice a more moderate form of Islam as a means of becoming integrated into mainstream American society.[19]

The MSA grew to number more than two hundred affiliated chapters at American and Canadian universities, and it allied itself with "both religious and secular social justice organizations to mobilize support for numerous domestic and international causes."[20] MSA no longer demonstrates Islamist leanings or any form of extremism, given the organization's enormous ethnic diversity, religiosity, and self-financing.[21] Additionally, the dramatic increase in the number of female participants has altered the topics discussed and activities promoted by the organization.[22] More than half of MSA's leadership now consists of women, and in 2004 Hadia Mubarak was elected as the first female national president of the organization.[23] While the MSA initially adhered to Wahhabi Islam's repudiation of gender mixing, it has slowly attempted to do away with gender segregation and become more inclusive of both genders.[24] Moreover, MSA has become more culturally heterogeneous by accepting Muslims from various sects and ethnic backgrounds.[25] While many activities of the MSA chapters throughout the United States still focus on issues such as establishing prayer rooms and halal food venues within university campuses, the majority of MSAs now also actively participate in community service events addressing homelessness, hunger, education, and youth violence.[26] Many MSA university chapters, including those at UC Berkeley, UCLA, Penn State, and the University of Michigan, also host Fast-A-Thons, in which non-Muslims are encouraged to fast during the month of Ramadan as a means of raising awareness not only about the Islamic faith but also about other issues, such as AIDS/HIV and Ebola.[27] Such actions demonstrate MSAs' willingness to connect to mainstream social causes and become more inclusive toward all Muslims, as well as non-Muslims.

In the 1980s Arab students from various universities involved with the MSA broke off from the organization and in 1989 officially created their own organization, the Muslim Arab Youth Association (MAYA) in Plainfield, Indiana. The goal of MAYA was to organize Islamic youth conferences and matrimonial services catering to Arab youth.[28] However, MAYA's activities indicate a more extremist position. For example, MAYA invited Sheikh Muhammed Siyam, a Hamas military leader, as the guest speaker for a 1994 conference in Los Angeles. Siyam reportedly stated, "I've been told to restrict what I say. I hope no one is recording me or taking any pictures, as none are allowed, because I'm going to speak the truth to you. It's simple. Finish off the Israelis. Kill them all! Exterminate them! No peace ever! Do not bother to talk politics," and the organization received more than $200,000 in donations that night.[29] Other Islamic militants invited to speak at MAYA events included Mustafa Mashhur, the Supreme Guide of the Egyptian Muslim Brotherhood; Musa Abu Marzook, a central Hamas leader currently living in Syria; and Yusuf al-Qaradawi, an Egyptian Muslim Brotherhood cleric based in Qatar.[30]

The Islamic Society of Northern America (ISNA), a Muslim umbrella organization for the MSA established in 1963, also relied on Saudi funding during its inception. With many founding members trained and educated in Saudi Arabia, ISNA initially promulgated Salafi and Wahhabi teachings.[31] By the 1990s, however, ISNA had cut ties with the Saudi kingdom in response to the Gulf War (and Saudi Arabia's decision to admit U.S. troops), and it began to adopt a more pluralistic religious stance that was inclusive of most Islamic sects. ISNA is now believed to be "the largest umbrella organization for the estimated 6 to 8 million Muslims embracing over 300 community organizations and professional organizations in North America."[32] Some analysts, including Michael Waller, Steven Emerson, and Stephen Schwartz, have repeatedly and controversially accused ISNA of being a front for Wahhabi indoctrination.[33] In 2003 Michael Waller testified before the U.S. Senate on ISNA's role in promoting Wahhabi Islam in U.S. prisons. Waller stated, "The Islamic Society of North America (ISNA) refers Muslim clerics to the U.S. Bureau of Prisons. The Islamic Society of North America is an influential front for the promotion of the Wahhabi political, ideological and theological infrastructure in the United States and Canada. . . . ISNA has connections to 50 to 79 percent of mosques on the North American continent."[34] Similarly, in 2003 Stephen Schwartz accused ISNA of being a conduit for Islamism in the United States.[35] Despite these accusations, and ISNA's prior financial support from Saudi Arabia, ISNA has never been convicted of inciting violence or engaging in terrorist activities. On the contrary, ISNA has repeatedly issued statements condemning violence, antisemitism, and attacks against non-Muslim groups.[36] It also focuses on improving interfaith relations and civic engagement beyond the Muslim community.

The North American Islamic Trust (NAIT) was created in 1973 as a financial institution to fund and often hold the real estate titles to mosques, Islamic centers, and other institutions.[37] NAIT's funding comes from Saudi Arabia and other states and has ties to the Muslim Brotherhood. In 2007 NAIT was named an unindicted co-conspirator in the terrorist charges brought against the Holy Land Foundation.[38]

The Institute of Islamic and Arabic Sciences in America (IIASA), established in Fairfax, Virginia, in 1989, was another Saudi-funded organization accused of promulgating an intolerant version of Islam that repudiated other Islamic sects, Christianity, and Judaism. IIASA was a branch of Imam Muhammad ibn Saudi Islamic University (IBSIU) in Riyadh and the Islamic University of Madinah.[39] The Saudi embassy fully funded the institute, so all the instructors were technically embassy employees. The institute provided "distant learning" in Arabic, Quranic studies, Hadith studies, the doctrines of Islam, and "educational psychology" to more than four hundred students.⁴⁰ The courses often taught the supremacy of Salafism and the fallibility of modern Islamic schools of thought. The course on educational psychology in particular was significant because it focused on pedagogical studies; thus, the goal was to train students to become teachers themselves. Native Arabic speakers were typically favored and often granted immediate acceptance. The institute also collaborated with mosques and prisons to provide imams and Muslim chaplains.⁴¹

In order to promote Wahhabi Islam, Saudi Arabia offered hundreds of scholarships to American Muslim students to study at the Islamic University of Madinah and its satellite school in the United States, the IIASA. Saudi recruiters would travel annually within the United States to look for influential youth who would study in Saudi Arabia and then return to the United States to create an Islamic youth movement based on Wahhabi teachings. Students had to be under the age of twenty-two, have Islamist leanings, and some experience in the Arabic language. Recipients of the scholarship received housing accommodations, food stipends, and a university education.⁴²

Numerous of these scholarship recipients have been tied to violent extremism. For example, Abu Ameenah Bilal Philips (born Dennis Bradley Philips) was one of the first Westerners to enroll in the Islamic University of Madinah with an IIASA scholarship. He then went on to receive his master's in Islamic theology (*aqida*) from King Saud University in Riyadh. Philips came under intense scrutiny after a speech he gave in which he appeared to condone suicide bombers:

> When you look at the mind of the suicide bomber, it's a different intention altogether. . . . The [enemy] is either too heavily armed, or they don't have the type of equipment that can deal with it, so the only other option they have is to try to get some people amongst them and then explode the charges that they have to try to destroy the equipment and to save the lives of their comrades. So this is not really considered to be suicide in the true sense. This is a military

action and human lives are sacrificed in that military action. This is really the bottom line for it and that's how we should look at it.[43]

On numerous occasions, Philips has been accused of inciting violence and recruiting people to engage in terrorist activities. He was banned from Australia in 2007 after national security agencies deemed him a security threat.[44] In 2010 the home secretary for the United Kingdom, Theresa May, also banned him for promoting "extremist views."[45] In 2014 in Prague, security officials raided several mosques and arrested the publisher of a book, *The Fundamentals of Tawheed*, written by Philips. Security officials claimed the book incited antisemitism, xenophobia, and violence against "inferior races." Philips defended the contents of the book and stated that millions of copies had been distributed to Muslim communities around the world.[46] In September 2014 Phillips was incarcerated in the Philippines for recruiting individuals to engage in terrorist activities and over his alleged links to terrorist groups—including the Islamic State (IS).[47] He was deported to Canada and later went to live in Qatar.

Abdullah Hakim Quick was another scholarship recipient, and he was the first American to graduate from the Islamic University of Madinah, in 1979. Quick, a Toronto-based Islamic scholar, has been accused of propagating antisemitic and homophobic views. He once gave a televised lecture in which he declared that the punishment for homosexuality was death.[48] The University of Toronto was also urged to cancel an eighteen-week course led by Quick after he reportedly made a comment about purifying Islam's "third holiest shrine from the 'filth of Christians and Jews.'"[49]

Ali Al-Tamimi also received a scholarship to attend the Islamic University of Madinah. Al-Tamimi was born and raised in Washington DC and was an Islamic lecturer who traveled around the world. He was the preacher and revered figure at the Center for Islamic Information and Education, also known as Dar al-Arqam, in Falls Church, Virginia, a center located in the same office complex as other prominent Saudi groups, including the Muslim World League and the International Islamic Relief Organization.[50]

Al-Tamimi helped radicalize what was to become known as the Virginia Jihad Network, whose eleven members were heavily influenced by Al-Tamimi's version of Salafi Islam and those within Al-Tamimi's circle. The group's primary association was with the Dar al-Arqan. The Benevolence International Foundation (BIF) was also instrumental in radicalizing the eleven members by showing jihadi videos. Lectures offered by BIF emphasized the Taliban's innocence and the duty of Muslims to help their Muslim brethren.[51]

In 2003 Al-Tamimi was named an unindicted co-conspirator in the case of the Virginia Jihad Network, in which these eleven American Muslim college students were accused of engaging in paramilitary training, including playing paintball, to prepare for "holy war."[52] The FBI received two tips from the local Muslim community that Al-Tamimi was conducting "military-style training" at his home. Shortly thereafter the FBI raided Al-Tamimi's home and found *fatwas* (Islamic decrees) by Saudi clerics and a four-page document titled "Suicide Attacks: Are They Suicide? A Sharia Viewpoint."[53] The content of the document argued that suicide was not *haram* (forbidden) if it was well intentioned and served Islam. The FBI also raided the homes of Mohammad Atique in Norristown, Pennsylvania, and Masoud Khan, in Gaithersburg, Maryland. FBI authorities retrieved an AK-47-style rifle, a shotgun, and a .45-caliber pistol, a document titled "The Terrorists Handbook," and pictures of the Washington Monument, the National Atomic Museum, and the FBI building.[54] Ten of eleven group members were "charged with forty-two counts in a seven-part conspiracy, including knowingly enlisting in armed hostility toward the United States, and the intentional participation in military activities against a foreign state with which the US is at peace," and they received sentences ranging from forty-six months to sixty-five years in prison. In 2004 Al-Tamimi was convicted on ten counts, including soliciting others to attend terrorist training camps in Afghanistan and contributing services to Afghanistan's former Taliban rulers.[55] He was sentenced to life in prison.

The Saudi embassy's Islamic Affairs Department managed IIASA and had an annual budget of more than $8 million with in excess of thirty staffers. The majority of the staffers were either Saudi-born or Saudi-trained religious scholars.[56] Besides offering scholarships, the institute built mosques, distributed Qurans, and brought in imams from the Middle East to lead prayers and *khutba* (sermons). Most of the imams and Islamic teachers were brought in from Saudi Arabia to teach and grant certificates recognized only by the Islamic University of Madinah.[57] Given the tremendous funding the Islamic University of Madinah and IIASA received from the Saudi kingdom, they had enormous influence over and presence in Islamic discourse in the United States. Because the curriculum centered on the teachings of Imam Muhammad ibn Abd al-Wahhab, much of the focus was on *tawhid* (the oneness of God), the *sunna* (followers of Prophet Muhammad), and the propagation of Islamism. Other concepts, such as *bid'ah* (any sort of deviation from the Quran) and *shirk* (believing in multiple gods or no god), as well as other opposing Islamic views, were disparaged.[58] The English version of the Quran that IIASA distributed was entitled *The Noble Quran*, and much of the commentary within the book reflected Wahhabi teachings.[59]

In 2004, amid accusations that IIASA was propagating radical Islamic teachings, the U.S. State Department revoked sixteen diplomatic visas of people associated with the institute. Eleven of the sixteen were Saudi citizens, and one of them was Ibrahim ibn al-Khlaib, a prominent activist of Saudi Salafism. Shortly thereafter, federal agents raided the institute and confiscated computers and documents.[60] Many American Muslim students who also attended the Islamic University of Madinah or IIASA were later accused of religious extremism and inciting violence. While a pro-Muslim organization, the Council on American-Islamic Relations, criticized the raid as a "fishing experiment for the government," Ali Abbas Al-Ahmed, founder and director of the Institute of Gulf Affairs, an independent think tank in Washington DC, maintained that IIASA was teaching a "militant" brand of Islam. Al-Ahmed stated, "In my mind, if this organization keeps running in this country, it will create a lot of Osama bin Ladens." He further contended, "The crux of their message is that this is a Christian-Jewish land and that we should hate those people."[61] Despite allegations against IIASA, no charges were brought against the institute. IIASA was the primary meeting place for the Virginia Jihad Network, mentioned earlier.

The Islamic Assembly of North America (IANA) was established in 1993 in Ann Arbor, Michigan, as a Salafi organization that focused on da'wa (missionary work), primarily in American prisons. According to the IANA website, more than 530 packages of Islamic content were disseminated to prison inmates, and they contained such items as "audiotapes on Islam, a Qur'an, and several books on Islamic thought."[62] The organization's annual operating budget was around $500,000, of which the Saudi government financed more than half, and the remainder came from private donors in the Gulf region. Salih al-Hussayen, one of the individual donors, gave more than $100,000 to IANA.[63] IANA was explicit with respect to its Salafi activism by stating on its website that IANA's primary goal was to engage "in a comprehensive form of Islam work . . . based on the principles of *Ahl al-Sunnah wa al-Jamma* [the people of the Prophet's traditions and the group] and the guidance of the pious forefathers."[64] To spread its message, IANA published two magazines: *Assirat al-Mustaqim* (The straight path) and *Al Asr* (The era). Both magazines extensively covered militant Islamist movements throughout the Muslim world. One issue of *Al Asr* published in May 2001 included three separate fatwas promoting terrorism. One of the fatwas came from Hamid al-Ali, a Kuwaiti Salafi cleric. It praised the efficacy of destroying a "vital enemy command post" and encouraged individuals to "crash one's plane on a crucial enemy target to cause great casualties."[65] Salih al-Hussayen's nephew, Sami Omar al-Hussayen, was the administrator for IANA's online jihadi publishing site. Al-Hussayen often broadcast the writings of prominent Salafi sheiks from Saudi Arabia, including Sheikh Safer al-Hawali, the author of an antisemitic and anti-American lecture entitled "The Intifada and the New Tartars." After a series of wire transfers (totaling more than $300,000), a suspicious bank teller notified federal authorities, who then began investigating al-Hussayen.[66] Al-Hussayen was later tried on charges of supporting terrorism through IANA's site. In the end he was not indicted on terrorism charges but on visa fraud charges. IANA eventually dissolved after scrutiny from federal agencies.

During the Afghan war, organizations sprouted throughout the United States with the purported aim of providing humanitarian assistance to Afghan civilians. One of these was the Benevolence International Foundation, the charity established in the early 1980s by Adel Batterjee and his well-connected family in Saudi Arabia. Its main headquarters was in Jeddah, and it was set up to offer humanitarian relief to Afghan victims during the Soviet invasion of Afghanistan. Although the Jeddah office closed down shortly after the war ended, the Chicago office in the United States remained open until 2002. Batterjee met Enaam Arnaout (also known as Abu Mahmud) in Peshawar in the 1980s, when Arnaout was working for another Saudi charity, the Muslim World League. When Batterjee officially resigned as executive director for BIF in 1993, Arnaout became his successor at the Chicago office of BIF. Batterjee remained active in the organization and continued to play a pivotal role in promulgating militant jihad in Muslim countries. Investigative reports later revealed that, unbeknown to donors, BIF had been diverting portions of the funds ($400,000 in U.S. dollars) to Bosnian mujahedeen groups, and Batterjee was one of the primary financiers.[67]

Arnaout also had a direct relationship with Osama bin Laden for more than a decade and provided a bin Laden operative, Mamduh Salim, the means to use Benevolence International as a guise to obtain his travel documents. Salim was accused of orchestrating the 1998 al-Qaeda attacks on the U.S. embassies in East Africa.[68] Muhammad Bayazid—another bin Laden operative who tried to acquire nuclear weapons for other al-Qaeda members—used BIF's Chicago address in his application for a driver's license. During a wiretapped telephone conversation between Adel Batterjee and Arnaout, Batterjee urged Arnaout to flee to Saudi Arabia to avoid further investigation by U.S. federal authorities into his involvement in terrorism.[69]

U.S. federal agents raided the BIF office in Sarajevo in March 2002 and uncovered the charity's definitive links to al-Qaeda militancy. A copy of the 1988 handwritten letter titled "Golden Chain" was found, and it listed more than twenty of bin Laden's financiers. In October 2002 Enaam Arnaout was indicted on seven charges of conspiracy and racketeering. The U.S. Treasury froze BIF bank accounts and seized its assets. In 2011 Arnaout was released from prison and took up residence in Illinois.[70] In 2015 Arnaout was facing trial to have his U.S. citizenship revoked. Batterjee, who moved to Jeddah, has yet to be tried for his connections to al-Qaeda.[71]

The al-Haramain Islamic Foundation, with a U.S. branch located in Ashland, Oregon, was another Saudi-funded organization accused of terrorist activities. In 2004 the U.S. government declared the organization a Specially Designated Global Terrorist group after its financial manager, Perouz Sedaghaty, was accused of concealing a $150,000 donation that al-Haramain had received in 2000 from Egypt to fund religious extremists in Chechnya.[72] In September 2010 Sedaghaty was convicted on two felony charges and sentenced to thirty-three months in federal prison for converting $130,000 of the donations to travelers checks and subsequently cashing them for Saudi royals at Al Rajhi Bank in order to smuggle the funds to Chechnya.[73]

The Council on American-Islamic Relations (CAIR), a Muslim civil liberties advocacy organization established in 1994 in Washington DC and later growing to include twenty-eight chapters across the United States, is also heavily financed by Saudi money. As Stephen Schwartz indicates, "in 1999, CAIR received $250,000 from the Jeddah-based Islamic Development Bank, an official Saudi financial institution."[74] CAIR also received $500,000 from Prince Alwaleed bin Talal of Saudi Arabia to help distribute the Quran and other Islamic books throughout the United States.[75] Despite its push for Muslim advocacy, CAIR has been mired in controversy. Critics of CAIR point out that at least five members have been convicted or deported for links to terrorist groups.[76] Randall "Ismael" Royer, a Muslim convert and CAIR's communications specialist and civil rights coordinator, was indicted on charges of conspiring to help Lashkar-e-Taiba, one of the largest and most proficient of the Kashmir-focused militant groups.[77] Royer later pled guilty to lesser, fire-related charges and was sentenced to twenty-two years in federal prison. Ghassan Elashi, the founder of the Texas chapter of CAIR and the Holy Land Foundation, was indicted in July 2009 on charges of money laundering and supporting terrorism by funneling $12 million to Hamas.[78] Rabih Haddad, a CAIR fundraiser, was arrested on terrorism-related charges and deported from the United States to Lebanon due to his affiliation with, as executive director, the Global Relief Foundation (GRF), a charity he co-founded. In October 2002 GRF was designated by the U.S. Treasury Department for financing al-Qaeda and other terrorist organizations.[79]

CAIR has repeatedly denounced terrorism and tried to dispel rumors it has been a front for Wahhabi Islam. The organization denies receiving foreign assistance, with the exception of the $500,000 it received from Prince Alwaleed bin Talal. The group indicated that the funds went toward a library project that was "designed to distribute a set of books on Islam, the majority of which were written by non-Muslim academics, to libraries so that people can learn more about Islam." The organization also states that it has aligned with law enforcement officials and engaged in antiterrorism campaigns to reduce the threat of homegrown Islamic terrorism.[80]

INSTITUTIONS

Besides supporting these organizations, Islamist financiers have sponsored mosques, centers, and other institutions. After 9/11, rumors and speculation ran wild. For example, according to Stephen Schwartz, Wahhabis took control of more than 84 percent of mosques in the

United States.[81] (This claim is likely drastically overstating the phenomenon, as detailed below.) He further contends that Saudi Arabia has spent more than $324 million on establishing Islamic institutions in the United States and thus their "control over mosques means control of property, buildings, appointment of imams, training of imams, content of preaching—including faxing of Friday sermons from Riyadh, Saudi Arabia—and of literature distributed in mosques and mosque bookstores, notices on bulletin boards, and organizational solicitation."[82] According to a Freedom House report, Saudi-funded Wahhabi literature was found at more than a dozen mosques, in Los Angeles, Oakland, Dallas, Houston, Chicago, Washington DC, and New York.[83] The *New York Times* reported that "records of the Saudi-controlled Muslim World League reveal that during a two-year span in the 1980s, the organization spent about $10 million in the United States on mosque construction."[84] Additionally, according to Ihsan Bagby, "radical 'nongovernmental Saudi sheiks' became very active in pushing a far more militant brand of Wahhabism than the government-appointed imams." Ihsan further contends, "These radicals cultivated American Muslims, who used Saudi money to build their own mosques."[85] While Saudi financing has been extensive, self-identifying Salafi mosques are few in number. According to a 2011 U.S. survey, there are about 2,106 mosques throughout the United States. Only 1 percent of the mosques surveyed adhered to Salafi Islam.[86] Some of these include al-Masjid al-Awaal (the First Mosque), founded in 1932 in Pittsburgh, Pennsylvania. The mosque follows a curriculum that includes teachings from Rabi' ibn Hadl al-Madkhali, a significant Salafi scholar from Saudi Arabia. Another Salafi mosque is Masjid al-Mu'min, in Los Angeles. Rather than focusing on political activism, many of the Salafi mosques focus on propagating Salafism among American Muslims.[87] Moreover, while these Salafist-influenced mosques might espouse Islamist ideas, only a handful of ties to terrorism have been discovered. Some of the more notable Saudi-funded mosques are described below.

Leaders and worshippers at the Islamic Society of Boston (ISB) mosque in Cambridge, Massachusetts, have repeatedly been suspected of funding and/or engaging in terrorism.[88] In December 2005 the Islamic Development Bank, a subsidiary of the Organization of the Islamic Cooperation (OIC), located in Jeddah, wired $250,000 to ISB, and in 2007 the ISB received an additional $1 million in funds from the Saudi Bank. Many of ISB's past leaders and members have been accused of "supporting Islamic terrorism and Islamist terrorism or indulging in virulently anti-American and anti-Semitic rhetoric."[89] In 2004 Abdurahman Alamoudi, the mosque's founder and first president, was sentenced to twenty-three years in prison for illegal transactions with the Libyan government and for his role in a Libyan conspiracy to assassinate then–Crown Prince Abdullah of Saudi Arabia.[90] In 2010 Aafia Siddiqui, an MIT neuroscientist turned al-Qaeda agent, was sentenced to eighty-six years in prison on charges of assault and attempted murder of a U.S. Army captain. Referred to as "Lady al-Qaeda," she was arrested in Afghanistan in 2008 for possession of sodium cyanide and maps of prominent New York buildings. She was also related to the 9/11 mastermind, Khalid Sheikh Mohammed.[91] Another worshipper at ISB was Tarek Mehanna, an American pharmacist who was sentenced to seventeen years in federal prison in 2012 for conspiring to provide material support to al-Qaeda and other terrorist groups. Federal investigators alleged that Mehanna "had traveled to Yemen to seek terrorist training and plotted to use automatic weapons to shoot up a mall in the Boston suburbs." ISB worshipper Ahmad Abousamra, now wanted by the FBI, was Mehanna's co-conspirator in the plot to kill Americans in a foreign country and to aid terrorists. He fled to Syria.[92] Tamerlan Tsarnaev and his brother, Dzhokar Tsarnaev, the 2015 Boston Marathon bombers, also attended the ISB.[93] While many of these individuals have been linked to the ISB mosque, no actual indictments have been made against the mosque, and it remains open.

The King Fahad Mosque, established in 1998 in Culver City, a suburb of Los Angeles, is the largest Saudi-financed mosque in the United

States. The Saudi king and his son, Prince Abdullah bin Abdulaziz, financed the mosque with between $2.1 million and $8 million in private donations. In 2003 Fahad al Thumairy, the chief imam of the King Fahad Mosque, was denied reentry to the United States by the State Department amid accusations he was connected with terrorist activities.[94] Other than that single incident, the King Fahad Mosque has not been accused of promoting extremism or terrorism. Moreover, the mosque no longer accepts foreign funding or imams from overseas. The mosque now includes classes on the Quran, interfaith programs, marriage services, and an Islamic research center.[95]

Formally known as the American Muslim Society, the mosque in Dearborn, Michigan, was established in 1938.[96] For twenty-plus years the mosque served as more of a place for social gatherings than for worship. With the 1965 repeal of the immigration quota, the Yemeni population in the city increased exponentially and so too did their influence in the mosque. By the 1980s the newcomers had taken control of the mosque away from the Lebanese and Syrian immigrants and declared that more conservative Islamic views would be enforced.[97] The mosque hired a Saudi-trained Yemeni imam to lead the prayer and give the khutba, or sermons. The mosque then expanded its hours to being open every day, not just for Friday prayers. Men and women had designated praying areas, and women were required to wear headscarves and enter through the back entrance. Matrimonial and other social celebrations were banned, as were co-ed Islamic classes. Saudi Arabia also funded the mosque's 2000 expansion, from twenty-four thousand to forty-eight thousand square feet, which allowed it to accommodate up to two thousand people.[98] The sound of the *adhan* (Islamic call to prayer) can be heard five times a day, "as bearded men with *gallabiyas*, white, ankle-length tunics, and white skull caps leave their houses nearby and walk to prayer," with women in abayas (ankle-length dresses, often in black) following behind.[99] There was contention between the mosque's board members and individuals from the community. Imam Mohammad Musa, who often clashed with Dearborn board members over their rigidity and extreme conservativeness, eventually left Dearborn after twenty years.[100] Although the mosque has maintained its culturally and religiously conservative tune, there are no connections to any terrorist incidents.[101] If anything, the mosque has made stronger attempts to reach outside of the community by organizing open houses where individuals can meet mosque attendees, observe the prayers, and learn more about the faith.[102]

The Koranic Literary Institute of Chicago (KLIC) was an Islamic institute that distributed Muslim textbooks throughout the United States. Yasin Abdullah Ezzedine al-Qadi, a wealthy Saudi businessman accused of supporting terrorism, was found to have transferred $820,000 from his Swiss bank account to the KLIC.[103] According to an affidavit by FBI agent Robert Wright, KLIC purchased land in Woodridge (south of Chicago) subsequent to the transaction. Wright claimed that "investment in the property was meant to produce income for terrorism in the Middle East."[104] The U.S. Justice Department also accused KLIC of lending "substantial assistance, through means of repeated and possibly illegal subterfuge and misrepresentation" to Mohammad Salah, a known Hamas operative. Mohammad Salah received $110,000 as a result of the investment from the property. In 1993 Salah was arrested in Israel with a large sum of cash and other "incriminating notes on meetings with Hamas cells."[105] In November 2002 Switzerland blocked twenty-three bank accounts belonging to al-Qadi because of his links to al-Qaeda. While "some of the accounts were under al-Qadi's relative's name, most were in the name of a company called Faisal Finances whose president, Prince Mohammad al-Faisal, is a member of the Saudi royal family." While the Saudi interior minister, Na'if bin Abdul Aziz, reiterated al-Qadi's innocence, the United States gave al-Qadi special designation as a global terrorist and froze all his assets.[106]

Many other mosques in the United States were initially funded by Middle East sources, but that changed after 9/11. According to Shakeel Syed, executive director of the Islamic Shura Council of Southern California, most mosques have begun rejecting foreign donations and are now funded entirely by local Muslims.[107] This is in part because of increased government scrutiny of foreign transactions from Islamic countries, along with reluctance by local Muslims about accepting donations from overseas.

There is also debate over the extent of Islamist influence with the American prison system. Officials and scholars have asserted that the supply of Wahhabi Islam is a pressing issue in U.S. prisons.[108] According to FBI director Robert Mueller's testimony to the U.S. Senate Intelligence Committee, "Foreign states and movements have been financing the promotion of radical, political Islam [Islamism] within America's armed forces and prisons."[109] Senator Charles Schumer (D-NY) also claimed that "these organizations have succeeded in ensuring that militant Wahhabism is the only form of Islam that is preached to the 12,000 Muslims in federal prisons. The imams flood the prisons with anti-government, pro-bin Laden videos, literature and sermon tapes."[110] Frank Gaffney, director of the Center for Security Policy, has made similar claims, saying that the Saudi government has made strenuous efforts to "recruit convicted felons in the U.S. prison system as cannon-fodder for the Wahhabist jihad."[111] FBI counterterrorism officials allege that "inmates are logical targets for terrorist recruitment because they may be pre-disposed to violence, feel disenfranchised from society, desire power and influence, seek revenge against those who incarcerated them, be hostile towards authority and the United States, or cling to a radical or extremist Islamic 'family.'"[112] Despite allegations of pervasive Saudi influence in U.S. prisons, members affiliated with the Islamic Assembly of North America (IANA) were the only ones convicted of spreading jihadi propaganda, as discussed in earlier sections.

The theory that foreign organizations emanating primarily from the Middle East are recruiting terrorists in U.S. prisons is certainly alarming; however, the evidence does not support these claims. According to a 2013 report by the Institute for Social Policy and Understanding, a think tank and research organization focusing on policy issues related to American Muslims, very few cases show that radicalization stemmed from Saudi-based charities or other foreign sources. The report further states that "die-hard extremists need little proselytizing from Wahhabi clerics from abroad. They are already prison radicals of the first order, many of whom are fully capable of radicalizing other inmates on their own."[113] According to an extensive two-year study of the U.S. prison system conducted by Mark Hamm, only a tiny fraction of inmate converts to Islam actually "turned radical beliefs into terrorist action."[114] Hamm further suggests that the biggest threat to U.S. security is not the large number of Muslims in the prison systems. Rather, the concern is the possibility of small groups of radicals who instigate terrorist acts upon their release. But even the chances of that are very slim. A 2004 report conducted by the Office of the Inspector General in the Justice Department acknowledged that there was a lack of evidence to demonstrate widespread terrorist radicalization or recruitment in U.S. prisons by Muslim chaplains, contractors, or volunteers. Rather, the concern was inmates radicalizing other inmates to adopt what is referred to as "prison Islam."[115]

Finally, there have been allegations of Saudi placements of Islamist literature in mosques and Islamic centers within the United States.[116] Yet, while some evidence was found, when taken in context, the number of Saudi texts was relatively low across thousands of venues and in comparison to all the other texts and materials found at other various locations. In fact, the largest collection of Islamist materials was found at the King Fahd Mosque (mentioned above), where there were only six Saudi-connected titles on the shelves.[117]

WHY IS THE U.S. DIFFERENT?

While there has been some supply of Islamism into the United States, this ideology has not achieved as much resonance among American Muslims as it has in the other cases studied. What explains why the U.S. experience with Islamism has been different from those of Indonesia, Pakistan, and Britain? The answer is likely a combination of demographic, financial, and ideological factors, as described below.

Whether these factors continue to minimize the Wahhabification of American Muslims remains to be seen.[118]

Demographically, American Muslims are a minority, as they are in Britain. Importantly, though, more than 30 percent of the American Muslims are African American and are generally opposed to Wahhabi and Salafi Islam.[119] In large part, American Muslims are highly committed to their Islamic faith but do not see any contradictions in practicing their religion and integrating their lives into a modern society. Unlike their European counterparts and in other Muslim majority countries, American Muslims are more likely to develop relationships with non-Muslims and those outside their cultural groups, and they typically do not see any imminent clash between Muslims and non-Muslims.[120] Stark differences in socioeconomic circumstances relative to their European Muslim counterparts also play a significant role in the religious tolerance within the American-Muslim population. While European Muslims dominate the unskilled or semiskilled class, many Muslim immigrants in the United States are educated, skilled, and established professionals in the medical, legal, and engineering fields.[121] American Muslims are also socially and economically invested in the United States.[122]

In financial terms, many U.S. Muslim organizations acquired greater independence in the 1990s. According to Yvonne Haddad, a historian of Islam at Georgetown University, "The Saudi influence weakened considerably in the 1990s, as many believers stopped being Muslims living in America and became American Muslims."[123] Muslim scholars, including Ilyas Ba-Yunus, have refuted the claim of Saudi Arabia's penetration and influence in the United States by pointing out that mosques are fiercely independent and cater to their own American Muslim constituents. Ba-Yunus has further argued that many U.S. mosques hire their own imams, who are often Western-educated and autonomous in what they preach during khutba.[124]

Perhaps the most important reason for the limited resonance of Islamism in the United States is that local Muslims and Islamic groups have "pushed back" ideologically against external suppliers. Christopher Heffelfinger posits that while Salafi influence has been strong in the American Muslim community, "the majority of Islamic advocacy organizations have directly opposed militancy and have increasingly tried to address the question of what it means to be a Muslim in America today."[125] Heffelfinger's assertion is consistent with a 2007 Pew study revealing that the majority of American Muslims (81 percent) overwhelmingly denounce suicide bombings and other forms of violence against civilians.[126] Moreover, they identify as moderate Muslims.[127]

Khaled Abou El Fadl, an Islamic scholar, criticized many American Muslim leaders for their Wahhabi-influenced interpretation of Islam. El Fadl has argued that Islamic jurisprudence encourages intellectual debate, yet the influx of "Wahhabi puritanism" among some American Muslims has stifled Islamic dialogue.[128] El Fadl's strong criticism of Wahhabism and "puritan Islam" gained traction among many college-educated American Muslims, especially after 9/11.[129] American Muslim intellectuals, including Hamza Yusuf, an American Muslim scholar and co-founder of Zaytuna College in Berkeley, California, began publicly challenging the authority of Saudi-influenced and funded organizations because they promulgated extremist rhetoric.[130] Other homegrown movements also emerged in response to the Salafi/Wahhabi teachings and included "those who promote[d] the 'traditional' madhahib, Ash'arism/Maturidism, and some form of 'orthodox' Sufism, including Hamza Yusuf, Nuh Ha Mem Keller, and Zaid Shakir."[131]

Post-9/11, the American Muslim community made even greater efforts to counter Islamic extremism by becoming active at both the national and grassroots levels and trying to educate non-Muslims in their communities about Islam. Many mosques also adopted a no-tolerance policy toward the expression of anti-American and antisemitic views.[132] The Muslim Public Affairs Council (MPAC), a national American Muslim advocacy and public policy organization, has been active in deterring radicalization in U.S. mosques. MPAC initiated the Safe Spaces Initiative, which would seek to identify individuals susceptible to violent extremism. According to Salam Al-Marayati, president of MPAC, the Safe Spaces Initiative is intended "to provide the nation's estimated 2,100 mosques with training and resources to help create an environment where Muslims feel free to discuss sensitive political topics."[133]

CONCLUSION

The future of Islamism in the United States remains an open question. As Paul Barrett contends, Muslims are currently facing crucial choices as they struggle for the "soul of their faith" in the United States.[134] At this juncture, moderate Islamic groups have prevailed in the United States while militant Islamists have been a small minority. Although many American Muslims currently reject terrorism, there is a small segment that accepts Islamist ideologies. Younger American Muslims are more likely than older American Muslims to hold a strong sense of Muslim identity and to assert that suicide bombings in defense of Islam can at times be justified.[135] This can, in part, be attributed to increased religious rhetoric being promulgated by Saudi-funded institutions that have historically condoned extremist activities and sponsored terrorism in the United States and abroad. After 9/11, Saudi-funded religious institutions have been extremely careful not to overtly promote violence; however, they condone antipathy toward the *kafir* (any Muslim labeled a nonbeliever) as well as non-Muslims and encourage self-segregation.[136] Marcia Hermansen has pointed to Saudi influence overpowering Islamic cultural elements, particularly among American Muslim youth. She suggests that the "identity Islam" propagated by Saudi Arabia is a "mindless rejection of 'the Other' and the creation of de-cultured, rule based space where one asserts Muslim 'difference' based on gender segregation, romantic recreations of madrasa experiences, and the most blatantly apologetic articulation of Islam."[137] Others, including Barrett, have alluded to Saudi penetration in the United States by postulating that Saudi money has "funded the training of hundreds and maybe thousands of Muslim clerics and teachers sent to America."[138] Moreover, while Arabs comprise only about one-quarter of the American Muslim population, the majority of Muslim leaders in the United States are Arab.[139] This is due primarily to reverence for the Arabic language throughout the Muslim world because the Quran is in Arabic. Thus, Salafism has been heavily promulgated by Arabs, with its ideological leadership being predominantly Arab. Furthermore, as El Fadl points out, Saudi Arabia continues to have the financial capacity to sponsor "puritan theology" throughout the Muslim and non-Muslim world. Even if Islamists do not overtly support militancy, the reality is that they perceive modernity to be a "culturally biased concept" and view ideas such as "human rights, minority rights, and religious freedom, pluralism, and democracy" as largely Western concepts.[140]

It remains to be seen, however, what the future will hold for the American Muslim community as conflict in the Middle East and U.S. policies will likely continue to frustrate and anger some Muslims. Despite significant strides toward religious tolerance and integration made by the American Muslim community, a small group of immigrants, particularly from the Middle East and South Asia, will continue to import the ultraorthodox and culturally conservative views practiced in those regions. Other factors to consider are the sense of alienation and persecution that some American Muslims felt after 9/11, given the heavier scrutiny and religious bigotry they experienced.[141] This in turn caused many Muslims to cling even more tightly to their Muslim identity, as evidenced by the increasing numbers of young Muslims attending Islamic schools, as well as the proliferation of Muslim Student Association (MSA) chapters on college campuses.[142]

To reiterate once more, not all fundamentalists condone or propagate violence. However, as Barrett argues, "an influx of those holding, and able to spread immoderate views will retard assimilation and create pockets of extreme ideology."[143]

CHAPTER 7

Countering an Ideology

Tolerance has been responsible for not a single civil war, whereas intolerance has covered the earth with corpses. —**Voltaire**, *Treatise on Tolerance*

The spread of Islamist ideology has been ongoing, especially since 1979, and is supported by Saudi Arabia, other Gulf states, wealthy individuals, and a host of private charities. Their financial support has helped create organizations, schools, mosques, and media in various countries. The spread of Islamist ideology has helped radicalize a small portion of the Muslim population, and an even smaller subset have joined terrorist groups and engaged in acts of terror. The supply of Islamism has not been the only factor, or even sometimes the most important factor, involved in increasing the Islamization of Muslim communities, but, as shown here, it has been an important piece of the puzzle. To recap, this text has traced the supply of Islamism from the events of 1979, to the changed incentives for Saudi Arabia and others, to the funds funneled through charities and other entities into local organizations and institutions (mosques, schools, etc.) that radicalized individuals, some of whom turned to violence and terrorism. The story of the supply of Islamism goes a long way in explaining why the world has seen a surge in Islamist violence.

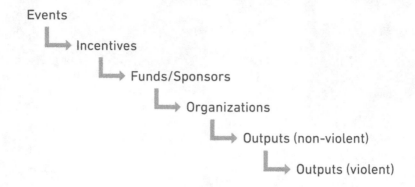

Fig. 1. Flowchart for the supply of Islam

EXTENSIONS

This causal process, while focused on the four case studies described in detail earlier, is by no means limited to these examples. The following few pages describe how this process has occurred in numerous other places, including countries in the Balkans, the Caucasus region, West Africa, East Africa, and western Europe.[1] Even these extensions of the phenomenon of the spread of Islamism do not encompass every case, nor does the rise of Islamism always come from the outside. For example, in Turkey, Islamism largely grew internally.[2]

Taking advantage of ethnic strife in the Balkans, Saudi charities poured money into the region. In Kosovo this supply of Islamism transformed a moderate and tolerant practice of Islam into one where 314 people left to join ISIS over a two-year time frame. After the war in the late 1990s, Saudi money—"from charities, private individuals, and government ministries"—helped build mosques, distribute literature, and support local Islamists.[3] Beyond just Kosovo, the Saudis are transferring hundreds of millions dollars to the Balkans to spread Wahhabism by funding a series of mosques, community centers, and charities.[4] In Bosnia, for example, since the 1990s Saudi money has helped build mosques, madrasas, and cultural centers, including the King Fahd

Mosque in Sarajevo.[5] In Albania dozens of Islamist NGOs, many of them mentioned throughout this book (IIRO, al-Haramain, WAMY, etc.) began in the 1990s to build mosques, schools, and Islamic centers and to provide students with scholarships for study in Saudi Arabia.[6] By one count, Saudi NGOs built two hundred mosques and donated a million copies of the Quran in the Albanian language.[7] In Macedonia, Wahhabist influence has similarly been tied to an influx of charities and funding for the construction of mosques and the propagation of Wahhabi ideology. As a consequence, Macedonia has seen confrontations, both violent and spiritual, between Wahhabi-influenced youth and more moderate Macedonian Muslims.[8]

In Chechnya the external supply of Wahhabism dramatically changed the scope and tenor of the conflict with Russia. The First Chechen War (1994–96) was largely dominated by ethnic rather than religious cleavages. Although some foreign fighters came to Chechnya, they had little impact on the tactics used or on the war in general.[9] In the late 1990s, though, Islamists began to see Chechnya as the new front line for jihad. Following the first war, Chechnya was in ruins, and in that environment "only money talked," and the foreign Islamists came with lots of money.[10] For example, "a Jordanian cleric named Khabib Abdurrakhman arrived in [neighboring Dagestan in] the early 1990s with a seemingly irresistible deal. To a hamlet made destitute by the collapse of the Soviet Union, Abdurrakhman brought a slaughtered cow and a free feast every week. He handed out $30 to every convert who came to his simple mosque."[11] Wahhabis set up mosques, schools, and training camps, including a camp run by Saudi-born Ibn al-Khattab in the Kavkaz (Caucasus) region.[12] Islamic militias funded by Saudi Arabia began introducing Islamic courts with the intention of enforcing sharia law in the cities and villages. Individual Islamists like Sheikh Abu Umar, from Saudi Arabia, arrived in Chechnya in 1995 to join the armed mujahedeen groups. He eventually became the chief Islamic judge and *mufti* in the region.[13] Charities like al-Haramain and the International Islamic Relief Organization (IIRO) supported these efforts as well as more explicitly terrorist activities.[14] With this influx of Wahhabism, the Second Chechen War (1999–2009) saw an increase in the scope and scale of terrorism, including suicide bombings and the notable attacks on the Moscow theater, the Moscow subway system, and the school in Beslan.[15]

In Africa there is a similar dynamic. Islam had a long tradition of moderation and amalgamation with local beliefs, until Islamism was exported to the region. Since the 1970s more than $40 billion has been sent to Africa from Middle East charities.[16] As David McCormack finds, "Islamists have become extremely adept at exploiting local conditions to advance their agenda through political and social warfare. . . . Islamism in Africa has resulted in the corrosion of moderate-Islamic and secular traditions."[17] The spread of Islamism has largely been conducted through direct government funding and through the same charities and organizations seen earlier, like the Muslim World League (MWL), the World Assembly of Muslim Youth (WAMY), the International Islamic Relief Organization, al-Haramain, and others, and they have opened up dozens of office, funded mosques, distributed Qurans, and more.[18]

In West Africa, Saudi Arabia has helped finance perhaps thousands of mosques, including "the King Faisal Mosque and Centre in Guinea, the King Faisal Mosque in Chad, the Bamako Mosque in Mali, and the Yaondi Mosque in Cameroon."[19] In Mali, Qatar has also "been involved in arming, funding, and providing direct military support for Islamists in Northern Mali. It has established madrasas, schools, and charities in northern Mali, pushing the Islamist message."[20] Saudi Arabia also directly funded Islamist groups like the Izala of Nigeria and Al-Falah of Senegal. In Nigeria, Islamism has taken hold of the largely Muslim north, with Boko Haram arising as the most prominent group since 2009. Yet, Islamist money and influence had been building support for decades.[21]

In East Africa the MWL distributed two million copies of the Quran in Sudan. In Somalia WAMY funded the Imam Nawawi educational complex. Saudi Arabia helped fund the King Fahd Charity Complex Plaza in Uganda, the International University of Africa in Sudan, and "innumerable madrassas" in Ethiopia. Saudi Arabia also directly funded Islamist groups like the Muslim Supreme Council in Uganda and the Muslim Association in Malawi.[22] In Somalia the al-Islah organization built schools, clinics, and community centers with money received from the MWL and al-Haramain.[23] There are also reports that some funds have been sent directly to terrorist groups. For example, al-Haramain sent money through its Somalia office to the Al-Itihad Al-Islamiya terrorist group.[24]

In western Europe the United Kingdom is not the only place facing an influx of Islamism. Saudi Arabia has built mosques, cultural centers, and schools not only in London and Edinburgh but also in Brussels, Geneva, Madrid, Rome, Gibraltar, Zagreb, Lisbon, Vienna, and more.[25] Coupled with a growing Muslim population over the last few decades, the supply of Islamism has gradually radicalized increasing numbers of people and institutions in Europe. In Germany, for example, the Salafist group True Religion passed out three hundred thousand copies of the Quran, with a goal of giving away twenty-five million copies. This group, accused of persuading more than one hundred people to join militant groups in Iraq and Syria, was banned by Germany.[26] In the Netherlands, Saudi charities like al-Haramain and al-Waqf helped create local institutions and build mosques in Amsterdam, Eindhoven, The Hague, and Tilburg. This external supply of Salafism turned what was a "minor current" into a much more popular strand of Islam. Most Salafis in the Netherlands are either apolitical or political and nonviolent, but a small subgroup, tied to the organizations and institutions mentioned above, turned to terrorism abroad and within the Netherlands.[27]

While the supply of Islamism has historically been maintained through the sponsorship of geographically localized proselytizing institutions, the use of social media for those purposes is now apparent. After studying Saudi clerical involvement on social platforms, Jonathan Schanzer and Steven Miller have reported widespread hostility to the West and non-Arabs. Clerics used popular platforms like Twitter, Facebook, and YouTube, as well as traditional websites. A member of the Saudi

Ministry of the Interior claimed that more than six thousand websites propagated extremism.[28] The online promotion of Islamism provides a cheaper and globally accessible alternative to the historical methods.[29] Some scholars argue that online access to ideologies by itself is insufficient to cause radicalization. Additionally, others argue that online ties are much weaker than physical, face-to-face ties, especially those based on kinship or friendship.[30]

COMPARISONS

All of these cases—from the primary four discussed in earlier chapters to the myriad examples described above—demonstrate certain commonalities as well as differences. In broad strokes we see similar patterns: some localized form of Islam is practiced; external Islamist influences enter a country and support and expand what are often minimal Islamist institutions within that country; external funds help build mosques, schools, and community centers; foreign imams come into the country and local citizens go to Saudi Arabia on scholarships; Islamist influence grows; and the state makes some effort at curbing at least the most violent form of this ideology.

The differences in all of these cases occur in the details but often have profound consequences. Clearly, a great deal of variation exists in terms of the type of Islam practiced at the local level. In one extreme, a country like Saudi Arabia (though not studied here), with its centuries-old ties between the ruling family and the Wahhabis, offers the most conducive environment for Islamism. Close to it is Pakistan, where Muslims form the majority of the population, where Islam is an integral component of national identity, and where some like-minded movements (Deobandis and Salafis) already had an Islamist foothold. Indonesia, Chechnya, and Bosnia are further along the spectrum, but all have Muslim majorities that practice Islam in a more syncretized and localized manner. Interestingly, all three of those countries (as well as Pakistan, Somalia, and others) experienced conflicts in which the construction of local and oppositional identities could have and often did use Islam as a cornerstone. At the far end of the spectrum are countries like the United Kingdom and United States, where Muslims are a minority. In these cases, however, the integration of Islam into a set of Western norms (or even its failure to integrate) has created opportunities for exploitation by advocating a harsh and unaccommodating version of Islam that refuses to acculturate or assimilate. For all these cases, the majority/minority status of Muslims, the nature of Islam practiced locally, and whether or not the country is involved in conflict all seem to shape the degree to which Islamism has been accepted by local populations.

Likewise, the funds supplied to export Islamism, as well as the institutions, preachers, and scholarships funded, vary across countries. Pakistan is again at one end of the spectrum, having had, for example, thousands of madrasas built with Gulf funds. The United States is probably at the other end of the spectrum, with just a handful of Wahhabi-supported mosques. Again, the variation probably depends on the nature of Islam practiced locally and the demographic status of Muslims in the country.

States have responded to the spread of Islamism in various ways. Some have welcomed it, like Pakistan. Others have tolerated it to the extent liberal democracies, like the United States and the United Kingdom, are able. Many have tried countering it with messages of tolerance, efforts at counterradicalization, and support for moderates, as Indonesia has. Yet Indonesia continues to struggle against the expansion of Islamism.[31] Many states have tried banning the most virulent organizations, arresting the most radical preachers, and shutting the mosques and schools funded by Islamists. Even Saudi Arabia, while exporting Wahhabism abroad, has taken steps to curtail its most violent permutations at home. Again, much of this variation depends on the individual country's political situation, its regime type, and its demographics.

COUNTERMEASURES

With regard to possible countermeasures, to a certain extent this is a story without a happy ending or easy fix. It will be difficult to put the genie back in the bottle. Nevertheless, appreciating how the supply of Islamism developed helps us understand some of the opportunities that are at hand to counteract this phenomenon.

What has been done to reverse this trend? How has the appeal of Islamic extremist ideology been countered in places like Indonesia, Pakistan, or elsewhere? What more could be done? We describe several possible courses of action, although none of them share the magical attributes of being both easy to implement and effective in their outcomes. It is useful to return to the narrative chain from earlier, linking incentives, external sponsors of funding, local organizations and institutions, and the nonviolent and violent outputs of these institutions. Each of these links and the chain can be addressed by countermeasures. Unfortunately, the aspects that are the easiest to address also seem to be the least likely to be effective in any systematic way. Likewise, the aspects that most need to be addressed are nearly impossible to change. In other words, there is no good answer to this phenomenon. Once Pandora's Box has been opened, it is nearly impossible to close.

Starting with the most immediate countermeasures, states can target the *violent outputs* of Islamist ideology. To counter those who have turned to jihad and terrorism, governments can arrest, prosecute, imprison, and deradicalize them. Examples abound in nearly every country, but drawing from the cases listed above, in Kosovo, for example, "the police have charged 67 people, arrested 14 imams, and shut down 19 Muslim organization for . . . inciting hatred and recruiting for terrorism."[32] In the Netherlands the government expelled three imams for inciting violence while preaching at mosques. Likewise, in Saudi Arabia authorities arrested three clerics who urged followers to wage jihad against the Saudi state in 2003 and 2004.[33] Again, the list of arrests and prosecutions of perpetrators and advocates of violence is enormous and beyond the scope of this book. Once states have arrested terrorism suspects, they can also engage in deradicalization efforts to try to moderate the ideological views of extremists, although these programs are frequently criticized for being ineffective.[34] Overall, targeting the violent outputs

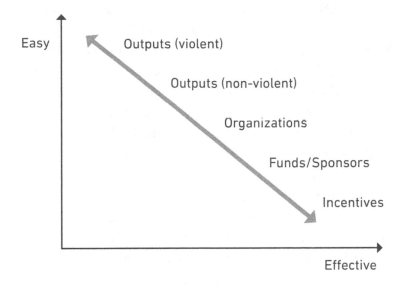

Easy

Outputs (violent)

Outputs (non-violent)

Organizations

Funds/Sponsors

Incentives

Effective

Fig. 2. Ease versus effectiveness of potential countermeasures
against terrorism

is relatively easy: those espousing and committing acts of violence are
fairly easy to identify (often too late, however, if violence has already
been committed). Yet, targeting this link in the chain is only the final
output of a much longer and larger process and does nothing to get at
the underlying dynamics. Nor does it stop the violence from occurring
in the first place. Because of this, targeting this link only mitigates the
symptoms and does nothing to cure the disease.

States can also target the *nonviolent outputs* of the supply of Islamism by promoting alternative, moderate ideologies to counter the
ideologies promulgated through Islamist schools and mosques. This
can take many forms, from promoting moderate views from within the
Muslim community to directly engaging and challenging the extremist views of the Islamists by engaging in "ideological competition."[35]
Again, these kinds of action have been taken to various degrees by
several states. For example, clerics in Saudi Arabia, Jordan, and Brit-

ain have publicly denounced the extremism of the terrorist organization known as the Islamic State in Iraq and Syria (ISIS).[36] In Britain the Prevent strategy aims to "change the nature of Muslim extremist communities . . . by engaging with 'moderate' and 'mainstream' organizations."[37] The Chanel program, under the auspices of the Prevent strategy, has actively intervened with potentially violent extremists. Also in Britain, groups like the Quilliam Foundation have directly challenged Islamists' interpretations of texts. In Germany, imams in Berlin visited with parents of youth threatening violence. In Denmark, local communities have shown resilience to Islamist ideologies through strong family networks, schools, and municipal youth clubs, as well as through actively engaged local police. In Amsterdam, local authorities tried to subsidize the construction of a "moderate" mosque, but their efforts backfired when the mosque directors refused to sign a declaration of "moderation."[38] In Indonesia, former president Abdurrahman Wahid and an American, C. Holland Taylor, created the LibForAll organization, which aims to promote "Muslims who endorse moderation, pluralism, and democracy."[39] In Pakistan, Khudi is a self-labeled "counter-extremism social movement" that aims to counter all forms of extremism through education and by directly debating proponents of extremism. In Nigeria, Yemen, and Pakistan, the U.S. State Department has sponsored television and media programs that provide alternatives to extremist ideologies. In Kosovo, moderates have created the website Foltash.com to counter Wahhabi interpretations of Islam.[40] In Australia, a government program works with schools to build "social cognitive resilience" to "prepare students to challenge the influence of violent extremism."[41] In an effort to support, coordinate, and fund many of these and similar initiatives, the United States has created the Global Counterterrorism Forum. Saudi Arabia has created the Global Center for Combating Extremist Ideology. It remains to be seen how impactful these initiatives will be.[42]

For all the efforts at promoting moderates and moderation, this approach suffers from several constraints. For example, the moderates are treated with distrust or seen as manipulated by the government, especially if the ties are obvious. In Britain the controversial Quilliam Foundation is viewed skeptically by many Muslims.[43] Furthermore, identifying true moderates is often difficult; governments have been "duped into regarding [Islamist groups] as representatives of 'moderate Muslims' simply because they do not engage in violence."[44] Additionally, the message needs to come out of existing narratives and moderate communities, when all too often the state tries to impose its own narrative on the targeted communities.[45] Furthermore, encouraging moderates to speak out against extremism has proven difficult because it puts them in the middle of an ideological battle in which they do not want to participate.[46] Nor are they as capable as the extremists in waging this fight. As Anna Simons argues, "moderates . . . cannot seize attention, let alone galvanize youth or sway public opinion, unless they are willing to speak or act with as much passion as partisans—and by definition they don't. . . . Moderates are never ruthless enough to defeat those bent on using violence to cleanse and purify."[47] Finally, sometimes the media may be perceived as inappropriate by the audience. Promulgating voices of moderation over the media only works if the targeted audience has access to the particular media outlet. This was a concern in Nigeria, for example, where a U.S.-sponsored television station had little impact because so few people owned televisions.[48]

Liberal states also face what Karl Popper coined "the paradox of tolerance" in addressing these extremist but not explicitly violent ideologies.[49] In a nutshell, how much intolerance should be tolerated? Are the activities of Islamists covered by protections of free speech? Can Islamist speech be monitored for security purposes or is it protected by free speech provisions? Should tolerant societies be willing to forcibly resist intolerance as a last resort, as Popper argued?[50] Free speech is well protected in most Western countries, but what about other countries still engaged in the process of democratization? Will they be willing to maintain protections for free speech if doing so reduces the state's security? In Africa, for example, McCormack argues that Islamists have been more successful in countries enjoying greater freedoms and democracy.[51] Faced with greater security threats, will they continue to tolerate speech that leads to extremism?

States can also target the *organizations* that provide the local supply of Islamism—the mosques, schools, centers, and so on. In the most direct sense, governments could close these institutions, prosecute their members, and restrict others from engaging in similar activities. For example, in Egypt the authorities banned unlicensed imams and preachers, particularly those affiliated with the Muslim Brotherhood, Salafists, and other Islamists who might be critical of the regime. Likewise, in Tunisia the government recognized that mosques were a key locus for radical recruitment and tried to control the messages being delivered in about four hundred Islamist-controlled mosques by replacing unauthorized imams with state-appointed preachers. In Indonesia, Pesantren al-Mukmin in Ngruki and Pesantren al-Islam have come under increased government scrutiny, while Luqmanul Hakiem in Malaysia has been closed. In France, after the attack on the *Charlie Hebdo* offices, the government closed twenty mosques for preaching extremism.[52] As mentioned earlier, Germany banned the Salafist organization known as True Religion.

In many countries the state cannot directly target these organizations because of legal protection of speech and religion, but they could still be monitored by government authorities.[53] For example, in the United Kingdom the Office for Standards in Education, Children's Services and Skills (Ofsted) monitors and regulates schools and other institutions. It has found instances of objectionable teaching and has required the promotion of "British values such as freedom, tolerance, and the rule of law."[54] Most prominently, the controversial Quilliam Foundation monitors Islamic organizations in the United Kingdom for extremist content. In Saudi Arabia "officials from the Ministry of Islamic Affairs monitored tens of thousands of the country's approximately 70,000 mosques, in addition to schools and websites."[55] In general, the effectiveness of this approach is limited. Shutting institutions and banning organizations likely leads to some short-term disruptions, but these organizations can mutate and reform. Additionally, where countries have strong laws protecting freedoms of speech and religion, the state has a more difficult time quashing nonviolent organizations. Even monitoring organizations has historically been restricted in the United States if the basis of the surveillance was tied to protected speech (i.e., speech not inciting violence).[56]

States can also target the *external funders*—charities and donors—that bring money into the country to set up local Islamist institutions. For example, since September 11 the United States has engaged in efforts to curtail the direct financing of terrorist networks. The United States unilaterally designated all branches of al-Haramain in 2008, including its headquarters in Saudi Arabia, for providing financial support to al-Qaeda. The United Nations Security Council, pursuant to resolutions 1267 and 1989, has also listed all branches of al-Haramain as being affiliated with al-Qaeda and has subjected them to sanctions.[57] After the 1998 U.S. embassy bombings in Dar es Salaam and Nairobi, "the Kenyan government banned five Islamic NGOs because of their alleged sympathies and funding of local Islamic fundamentalists. Those banned included Mercy Relief International, the Al-Haramain Islamic Foundation, Help African People, the IIRO and the Ibrahim Bin Abdul Aziz Al Ibrahim Foundation."[58] In Kosovo, authorities shut down the Saudi Joint Relief Committee for Kosovo, "whose name still appears on many of the mosques built since the war," as well as al-Haramain, when it became known as a front for al-Qaeda.[59]

While these efforts at targeting organizations and charities directly tied with terrorism have met with mixed success, going after the funding that *indirectly* leads to terrorism (through the promotion of extremist ideologies) is even more difficult.[60] As noted earlier, much of the money is funneled through Islamic charities, many of which are legitimate and do important charitable work.[61] Stopping the flow of funds to these groups would be complicated and controversial and likely reduce the flow of legitimate charitable giving. However, Saudi Arabia itself has started to monitor and regulate the flow of money coming out of charities.[62] Indonesia too has begun to more closely track the charitable contributions coming into the country. Making this course of action more difficult is that these charities are adaptive; when Kosovo banned al-Haramain, its staff and equipment were transferred to Al Waqf al Islami and continued to function.[63]

Indirectly, and not as a result of any policy, the funds available for countries, charities, and individuals to spread Islamism might decrease as oil revenues in the Gulf states decline. However, this is unlikely, as some estimates show they have enough proven reserves to last one hundred years.[64] Prices may fluctuate from year to year, but with futures markets and ample reserves, Saudi Arabia can weather much of any volatility.[65]

Finally, the *incentives* to spread Islamism could be undermined. The Saudi-Wahhabi connection is the most essential element to the global supply of Islamism. Arguably, all the other possible courses of action are likely to fail unless there is a decoupling of the centuries-old alliance between the Saudis and Wahhabis.[66] As Mohammad Zarif contends, "it is not the supposed ancient sectarian conflict between Sunnis and Shiites but the contest between Wahhabism and mainstream Islam that will have the most profound consequences for the region and beyond."[67] This course of action would be the most consequential but also the least likely to occur, although at least there has been some acknowledgment by the Saudis of their role in the rise of Islamist terrorism.[68]

To think that outsiders could play any role in this decoupling is probably foolish; instead, the Saudis themselves must be willing to undertake this process.[69] Historically, Wahhabism was contested by religious scholars in Saudi Arabia and elsewhere, suggesting it could be contested yet again. Efforts at decoupling Saudi Arabia from Wahhabism may come internally from the ground up.[70] According to Madawi Al-Rasheed, there is a growing but still struggling grassroots "modernist" movement in Saudi Arabia. Called Tanwiris (meaning promoters of enlightenment, but used pejoratively by Salafis), these modernists seek "a civil state that does not patronise and instrumentalize religion to justify inertia and repression."[71] They endorse a reinterpretation of Islamic political theology, advocate for participatory democracy, and reject theocracy. Not surprisingly, they have suffered at the hands of the Saudi state. More recently, there were some preliminary signs that Crown Prince Mohammed bin Salman might push further to modernize the kingdom and marginalize the Wahhabi religious establishment.[72] If the crown prince succeeds, the impact would be felt beyond just Saudi Arabia; as Kamel Daoud argues, if Saudi Arabia, "the motherland of fatwas, undertakes reforms, Islamists throughout the world will have to follow suit or risk winding up on the wrong side of orthodoxy."[73]

In the past the Saudi state has undertaken some efforts to curb extreme Wahhabism. After 9/11 and the 2003 Riyadh bombings, the Saudis did begin to target extremists and question the role of Wahhabism in Saudi Arabian life and politics. The Saudi government became less tolerant of inflammatory rhetoric, purged two thousand clerics, established more control over charities, tried to block the transmission of cash outside its borders, and cooperated more with international institutions. All of these efforts were in the right direction, but they were not always fully supported and implemented.[74] As Cole Bunzel argues, "the limited revision of Wahhabism that took place in the wake of the AQAP [Al-Qaeda in the Arabian Peninsula] campaign of 2003 to 2007 was largely superficial."[75]

FINAL THOUGHTS

In the end, whether Islamism (and all of its violent variants) continues its ascendance or falls into retreat will be a struggle between the forces of tolerance on one side and of intolerance on the other. On the side of intolerance there are individuals who believe not only that their ideology or way of life is correct but also that all others who do not follow along must be punished and even killed. On the side of tolerance there are individuals who strongly believe in their own views but accept the diversity of beliefs among others. This is not a new fight; intolerant ideologues have always been a dangerous threat.[76] But intolerance, taken to its logical extreme, can only end in death for everyone except followers of the last ideology standing. Voltaire, writing in the 1700s when branches of Christianity were killing each other, recognized this in his plea for tolerance. Summarizing Voltaire's philosophy, Simon Harvey writes, "There are very few things that we can know for certain, particularly in matters which concern the ultimate meaning of things.... Since we cannot be sure about absolute truths, we should not seek to impose our answers to imponderable questions on fellow human beings who may not agree with us. The only civilized stance therefore is one of tolerance, opposed to all forms of dogmatism."[77]

Notes

1. THE SUPPLY OF AN IDEOLOGY

1. Rapoport, "Four Waves of Modern Terrorism." As Mark Juergensmeyer notes, "In 1980 the U.S. State Department roster of international terrorist groups listed scarcely a single religious organization. Almost twenty years later, at the end of the twentieth century, over half were religious." Juergensmeyer, *Terror in the Mind of God*, 6.
2. As characterized in Cronin, "Behind the Curve," 41–42. Robert Pape, in *Dying to Win*, finds that even though suicide terrorism is not associated with any one religion per se, about half of all suicide attacks from 1980 to 1993 were carried out by Islamic extremists.
3. Rapoport, "Four Waves of Modern Terrorism."
4. For examples of the approach that identifies the evolution of ideology, see Gerges, *Far Enemy*; and Kepel, *Jihad*.
5. Al-Rasheed, "Minaret and the Palace," 200.
6. For more on root causes, see Davis and Cragin, *Social Sciences for Counterterrorism*; Cronin, "Sources of Contemporary Terrorism"; and Breen, *Violent Islamism in Egypt*. Breen argues that the central factors leading to the rise of radicalization in the 1970s and onward were "modernization, Western encroachment, tyrannical rule and corruption by the national elite, gross inequality, poverty, and lack of economic development" (10).
7. Hegghammer, *Jihad in Saudi Arabia*.

8. Note that Hegghammer recognizes the importance of the "supply" of ideology *in combination* with these violent conflicts: "the rise of populist pan-Islamism in the 1980s was above all a result of the accumulated propaganda effort of the international Islamic organisations, which had been working relentlessly since the 1970s." Hegghammer, *Jihad in Saudi Arabia*, 21.

9. Hegghammer, *Jihad in Saudi Arabia*, 31.

10. Ayaan Hirsi Ali points to one group of scholars for whom Islamic religion plays a secondary role to the "root causes" of poverty and corruption for terrorism. See A. Ali, *Challenge of Dawa*, 14.

11. McAdam, Tarrow, and Tilly, *Dynamics of Contention*. See also Wiktorowicz, *Islamic Activism*, 6–16; and Robinson, "Hamas as Social Movement," 116.

12. Exceptions are Gold, *Hatred's Kingdom*; and Schwartz, *Two Faces of Islam*. Also, state sponsorship of terrorism would fall into the supply side and has been well studied.

13. See the recommendations from Windsor, "Promoting Democracy Can Combat Terrorism"; Mousseau, "Market Civilization and Its Clash with Terror"; and Pape, *Dying to Win*.

14. Sageman, *Understanding Terror Networks*, vii. For other examples, see Wright, *Looming Tower*; Schwartz, *Two Faces of Islam*; Kepel, *Jihad*; Mamdani, *Good Muslim, Bad Muslim*; Lewis, *Crisis of Islam*; Bin Ali, *Roots of Religious Extremism*; Hegghammer, *Jihad in Saudi Arabia*; and Bale, "Islamism and Totalitarianism." On the spread of terrorist ideologies through propaganda, see Ingram, "Analysis of *Inspire* and *Dabiq*."

15. As the noted Islamist critic Ayaan Hirsi Ali argues, "in focusing only on acts of violence, we have ignored the ideology that justifies, promotes, celebrates, and encourages these acts." A. Ali, *Challenge of Dawa*, 15.

16. Lynch, *Sunni and Shi'a Terrorism*.

17. Khaled Abou El Fadl has discussed the advantages and disadvantages of using various labels for this strand of Islamic ideology, including "fundamentalists," "militants," "extremists," "radicals," "fanatics," "jihadists," and "Islamists." He ultimately concludes that the best label is "puritans," although note that the subtitle of his book includes the term "extremists." El Fadl, *Great Theft*, 16–20. Henri Lauzière in his *Making of Salafism* labels this strand a purist Salafism, in contrast to a modernist Salafism. See also "Islamism" and "Wahhabism," in Sfeir, *Columbia World Dictionary of Islamism*, 170–71; Hegghammer, *Jihad in Saudi Arabia*, 1–9; Meijer, *Global Salafism*, 1–32; and Haykel, "On the Nature of

Salafi Thought and Action." For a thorough history of Wahhabism, see Commins, *Mission and the Kingdom*.

18. Denoeux, "Forgotten Swamp."

19. Bale, "Islamism and Totalitarianism."

20. Hassan, "Danger of Takfir."

21. Hegghammer, *Jihad in Saudi Arabia*. In contrast to the present work, Hegghammer focuses explicitly on the violent forms of pan-Islamism and asks a similar question: Why has violent Islamism spread since the late 1970s?

22. Wiktorowicz, "Anatomy of the Salafi Movement."

23. John Bradley notes that, for Saudi youth, their "shallow understanding of Islam, taught by hard-line Wahhabi teachers and clerics, sits in their minds like a highly combustible tinder box, just waiting for a loose spark to set it alight." Bradley, *Saudi Arabia Exposed*, 96.

24. Simon Ross Valentine notes that "the commonalities between Wahhabi and *jihadist* ideology are striking." Valentine, *Force and Fanaticism*, 239.

25. Ameena Hussein, "Fighting for the Soul of Islam in Sri Lanka," *New York Times*, May 2, 2019.

26. Hannah Beech, "Sri Lanka Attacks: Hometown of Accused Mastermind Was Fertile Ground for Extremism," *New York Times*, April 28, 2019.

27. David Rapoport in "It Is Waves, Not Strains," argues there were four key events in 1979: the three discussed here, as well as the Camp David treaty, which we address as a secondary event later. Valentine discusses the same three events in *Force and Fanaticism*, 241–42. Caryl, "1979," also points to this year as a key inflection point for numerous trends and changes in international politics.

28. "Saudi Government Paper: Billions Spent by Saudi Royal Family to Spread Islam to Every Corner of the Earth," Special Dispatch No. 360, MEMRI TV, March 27, 2002, https://www.memri.org/reports/saudi-government-paper-billions-spent-saudi-royal-family-spread-islam-every-corner-earth.

29. See, for example, Lacroix, "Understanding Stability and Dissent in the Kingdom"; Al-Rasheed, *Contesting the Saudi State*; Valentine, *Force and Fanaticism*; and Center for Religious Freedom, *Saudi Arabia's Curriculum of Intolerance*.

30. For example, see AbuKhalil, "Determinants and Characteristics of the Saudi Role in Lebanon"; Bonnefoy, "Salafism in Yemen"; and Shehabi, "Role of Religious Ideology in the Expansionist Policies of Saudi Arabia."

31. This is not to say the export of Wahhabism to Saudi Arabia's immediate neighbors was "easy." See the sources in the preceding note for more details on the contested expansion of Wahhabism.

32. For examples of different bodies of literature, see Lesch, *1979*, which discusses the events of 1979; Gold, *Hatred's Kingdom*, and Schwartz, *Two Faces of Islam*, which discusses the foundations of Islam and the role of the modern Wahhabis in spreading an extremist variant. Juergensmeyer, *Terror in the Mind of God*, examines the role of religion in terrorism.

33. Al-Rasheed, *Kingdom without Borders*, comes closest to painting a similar picture. Various chapters look at similar pieces: Saudi influence in the Arabian Peninsula, the greater Middle East, other Muslim countries, and even the United States; the roots and contestations of Wahhabist interpretations of Islam; and Saudi efforts in the media realm. What these chapters, including the chapter on Indonesia, do not do is fully and systematically connect the dots from Saudi exportation of Wahhabism to the terrorism that has at times followed in its wake.

2. EXPORTING ISLAMISM

1. Kepel, *Jihad*, 24.
2. For an overview of the Iranian Revolution, see Sick, *All Fall Down*; Keddie, *Roots of Revolution*; and Amuzegar, *Dynamics of the Iranian Revolution*.
3. Lesch, *1979*, 30.
4. For more on Khomeini and his ideology, see Abrahamian, *Khomeinism*; and Kepel, *Jihad*, 36.
5. Barton, "Historical Development of Jihadi Islamist Thought in Indonesia," 41; Singh, *Talibanization of Southeast Asia*, 58, 77; International Crisis Group, "Al-Qaeda in Southeast Asia."
6. Robinson, "Hamas as Social Movement," 124–25; N. Hasan, *Laskar Jihad*, 24; Lesch, *1979*, 58; N. Hasan, *Laskar Jihad*, 38; Kepel, *Jihad*, 106 (see also 118).
7. N. Hasan, "Salafi Movement in Indonesia"; N. Hasan, *Laskar Jihad*, 38.
8. International Crisis Group, *Recycling Militants in Indonesia*, 13.
9. Burke, *Al-Qaeda*, 109. For more on this rivalry, see Mabon, *Saudi Arabia and Iran*.
10. See Bradley, *Saudi Arabia Exposed*, 81–83; N. Hasan, *Laskar Jihad*, 39; N. Hasan, "Salafi Movement in Indonesia," 87; Hegghammer, *Jihad in Saudi Arabia*, 23; Sageman, *Leaderless Jihad*, 105; Hardy, "Ambivalent

Ally"; and Ben Hubbard and Mayy El Sheikh, "WikiLeaks Shows a Saudi Obsession with Iran," *New York Times*, July 16, 2015.

11. For the most thorough account of the siege, see Trofimov, *Siege of Mecca*. The exact number of assailants is disputed. Bernard Lewis (*Crisis of Islam*, 82) says 1,000. David Lesch (*1979*, 60) says 225. Dore Gold (*Hatred's Kingdom*, 106) says several hundred. Jason Burke (*Al-Qaeda*, 56) says 400.

12. Trofimov, *Siege of Mecca*, 33; Lesch, *1979*, 60; Gold, *Hatred's Kingdom*, 107, 108.

13. Trofimov, *Siege of Mecca*, 86.

14. Trofimov, *Siege of Mecca*, 100, 239; Gold, *Hatred's Kingdom*, 108; Burke, *Al-Qaeda*, 56; Lewis, *Crisis of Islam*, 82.

15. Kepel, *Jihad*, 119.

16. Lesch, *1979*, 60.

17. Kepel, *Jihad*, 120; Burke, *Al-Qaeda*, 59; Singh, *Talibanization of Southeast Asia*, 9; Means, *Political Islam in Southeast Asia*, 160; "Saudi Arabia Turns against Political Islam," *The Economist*, June 23, 2018. Hegghammer points out that the internal Wahhabization was promoted by the Najdi Wahhabis, while the external spread of Islamism was promoted by the Hijazi-based organizations. Hegghammer, *Jihad in Saudi Arabia*, 24. See also Center for Religious Freedom, *Saudi Arabia's Curriculum of Intolerance*; Schwartz, *Two Faces of Islam*, xi; and Wahid, *Illusion of an Islamic State*, introduction.

18. For more on the religious divisions and opposition to Wahhabism within Saudi Arabia, see Bradley, *Saudi Arabia Exposed*, 58-60.

19. Gold, *Hatred's Kingdom*, 109 (al-Hattlan quote), 110.

20. Trofimov, *Siege of Mecca*, 100.

21. For histories of the Soviet intervention in Afghanistan, see Bradsher, *Afghan Communism and Soviet Intervention*; Goodson, *Afghanistan's Endless War*, esp. chap. 3; Galeotti, *Afghanistan*; and Lesch, *1979*, 45-56.

22. See Borer, *Superpowers Defeated*.

23. See, for example, Crile, *Charlie Wilson's War*.

24. Lesch, *1979*, 94. The civil war continued for years after the Soviets left. The Taliban finally established control of the country, ruling from the mid-1990s until 2001.

25. Sageman, *Understanding Terror Networks*, 2; Wright, *Looming Tower*, 108-9; Al-Rasheed, "Minaret and the Palace"; Crile, *Charlie Wilson's War*, 522.

26. Lesch, *1979*, 105; V. Brown and Rassler, *Fountainhead of Jihad*; Singh, *Talibanization of Southeast Asia*, 58-59. Samuel Huntington says twenty-

five thousand Arabs went through Pakistan to fight in Afghanistan. Huntington, *Clash of Civilizations and the Remaking of World Order*, 247.

27. Bergen, *Holy War, Inc.*, 59, 71; Katzman, *Al Qaeda*. Burke (*Al-Qaeda*, 70) posits that the Saudis matched the U.S. aid more or less dollar for dollar. Huntington (*Clash of Civilizations*, 247) has a little more detail of the breakdown for some years and claims the Saudis by themselves spent more than $3 billion on the war. See also Hegghammer, *Jihad in Saudi Arabia*, 24–30, 38–48.

28. Stern, *Terror in the Name of God*, 117.

29. Mamdani, *Good Muslim, Bad Muslim*, 154.

30. See V. Brown and Rassler, *Fountainhead of Jihad*.

31. Mamdani, *Good Muslim, Bad Muslim*, 126.

32. Burke, *Al-Qaeda*, 93. Mahmood Mamdani cites Tariq Ali, who estimates there were 2,500 madrasas, with 225,000 students graduating from them every year. Most of these students, though, stayed and fought in Pakistan's conflicts and did not go to Afghanistan. Mamdani, *Good Muslim, Bad Muslim*, 138.

33. Singh, *Talibanization of Southeast Asia*, 58; Means, *Political Islam in Southeast Asia*, 160.

34. Gold, *Hatred's Kingdom*, 129.

35. Schwartz, *Two Faces of Islam*, 167–69; Kepel, *Jihad*, 142; Burke, *Al-Qaeda*, 70–71; Singh, *Talibanization of Southeast Asia*, 21.

36. Barton, "Jihadi Islamist Thought in Indonesia," 43. See also International Crisis Group, *Jemaah Islamiyah in Southeast Asia*, 5.

37. Gold, *Hatred's Kingdom*, 97, 116; Burke, *Al-Qaeda*, 104.

38. Gold, *Hatred's Kingdom*, 131.

39. Not mentioned but also part of the story is the 1991 Gulf War, which forced Saudi Arabia to once again demonstrate its Wahhabi credentials in the face of criticism for letting foreign troops onto its soil. N. Hasan, *Laskar Jihad*, 58–60; U.S. Institute of Peace, *Jihadi Threat*.

40. Singh, *Talibanization of Southeast Asia*, 13; Dreyfuss, *Devil's Game*, 145.

41. Lesch, *1979*, 2.

42. Schwartz, *Two Faces of Islam*, 135, 151; Lesch, *1979*, 109; Kepel, *Jihad*, 61, 69; Gold, *Hatred's Kingdom*, 119; Al-Rasheed, "Introduction," 10.

43. Gold, *Hatred's Kingdom*, 87.

44. Lewis, *Crisis of Islam*, 128.

45. Kepel, *Jihad*, 103 (see also 98, 101).

46. Crile, *Charlie Wilson's War*.

47. For more on Camp David, see Lesch, *1979*, 34–45.

48. Determining precise funding numbers is difficult because of limited access to Saudi primary sources. AbuKhalil, "Determinants and Characteristics of the Saudi Role in Lebanon," 79.

49. For more on the early history of Wahhab and Saud, see Commins, *Wahhabi Mission and Saudi Arabia*; Bradley, *Saudi Arabia Exposed*, 6–10; El Fadl, *Great Theft*, 45–74; Kepel, *Jihad*, 50; Gold, *Hatred's Kingdom*, 17–21; and Allen, *God's Terrorists*, 42–68.

50. Schwartz, *Two Faces of Islam*, 81.

51. Gold, *Hatred's Kingdom*, 21.

52. Schwartz, *Two Faces of Islam*, 82.

53. Bradley, *Saudi Arabia Exposed*, 10; Schwartz, *Two Faces of Islam*, 83, 101. The second Saudi state existed from 1824 to 1891.

54. Gold, *Hatred's Kingdom*, 63.

55. Gold, *Hatred's Kingdom*, 73–74.

56. Gold, *Hatred's Kingdom*, 77. John Bradley notes that Faisal also had some relatively liberal positions on education and slavery. Bradley, *Saudi Arabia Exposed*, 20.

57. Burke, *Al-Qaeda*, 44; Gold, *Hatred's Kingdom*, 77.

58. Schwartz, *Two Faces of Islam*, 120.

59. From a study cited in Gold, *Hatred's Kingdom*, 79. See also N. Hasan, *Laskar Jihad*, 52. For more on the diversity of political opinions in Saudi Arabia, see Bradley, *Saudi Arabia Exposed*.

60. Trofimov, *Siege of Mecca*, 242; Gold, *Hatred's Kingdom*, 126; Woolsey, foreword to *Saudi Publications on Hate Ideology Invade American Mosques*; Al-Rasheed, "Introduction."

61. Burke, *Al-Qaeda*, 60.

62. David E. Kaplan, "Saudi Connection: How Billions in Oil Money Spawned a Global Terror Network," *U.S. News and World Report*, December 2003. Alex Alexiev argues in "Saudi Arabia" that others have made estimates of $76 billion to $87 billion per year. Ayaan Hirsi Ali cites estimates of $87 billion and $110 billion. A. Ali, *Challenge of Dawa*, 18.

63. Frum and Perle, *End to Evil*, 132. The origin of these figures is an article in a Saudi government weekly, *Ain Al-Yaqeen*, from March 1, 2002, available as "Saudi Government Paper: Billions Spent by Saudi Royal Family to Spread Islam to Every Corner of the Earth," Special Dispatch No. 360, MEMRI TV, March 27, 2002, https://www.memri.org/reports/saudi-government-paper-billions-spent-saudi-royal-family-spread-islam-every-corner-earth.

64. Kepel, *Jihad*, 72.

65. El Fadl, *Great Theft*, 70, 73–74.

66. Kepel, *Jihad*, 144; Al-Rasheed, "Introduction," 4, 9. According to Hegghammer, the Saudi religious establishment is more decentralized and segmented than commonly thought. Hegghammer, "Rise of Muslim Foreign Fighters," 82.

67. Frum and Perle, *End to Evil*, 154, 259; Schwartz, *Two Faces of Islam*, 199–200.

68. Kepel, *Jihad*, 67.

69. Burke, *Al-Qaeda*, 73, 145 (quote).

70. Burke, *Al-Qaeda*, 224.

71. Burke, *Al-Qaeda*, 230; Kepel, *Jihad*, 93 (quote).

72. Burke, *Al-Qaeda*, 203; Gold, *Hatred's Kingdom*, 126; Kepel, *Jihad*, 194 (quote).

73. Van Bruinessen, "Indonesian Muslims and Their Place in the Larger World of Islam," 5.

74. Simon Henderson, "Institutionalized Islam: Saudi Arabia's Islamic Policies and the Threat They Pose," testimony before the U.S. Senate Committee on the Judiciary, Subcommittee on Terrorism, Technology, and Homeland Security, September 10, 2003, https://www.judiciary.senate.gov/imo/media/doc/henderson_testimony_09_10_03.pdf; Burr and Collins, *Alms for Jihad*, 33; N. Hasan, "Salafi Movement in Indonesia," 86.

75. Muslim World League, http://www.muslimworldleague.org/mwlwbsite_eng/index.htm.

76. N. Hasan, *Laskar Jihad*, 37; Burr and Collins, *Alms for Jihad*, 33.

77. Al-Rasheed, "Saudi Religious Transnationalism in London," 154.

78. Burr and Collins, *Alms for Jihad*, 39.

79. U.S. Department of the Treasury Press Release, "Treasury Designates Al-Haramain Islamic Foundation," June 19, 2008, https://www.treasury.gov/press-center/press-releases/Pages/hp1043.aspx; United Nations Security Council, "Security Council Committee Pursuant to Resolutions 1267 (1999) 1989 (2011) and 2253 (2015) concerning Islamic State in Iraq and the Levant (Da'esh), Al-Qaida and Associated Individuals, Groups, Undertakings and Entities," https://www.un.org/securitycouncil/sanctions/1267.

80. Burr and Collins, *Alms for Jihad*, 37; U.S. Department of the Treasury, "Additional Background Information on Charities Designated under Executive Order 13224," https://www.treasury.gov/resource-center/terrorist-illicit-finance/Pages/protecting-charities_execorder_13224-i.aspx.

81. Pew Research Center, *Muslim Networks and Movements in Western Europe*, 27, 28.
82. Pew Research Center, *Muslim Networks and Movements in Western Europe*, 29, 31.
83. The importance of local dynamics is highlighted in Bonnefoy, "Salafism in Yemen."
84. Shehabi, "Role of Religious Ideology in the Expansionist Policies of Saudi Arabia," 183.

3. ISLAMISM IN INDONESIA

1. "Struggle for the Soul of Islam: Inside Indonesia," PBS, http://www.pbs .org/weta/crossroads/about/show_indonesia.html.
2. Means, *Political Islam in Southeast Asia*, 159.
3. Singh, *Talibanization of Southeast Asia*, xi, 2 (quote); Barton, "Historical Development of Jihadi Islamist Thought in Indonesia," 31; N. Hasan, *Laskar Jihad*, 31. See also N. Hasan, "Salafi Movement in Indonesia," 83; and N. Hasan, "Saudi Expansion, the Salafi Campaign, and Arabised Islam in Indonesia."
4. Solenn Honorine, "Indonesia: A Different Kind of Muslim Nation," *Newsweek*, March 22, 2010, 7.
5. Mark Woodward, "Turning up the Heat on Wahhabi Colonialism," Arizona State University Center for Strategic Communication (blog), September 2, 2009, http://csc.asu.edu/2009/09/02/turning-up-the-heat -on-wahhabi-colonialism/.
6. Wanandi, "Islam in Indonesia."
7. Martin Van Bruinessen has observed that "the high visibility of Indonesian Arabs in leading positions in radical movements seem[s] to point to their role as middlemen in a process of Arabization of Indonesian Islam." Van Bruinessen, "What Happened to the Smiling Face of Indonesian Islam?," 5. See also Bubalo and Fealy, "Joining the Caravan?," 50.
8. Wanandi, "Islam in Indonesia," 105; International Crisis Group, *Indonesia Backgrounder*; N. Hasan, "Saudi Expansion, the Salafi Campaign, and Arabised Islam in Indonesia," 265.
9. Wanandi, "Islam in Indonesia," 105–6.
10. Van Bruinessen, "*Ghazwul Fikri* or Arabization?," 5–6. Muhammidiyah and Nahdlatul Ulama are still the leading Muslim organizations in Indonesia today, with the majority of the Indonesian population belonging to either one or the other organization, which makes them two of the largest Muslim organizations in the world.

11. Van Bruinessen, "*Ghazwul Fikri* or Arabization?," 2 (quote), 6.

12. Fealy and Borgu, *Local Jihad*, 19.

13. Van Bruinessen, "*Ghazwul Fikri* or Arabization?," 10; Hosen, "Religion and the Indonesian Constitution," 36.

14. Woodward et al., *New Cultural Path for Indonesia's Islamist PKS?*

15. Van Bruinessen, "*Ghazwul Fikri* or Arabization?," 9.

16. The five principles of the Pancasila are belief in the one and only God; just and civilized humanity; the unity of Indonesia; democracy led by the wisdom of deliberations among representatives; and social justice for the whole of the people of Indonesia. Freedom of religion is guaranteed in Article 29 (2) of the Constitution, but the blasphemy laws adopted in 1965 recognize only six official religions—Islam, Catholicism, Protestantism, Buddhism, Hinduism, and Confucianism.

17. Van Bruinessen, "*Ghazwul Fikri* or Arabization?," 6, 9.

18. Van Bruinessen, "Genealogies of Islamic Radicalism in Indonesia," 117–54.

19. Van Bruinessen, "What Happened to the Smiling Face of Indonesian Islam?," 1.

20. Wanandi, "Islam in Indonesia," 107.

21. Abuza, "Muslims, Politics and Violence in Indonesia," 7; Ananta, *Indonesian Crisis*, 229.

22. Wanandi, "Islam in Indonesia," 107; Van Bruinessen, "*Ghazwul Fikri* or Arabization?," 17.

23. N. Hasan, "Salafi Movement in Indonesia," 83; Van Bruinessen, "What Happened to the Smiling Face of Indonesian Islam?," 2.

24. Abuza, "Muslims, Politics and Violence in Indonesia," 6–7.

25. During the Saudi king's 2017 visit, he announced a billion-dollar aid package, unlimited flights between Saudi Arabia and Indonesia, and the allotment of fifty thousand extra spots per year for Indonesian pilgrims to make the *hajj* to Mecca and Medina. See Mohshin Habib, "Saudi Arabia's 'Lavish' Gift to Indonesia: Radical Islam," Gatestone Institute, April 29, 2017, https://www.gatestoneinstitute.org/10228/indonesia-saudi-arabia.

26. Means, *Political Islam in Southeast Asia*, 160; International Crisis Group, *Jemaah Islamiyah in Southeast Asia*, 3; Barton, "Historical Development of Jihadi Islamist Thought in Indonesia," 43.

27. Barton, "Historical Development of Jihadi Islamist Thought in Indonesia," 37; N. Hasan, *Laskar Jihad*, 39.

28. Woodward and Rohmaniyah, "Contesting New Media."

29. Antara News, "Indonesia and Muslim World League Launch Islamic Media Website," December 24, 2012, https://en.antaranews.com/news

/86356/indonesia-and-muslim-world-league-launch-islamic-media
-website. Antara is Indonesia's state-run national news agency.

30. N. Hasan, *Laskar Jihad*, 55, 56.

31. International Crisis Group, *Jemaah Islamiyah in Southeast Asia*, 13–14; N. Hasan, *Laskar Jihad*, 57.

32. Abuza, "Funding Terrorism in Southeast Asia," 31. Dwikarna was subsequently detained at Manila's international airport after the Makassar bombings and found to be carrying C-4 explosives in his suitcase.

33. U.S. Department of the Treasury Press Release, "Treasury Announces Joint Action with Saudi Arabia against Four Branches of Al-Haramain in the Fight against Terrorist Financing," January 22, 2004, https://www
.treasury.gov/press-center/press-releases/Pages/js1108.aspx.

34. Hasan, *Laskar Jihad*, 41–42; David E. Kaplan, "Saudi Connection: How Billions in Oil Money Spawned a Global Terror Network," *U.S. News and World Report*, December 2003.

35. U.S. Department of the Treasury, "Protecting Charitable Organizations," http://www.treasury.gov/resource-center/terrorist-illicit-finance
/Pages/protecting-charities_execorder_13224-i.aspx.

36. N. Hasan, *Laskar Jihad*, 42, 55, 57.

37. N. Hasan, *Laskar Jihad*, 57; U.S. Department of Treasury, "Kuwaiti Charity Designated for Bankrolling al Qaida Network," June 13, 2008, https://
www.treasury.gov/press-center/press-releases/Pages/hp1023.aspx.

38. Bubalo and Fealy, "Joining the Caravan?," 61.

39. Adianto Simamora, "Bomb Funding Brought from Middle East by Couriers," *Jakarta Post*, August 20, 2009. As the cited article notes, Indonesia's chief of counterterrorism, Ansyaad Mbai, observed after the attacks that "the problem is that the money was not transferred via banks. . . . They [the sponsors] understand the government could freeze any money if it was transferred through the banking system. Therefore they use couriers to channel the funds."

40. Singh, *Talibanization of Southeast Asia*, 29–31; Barton, "Historical Development of Jihadi Islamist Thought in Indonesia," 34–36.

41. International Crisis Group, *Recycling Militants in Indonesia*, 2.

42. Van Bruinessen, "*Ghazwul Fikri* or Arabization?," 15; International Crisis Group, *Recycling Militants in Indonesia*, 3.

43. International Crisis Group, *Recycling Militants in Indonesia*, 2.

44. International Crisis Group, *Recycling Militants in Indonesia*, 5, 7.

45. Barton, "Historical Development of Jihadi Islamist Thought in Indonesia," 40.

46. Quoted in Andrew Higgins, "Indonesia Steps Up Pressure on Islamist Militants," *Washington Post Foreign Service*, May 13, 2010.

47. International Crisis Group, *Recycling Militants in Indonesia*, 24.

48. Singh, *Talibanization of Southeast Asia*, 62; International Crisis Group, *Recycling Militants in Indonesia*, 31.

49. International Crisis Group, *Recycling Militants in Indonesia*, 15; International Crisis Group, "Indonesia: Jemaah Islamiyah's Current Status," 14.

50. Barton, "Historical Development of Jihadi Islamist Thought in Indonesia," 37; N. Hasan, *Laskar Jihad*, 39.

51. Van Bruinessen, "Indonesian Muslims and Their Place in the Larger World of Islam," 5; N. Hasan, *Laskar Jihad*, 40.

52. N. Hasan, *Laskar Jihad*, 43; N. Hasan, "Salafi Movement in Indonesia," 88.

53. N. Hasan, *Laskar Jihad*, 41–42; Van Bruinessen, "Indonesian Muslims and Their Place in the Larger World of Islam," 6.

54. N. Hasan, *Laskar Jihad*, 42, 43; International Crisis Group, *Indonesia Backgrounder*, 6–7.

55. Dewan Dakwah Islamiyah Indonesia, https://dewandakwah.or.id/.

56. Barton, "Historical Development of Jihadi Islamist Thought in Indonesia," 38; Singh, *Talibanization of Southeast Asia*, 46 (quotes).

57. International Crisis Group, *Indonesia Backgrounder*, 7.

58. Others are listed in Barton, "Historical Development of Jihadi Islamist Thought in Indonesia," 37. See also Singh, *Talibanization of Southeast Asia*, 46; and N. Hasan, "Salafi Movement in Indonesia," 89–91.

59 N. Hasan, *Laskar Jihad*, 47–51; International Crisis Group, *Indonesia Backgrounder*, 8.

60. Woodward et al., *New Cultural Path for Indonesia's Islamist PKS?*, 5.

61. Quoted in Wahid, *Illusion of an Islamic State*, 194–95. Universities included the University of Indonesia (UI) in Jakarta, the Institute of Agriculture in Bogor (IPB), the Institute of Technology in Bandung (ITB), Gadjah Mada University (UGM) in Yogyakarta, Airlangga University in Surabaya, Brawijaya University in Malang, and the Hasanuddin University in Makassar.

62. Dhume, "Indonesian Democracy's Enemy Within."

63. N. Hasan, "Salafi Movement in Indonesia," 88.

64. International Crisis Group, *Indonesia Backgrounder*, 8.

65. On JI's Afghanistan experience, see Barton, "Historical Development of Jihadi Islamist Thought in Indonesia," 40–43; and International Crisis Group, *Jemaah Islamiyah in Southeast Asia*, 2–10. The latter source (7–

10) actually lists all the JI-affiliated men who went to Afghanistan in the 1980s and 1990s.

66. Barton, *Indonesia's Struggle*, 15.

67. International Crisis Group, *Jemaah Islamiyah in Southeast Asia*, 6; Singh, *Talibanization of Southeast Asia*, 52.

68. Barton, "Historical Development of Jihadi Islamist Thought in Indonesia," 44. JI was created in 1997 according to Singh, *Talibanization of Southeast Asia*, 52. For more on JI's organizational structure, see Singh, *Talibanization of Southeast Asia*, 65-76; and International Crisis Group, *Jemaah Islamiyah in Southeast Asia*, 11.

69. Barton, "Historical Development of Jihadi Islamist Thought in Indonesia," 45. For more on JI's ideology, see Singh, *Talibanization of Southeast Asia*, 76-77.

70. Barton, "Historical Development of Jihadi Islamist Thought in Indonesia," 45-46.

71. International Crisis Group, *How Indonesian Extremists Regroup*.

72. Barton, *Indonesia's Struggle*, 15-16.

73. International Crisis Group, "Indonesia: The Dark Side of Jema'ah Ansharut Tauhid," 4.

74. International Crisis Group, "Indonesia: The Dark Side of Jema'ah Ansharut Tauhid," 1.

75. N. Hasan, *Laskar Jihad*, 53-54.

76. N. Hasan, *Laskar Jihad*, 54 (quote), 55.

77. International Crisis Group, *Indonesia Backgrounder*, 21.

78. Singh, *Talibanization of Southeast Asia*, 47.

79. Martin van Bruinessen, "The Violent Fringes of Indonesia's Radical Islam," *ISIM Newsletter*, January 2002, 7, accessed at https://www .researchgate.net/publication/27703090_The_violent_fringes_of _Indonesia's_Islam/link/58b8024b45851591c5d7c22f/download.

80. N. Hasan, *Laskar Jihad*, 17, 217; Barton, "Historical Development of Jihadi Islamist Thought in Indonesia," 38.

81. N. Hasan, *Laskar Jihad*, 18, 54.

82. International Crisis Group, *Jemaah Islamiyah in Southeast Asia*, 14.

83. International Crisis Group, *Indonesia Backgrounder*, 24; Wahdah Islamiyah, https://wahdah.or.id/.

84. International Crisis Group, *Jemaah Islamiyah in Southeast Asia*, 14 (quote). For more on MMI, see International Crisis Group, "Al-Qaeda in Southeast Asia," 17.

85. International Crisis Group, *Jemaah Islamiyah in Southeast Asia*, 13-15.

86. International Crisis Group, *Indonesia Backgrounder*, 23.

87. N. Hasan, *Laskar Jihad*, 55–56.

88. International Crisis Group, *Indonesia Backgrounder*, 23; N. Hasan, *Laskar Jihad*, 57.

89. Bubalo and Fealy, "Joining the Caravan?," 60.

90. International Crisis Group, *Indonesia Backgrounder*, 25.

91. N. Hasan, "Salafi Madrasas of Indonesia," 247.

92. On numbers of pesantren and students, see Means, *Political Islam in Southeast Asia*, 161 (37,363 pesantren); and International Crisis Group, *Jemaah Islamiyah in Southeast Asia* (14,000 students). An ICG briefing says about 20 pesantren are tied to JI. International Crisis Group, "Indonesia: Jemaah Islamiyah's Current Status," 5. According to one author, JI targeted 141 for radicalization. Singh, *Talibanization of Southeast Asia*, 145. For more on the mainstream madrasas/pesantren, see Pallavi Aiyar, "In Indonesia, Madrasas of Moderation," *New York Times*, February 10, 2015.

93. Noor, "Ngruki Revisited."

94. International Crisis Group, *Terrorism in Indonesia*, 4, 7; Barton, "Historical Development of Jihadi Islamist Thought in Indonesia," 37.

95. Noor, "Ngruki Revisited"; International Crisis Group, *Jemaah Islamiyah in Southeast Asia*, 26.

96. International Crisis Group, *Terrorism in Indonesia*, 2.

97. International Crisis Group, *Terrorism in Indonesia*, 2, 4. Magouirk, Atran, and Sageman, "Connecting Terrorist Networks"; and Magouirk, "Connecting a Thousand Points of Hatred," all discuss the pesantren, and specifically Luqmanul Hakiem, as being important for the indoctrination of ideology *and* for associations created among individuals.

98. International Crisis Group, *Jemaah Islamiyah in Southeast Asia*, 26.

99. International Crisis Group, *Terrorism in Indonesia*, 7. For the rest of the list of pesantren associated with JI, see International Crisis Group, "Indonesia: Jemaah Islamiyah's Current Status," 4.

100. International Crisis Group, "Indonesia: Radicalization of the 'Palembang Group.'"

101. Barton, "Historical Development of Jihadi Islamist Thought in Indonesia," 37–38.

102. Van Bruinessen, "Traditionalist and Islamist Pesantrens in Contemporary Indonesia," 235, 237.

103. N. Hasan, "Salafi Madrasas of Indonesia," 247 (quote), 260.

104. N. Hasan, "Salafi Madrasas of Indonesia," 254, 255 (quote).

105. N. Hasan, "Salafi Madrasas of Indonesia," 257, 261 (quote).

106. N. Hasan, "Salafi Madrasas of Indonesia," 258–59.
107. Barton, "Historical Development of Jihadi Islamist Thought in Indonesia," 39; N. Hasan, *Laskar Jihad*, 43, 53.
108. International Crisis Group, "Al-Qaeda in Southeast Asia," 9; International Crisis Group, *Recycling Militants in Indonesia*, 16; International Crisis Group, "Indonesia: Jemaah Islamiyah's Current Status," 8, 10.
109. International Crisis Group, *Indonesia: Jemaah Islamiyah's Publishing Industry*, 9–10.
110. Adam Gartrell, "Saudi Cleared over Jakarta Hotel Attacks," *Sydney Morning Herald*, June 28, 2010, https://www.smh.com.au/world/saudi -cleared-over-jakarta-hotel-attacks-20100628-zevt.html.
111. Quote from Wahid, *Illusion of an Islamic State*, 203.
112. Bubalo and Fealy, "Joining the Caravan?," 61, 62, 75.
113. Wahid, *Illusion of an Islamic State*, 227.
114. International Crisis Group, *Indonesia: Jemaah Islamiyah's Publishing Industry*, 2; Barton, "Historical Development of Jihadi Islamist Thought in Indonesia," 38, 50; van Bruinessen, "Wahhabi Influences in Indonesia, Real and Imagined."
115. Bubalo and Fealy, "Joining the Caravan?," 62; International Crisis Group, *Indonesia: Jemaah Islamiyah's Publishing Industry*, 2.
116. International Crisis Group, *Indonesia: Jemaah Islamiyah's Publishing Industry*, 9.
117. Bubalo and Fealy, "Joining the Caravan?," 62.
118. N. Hasan, *Laskar Jihad*, 49, 54.
119. Barton, "Historical Development of Jihadi Islamist Thought in Indonesia," 39; International Crisis Group, *Indonesia: Jemaah Islamiyah's Publishing Industry*, 9–10.
120. Van Bruinessen, "Traditionalist and Islamist Pesantrens in Contemporary Indonesia," 235; International Crisis Group, *Indonesia: Jemaah Islamiyah's Publishing Industry*, 2.
121. Barton, "Historical Development of Jihadi Islamist Thought in Indonesia," 40, 51; International Crisis Group, "Indonesia: Jemaah Islamiyah's Current Status," 7. For other publishers, see N. Hasan, *Laskar Jihad*, 146.
122. International Crisis Group, *Indonesia: Jemaah Islamiyah's Publishing Industry*, 13.
123. International Crisis Group, *Indonesia: Jemaah Islamiyah's Publishing Industry*, 3.
124. International Crisis Group, *Indonesia: Jemaah Islamiyah's Publishing Industry*, 8.

125. Honorine, "Indonesia," 7.

126. Osman, "Reviving the Caliphate in the *Nusantara*," 607.

127. Haeril Halim and Fadli, "Salafi Movement Gains Ground in the Public Sphere," *Jakarta Post*, September 6, 2016, http://www.thejakartapost.com/news/2016/09/02/salafi-movement-gains-ground-in-public-sphere.html; Krithika Varagur, "Salafi Movement Grows on Indonesia's Batam Island," *Voice of America*, March 14, 2017, https://www.voanews.com/a/salafi-movement-grows-on-indonesias-batam-island/3764858.html.

128. Wahid, *Illusion of an Islamic State*, 17.

129. Woodward et al., *New Cultural Path for Indonesia's Islamist PKS?*, 2, 6.

130. Sadanand Dhume, "Indonesian Democracy's Enemy Within," Yale-Global Online, December 1, 2005, https://yaleglobal.yale.edu/content/indonesian-democracys-enemy-within.

131. Woodward et al., *New Cultural Path for Indonesia's Islamist PKS?*, 18.

132. Wahid, *Illusion of an Islamic State*, 229, 230 (quote).

133. Fealy and Borgu, "Local Jihad," 41; Osman, "Reviving the Caliphate in the *Nusantara*," 602 (quote).

134. Osman, "Reviving the Caliphate in the *Nusantara*," 609–10, 614.

135. International Crisis Group, "Indonesia: Implications of the Ahmadiyah Decree," 12, 13.

136. Megawati Wijaya, "Secular Revenge in Indonesia," *Asia Times Online*, February 25, 2012, http://www.atimes.com/atimes/Southeast_Asia/NB25Ae02.html.

137. International Crisis Group, "Indonesia: Implications of the Ahmadiyah Decree," 13–14.

138. Wahid, *Illusion of an Islamic State*, 192.

139. Wahid, *Illusion of an Islamic State*, 196, 201, 224 (quote), 225–26, 226.

140. Wahid, *Illusion of an Islamic State*, 204.

141. Wahid, *Illusion of an Islamic State*, 203.

142. Wahid, *Illusion of an Islamic State*, 206–7 (quote), 210.

143. Wahid, *Illusion of an Islamic State*, 214, 215.

144. Joe Cochrane, "Extremists 'Infiltrating' Mainstream," *Jakarta Globe*, April 3, 2009.

145. N. Hasan, "Saudi Expansion, the Salafi Campaign and Arabised Islam in Indonesia," 278.

4. ISLAMISM IN PAKISTAN

1. Haider, "Ideologically Adrift," 128.

2. Haqqani, "Ideologies of South Asian Jihadi Groups," 24.

3. Other scholars also attribute the import of Islamism into Pakistan as a response to the emergence of British colonialism: "global religious ferment, fueled in part by the understanding that the 'intolerance ingrained in modernity [is a] source of countertolerance.'" Khuri, *Freedom, Modernity, and Islam*, 27.

4. The Arabic word *jihad* translates as "to struggle or to persevere" but can be interpreted in two distinct ways: armed struggle or inner struggle. Pakistani Islamists refer to jihad as a militant struggle against nonbelievers, whereas moderate Muslims refer to it as a personal struggle that does not involve violence.

5. Abayas are traditionally worn by Saudi women. Hoodbhoy, "Pakistan."

6. Fair, Malhotra and Shapiro, "Islam, Militancy, and Politics in Pakistan."

7. Islam first arrived briefly in the Sindh region of modern-day Pakistan in AD 712 with Mohammad bin Qasim, an Arab general. His transitory claim to power, however, minimally impacted the predominantly Hindu-practicing society. H. Abbas, *Pakistan's Drift to Extremism*, 3.

8. Sahni, "Pakistan," 350.

9. The Barelvi school of thought originated in the nineteenth century in British India and is a subset of Sunni Islam. The Barelvis were heavily influenced by Sufi traditions and extremely tolerant of "diverse local Islamic traditions." H. Abbas, *Pakistan's Drift to Extremism*, 103, 252. Segments of the population also adhere to the Hanafi school of Sunni theology, which is one of the most liberal of all four Sunni denominations (others include Shafi'i, Maliki, and Hanbali). El Fadl, *Great Theft*, 152–53; Bokhari, "Radicalization, Political Violence, and Militancy," 84.

10. Omar Waraich, "Why Pakistan's Taliban Target the Muslim Majority," *Time*, April 7, 2011, http://content.time.com/time/world/article/0,8599,2063794,00.html.

11. The Deobandi school of thought began in 1867 at a madrasa in Uttar Pradesh, in British-controlled India, as a reactionary response to the educational model forced onto the largely Muslim population by the British, and it focused primarily on the rise of the Sunni denomination of Islam. The Wahhabi movement originated in Najd, which lies on the Arabian Peninsula, in the eighteenth century and had its doctrinal roots in the Hanbali *fiqh* (school of jurisprudence). The Hanbali school of thought is the strictest and most conservative school in Islamic jurisprudence. El Fadl, *Great Theft*, 152–53. Salafism was a reform movement begun in the nineteenth century by Jamal al-Din al-Afghani. Afghani called for a return to the pure form of Islam. Salafism's original inten-

tion was to assist Muslims in transitioning to modern society. However, Salafism has now come to be associated with a more orthodox goal of purifying Islam from external influences (both from traditional Muslim society and the West). Second-generation Salafis have deviated entirely from their predecessors and are now inextricably linked to Wahhabis. Roy, *Globalised Islam*, 233.

12. Fair, Malhotra, and Shapiro, "Islam, Militancy, and Politics in Pakistan," 517.

13. Shias primarily differ from Sunnis by venerating Hussein ibn Ali, the fourth caliph and grandson of the Prophet Muhammad, and regarding him as the true successor to the Prophet Muhammad. According to most Sunni fundamentalists, both Shias and Ahmadis are considered heretics because of their deviation from Islamic orthodoxy. Haqqani, "Ideologies of South Asian Jihadi Groups," 24. Muharram is in reference to the month in which Hussein ibn Ali was martyred in Ashura (literally meaning the "tenth" day of Muharram) at Karbala in 680 CE.

14. Zia ul-Haq also significantly contributed to Deobandism's transformation into a jihadi-based movement. Roy, *Globalised Islam*, 236.

15. There are five pillars in Islam: (1) belief in one God (Allah) and the Prophet Muhammad, (2) prayer, (3) fasting, (4) almsgiving, and (5) pilgrimage to Mecca and Medina in Saudi Arabia. Burki, "Creeping Wahhabization Pukhtunkhwa," 154, 162; Roy, *Globalised Islam*, 236.

16. Burki, "Creeping Wahhabization Pukhtunkhwa," 158, 172. *Ijtihad* is defined in Wehr, *Dictionary of Modern Written Arabic*, 143.

17. Al-Rasheed, *Kingdom without Borders*, 295; Burki, "Creeping Wahhabization Pukhtunkhwa," 172.

18. Burki, "Creeping Wahhabization Pukhtunkhwa," 158.

19. Wahhabi Muslims failed to recognize the importance that Pashtuns placed on existing tribal mores and customs related to the Pashtunwali code—*nang* (honor), *namous* (honor of female family members), *badal* (revenge), *ghayrat* (courage), and *melmastia* (hospitality). Burki, "Creeping Wahhabization Pukhtunkhwa," 162.

20. Burki, "Creeping Wahhabization Pukhtunkhwa," 154, 162, 175.

21. H. Abbas, *Pakistan's Drift to Extremism*, 212.

22. Abou Zahab, "Salafism in Pakistan," 130.

23. Haider, "Islam and the Early History of Pakistan"; Aslan, *No God but God*, 219.

24. The Two-Nation Theory, which asserts that religion constitutes nationality, became the founding principle for the Pakistani movement to establish a country for Muslims out of British India, which finally occurred in 1947.

25. During Jinnah's first presidential address, in 1947, he declared, "You are free; you are free to go to your temples. You are free to go to your mosque or to any other places of worship in this State of Pakistan. You may belong to any religion, caste, creed." Muhammad Ali Jinnah's First Presidential Address to the Constituent Assembly of Pakistan, August 11, 1947, http://www.columbia.edu/itc/mealac/pritchett/00islamlinks/txt _jinnah_assembly_1947.html.

26. H. Abbas, *Pakistan's Drift to Extremism*, 30; Cohen, *Idea of Pakistan*, 162 (quote).

27. T. Ali, *Clash of Fundamentalisms*, 176.

28. Kfir, "Islam in Post-9/11 Pakistan," 61; H. Abbas, *Pakistan's Drift to Extremism*, 30 (quote).

29. A common assertion exists that the Pakistani military always had a close relationship with Islamist groups—the "military-mullah nexus"—but that did not transpire under Khan. Nawaz, *Crossed Swords*, xxviii; Kfir, "Islam in Post-9/11 Pakistan," 61.

30. Ayub Khan wanted to "manufacture an ideology for Pakistan, one that glorified the army as the state's key institution." Cohen, *Idea of Pakistan*, 67, 168.

31. Mawdudi established JI in 1941 as an "an Islamist revivalist movement to promote Islamic values and practices" in Pakistan. JI was staunchly opposed to Jinnah's secular party from the very beginning, primarily because of Jinnah's failure to incorporate Islamic ideology during the framing of Pakistan's constitution. Lodhi, *Pakistan*, 144 (quote); Nawaz, *Crossed Swords*, xxviii.

32. V. Nasr, *International Relations of an Islamist Movement*, 35.

33. V. Nasr, *International Relations of an Islamist Movement*, 35; T. Ali, *Clash of Fundamentalisms*, 176.

34. V. Nasr, *International Relations of an Islamist Movement*, 35; H. Abbas, *Pakistan's Drift to Extremism*, 31 (quotes).

35. Cohen, *Idea of Pakistan*, 166; Sahni, "Pakistan," 357.

36. International Crisis Group, *Pakistan: Madrasas, Extremism and the Military*, 7.

37. "Cleansing Hindus from the Land of the Pure," Hindu Human Rights, April 27, 2012, http://www.hinduhumanrights.info/cleansing-hindus -from-pakistan-the-land-of-the-pure/; Cohen, *Idea of Pakistan*, 170.

38. "1973 Constitution of Pakistan," http://www.pakistani.org/pakistan /constitution/part9.html.

39. Kepel, *Jihad*, 100–101; Peter Niesewand, "Bhutto Is Hanged in Pakistan," *Washington Post*, April 4, 1947.

40. H. Khan, *Constitutional and Political History of Pakistan*, 579; Nawaz, *Crossed Swords*, 384–85. After seizing control, Zia ul-Haq proclaimed that "Pakistan was created in the name of Islam [and] will continue to survive only if it sticks to Islam. That is why I consider the introduction of the Islamic system an essential prerequisite to the country." Quoted in Talbot, *Pakistan*, 251.

41. The Hudood Ordinances were based on a skewed understanding of Islamic injunctions. Fair, Malhotra, and Shapiro, "Islam, Militancy, and Politics in Pakistan," 514.

42. Roy, *Globalised Islam*, 291.

43. Zia ul-Haq went so far as to adopt the slogan of the right-wing Pakistan National Alliance: Nizam-e-Mustafa (Social Order of the Prophet). Lodhi, *Pakistan*, 121.

44. It is important to recognize that the United States was also complicit in propping up religious radicalism in the region at this time. Between 1984 and 1994, the U.S. Agency for International Development provided more than $51 million to the University of Nebraska at Omaha to create textbooks that included violent pictures and Islamist teachings in effort to inconspicuously bolster anti-Soviet sentiments. Joe Stephens and David B. Ottaway, "From U.S., the ABC's of Jihad," *Washington Post*, March 23, 2002, http://www.ratical.org/ratville/CAH/USjihadABCs.html; Lodhi, *Pakistan*, 121.

45. Addelton, "Impact of the Gulf on Migration," 520; Al-Rasheed, *Kingdom without Borders*, 71.

46. Fair, Malhotra, and Shapiro, "Islam, Militancy, and Politics in Pakistan," 506.

47. S. Nasr, "Islam, the State, and the Rise of Sectarian Militancy," 92; Roy, *Globalised Islam*, 291. Afghanistan bore the brunt of the Saudi-Pakistani scheme to counter Soviet influence by funding the most lethal and hardline mujahedeen groups stationed in Pakistan and trained by the ISI. Islamism only penetrated the region after the war and with the emergence of the Taliban, which Saudi Arabia and Pakistan heavily backed in its rise to power. Abdul Rasul Sayaf and Gulbiddin Hikmatyar, both Islamic fundamentalists, were the largest recipients of Saudi money. Sayaf had studied at Al-Azhar University in Cairo and later established the Afghan Muslim Brotherhood (Akhwan-ul-Muslimeen) with Hikmatyar in 1969. He later had created Ittehad-e-Islami (Islamic Unity), a Wahhabi party, in Peshawar. Zaidi, *Insights on Security in Pakistan*, 74.

48. S. Nasr, "Islam, the State, and the Rise of Sectarian Militancy," 291.

49. In May 2009 the U.S. secretary of state, Hillary Clinton, did apologize to Pakistan for its abandonment in the 1990s.

50. Haider, "Ideologically Adrift," 125.

51. V. Nasr, *Shia Revival*, 167.

52. Bhutto's mother, Begum Nusrat Bhutto, was from Iran. Maitra, "Benazir Bhutto Visit Removes Saudi Doubts."

53. Cohen, *Idea of Pakistan*, 171.

54. Benazir Bhutto was later assassinated, on December 27, 2007, while leaving a campaign rally for the Pakistan Peoples Party at Liaquat National Bagh in the run-up to the January 2008 parliamentary elections.

55. T. Ali, *Clash of Fundamentalisms*, 191.

56. Musharraf retained his position as army chief until late 2007.

57. Nawaz, *Crossed Swords*, 532.

58. Aryn Baker, "Storming the Red Mosque," *Time*, July 10, 2007, http://content.time.com/time/world/article/0,8599,1641630,00.html.

59. "Scores Killed in Pakistani Attacks," BBC News, July 19, 2007, http://news.bbc.co.uk/2/hi/south_asia/6905808.stm.

60. Zia ul-Haq also heavily supported Deobandi madrasas. Sahni, "Pakistan," 349. According to Antoine Sfeir, the Ahle Hadith bears many similarities to Wahhabism and is often called that. "Ahl-i Hadith," in Sfeir, *Columbia World Dictionary of Islam*, 27.

61. Sahni, "Pakistan," 349.

62. Rānā, *A to Z of Jehadi Organizations in Pakistan*, 295–305; Khaled Ahmed, "The Power of the Ahle Hadith," *Friday Times*, July 12–18, 2002.

63. B. Ali, "Religious and Political Dynamics of Jamiat Ahle-Hadith in Pakistan," 2.

64. Abou Zahab, "Salafism in Pakistan," 131.

65. Abou Zahab, "Salafism in Pakistan," 131.

66. Cohen, *Idea of Pakistan*, 181.

67. Abou Zahab, "Salafism in Pakistan," 131.

68. Jamaat-ud-Dawa was formerly known as Markaz Dawa wa'l-Irshad. The Musharraf government banned the group in 2002 for funding militant groups, but it reappeared as JuD.

69. Abou Zahab, "Salafism in Pakistan," 133; H. Abbas, *Pakistan's Drift to Extremism*, 212.

70. Jamaat-ud-Dawa, http://jamatdawa.org/en/ (website is no longer active).

71. Quoted in Abou Zahab, "Salafism in Pakistan," 136.

72. Abou Zahab, "Salafism in Pakistan," 35–36.

73. "Pakistan Seals Jamaat-ud-Dawa Headquarters, Detains More Than 120 Suspected Militants," *Economic Times*, March 7, 2019.

74. LeT was initially founded in 1987 during the Afghan war, but it later refocused its jihadi operations on India-administered Kashmir. "My Story: By Hafiz Saeed," *Indian Express*, April 8, 2012, http://archive .indianexpress.com/news/my-story-by-hafiz-saeed/933846/0.

75. Abou Zahab, "Salafism in Pakistan," 36.

76. T. Ali, *Clash of Fundamentalisms*, 199.

77. Rānā, *A to Z of Jehadi Organizations in Pakistan*, 335.

78. Abou Zahab and Roy, *Islamist Networks*, 37.

79. Rānā, *A to Z of Jehadi Organizations in Pakistan*, 335; Abou Zahab and Roy, *Islamist Networks*, 40.

80. Tellis, "Menace That Is Lashkar-e-Taiba," 1.

81. "Lashkar-e-Taiba," Counter Extremism Project, 2018, https://www .counterextremism.com/threat/lashkar-e-taiba; "Lashkar-e-Taiba," Mapping Militant Organizations, Center for International Security and Cooperation, Stanford University, https://cisac.fsi.stanford.edu /mappingmilitants/profiles/lashkar-e-taiba#note2.

82. Declan Walsh, "Wikileaks Cables Portray Saudi Arabia as a Cash Machine for Terrorists," *The Guardian*, December 5, 2010.

83. Prepared Testimony of Steven Emerson and Jonathan Levin before the U.S. Senate Committee on Governmental Affairs, 108th Cong., 1st sess., July 31, 2003.

84. Tellis, "Menace That Is Lashkar-e-Taiba," 12.

85. "US Embassy Cables: Lashkar-e-Taiba Terrorists Raise Funds in Saudi Arabia," *The Guardian*, December 5, 2010, https://www.theguardian .com/world/us-embassy-cables-documents/220186.

86. International Crisis Group, *Pakistan: Madrasas, Extremism and the Military*, 13–14. The ISI has also been accused of financially supporting LeT "as a foreign policy tool." Saba Imtiaz, "US Suspected ISI, Military of Supporting LeT, JuD," *Express Tribune* (Pakistan), December 5, 2010, https://tribune.com.pk/story/86150/wikileaks-us-suspected-isi-military -of-supporting-let-jud/.

87. H. Abbas, *Pakistan's Drift to Extremism*, 204; Yusuf, *Sectarian Violence*, 4.

88. Lodhi, *Pakistan*, 123; Fair, Malhotra, and Shapiro, "Islam, Militancy, and Politics in Pakistan," 506.

89. Abou Zahab and Roy, *Islamist Networks*, 22, 24, 25.

90. Schmidt, *Unraveling*, 129.

91. "Lashkar-e-Taiba," Mapping Militant Organizations, Center for International Security and Cooperation, Stanford University.

92. Waqar Gillani, "Pakistan: Bail for Terror Suspect," *New York Times*, July 14, 2011, http://www.nytimes.com/2011/07/15/world/asia/15briefs -BAILFORTERRO_BRF.html?_r=0.

93. Mir, *Fluttering Flag of Jehad*, 231; V. Nasr, *Shia Revival*, 166.

94. Meredith Bennett-Smith, "Qari Abdul Hayee, Daniel Pearl Murder Suspect, Arrested in Pakistan," *HuffPost*, March 18, 2013, https://www .huffpost.com/entry/daniel-pearl-murder-suspect-arrested-qari-abdul -hayee_n_2903167.

95. Hussain, *Frontline Pakistan*, 94.

96. Hussain, *Frontline Pakistan*, 67.

97. V. Nasr, *Shia Revival*, 168; Yusuf, *Sectarian Violence*, 4.

98. Many JeM recruits received training in LeJ camps. "Jaish-e-Mohammad," Mapping Militant Organizations, Center for International Security and Cooperation, Stanford University, https://cisac.fsi.stanford .edu/mappingmilitants/profiles/jaish-e-mohammed#note41.

99. "Al-Rashid Trust," South Asia Terrorism Portal, http://www.satp.org /satporgtp/countries/pakistan/terroristoutfits/Al-Rashid_Trust.htm.

100. Hussain, *Frontline Pakistan*, 67; V. Nasr, *Shia Revival*, 164.

101. Hussain, *Frontline Pakistan*, 67.

102. "Lashkar-e-Taiba," "Mapping Militant Organizations," Center for International Security and Cooperation, Stanford University.

103. Christine Fair (*Madrassah Challenge*, 50) shows the growth from 464 schools in 1960 to 6,741 in 2000. For similar numbers, see Abou Zahab, "Salafism in Pakistan," 133; and Riaz, "Global Jihad, Sectarianism and the Madrassahs in Pakistan," 8. See Fair, *Madrassah Challenge*, in its entirety, for an overview of madsrasas in Pakistan. Note that Pakistani institutions are often spelled *maddrassah* for the singular and *madaris* for plural.

104. Other madrasas are run by the Tanzim-ul-Madaras (Barelvi), Wafaq-ul-Madaras (Deobandi), Wafaq-ul-Madaras (Shia), and Rabita-ul-Madaris (Jamaat-e-Islami) schools of thought. Ashfaq Yusufzai, "Pakistan: Violence Arising from Madrasas," *Global Information Network*, October 22, 2012.

105. Schanzer and Miller, *Facebook Fatwa*, 18; Asit Jolly, "The Wahhabi Invasion: Saudi Charities and Private Donors Pump in Huge Funds through Hawala Channels," *India Today*, January 2, 2012.

106. Riaz, "Global Jihad, Sectarianism and the Madrassahs in Pakistan," 5.

107. "Interview with Vali Nasr," *Frontline*, October 25, 2001, https://www.pbs .org/wgbh/pages/frontline/shows/saudi/interviews/nasr.html.

108. Ahle Hadith madrasas often provide classes in English, mathematics, and science so long as the teachings do not go against Islamic values. "2008: Extremist Recruitment," *Dawn*, May 22, 2011, https://dawn.com /2011/05/22/2008-extremist-recruitment-on-the-rise-in-south-punjab -madrassahs/.

109. Younger children between the ages of eight to twelve tend to be favored. "2008: Extremist Recruitment," *Dawn*, May 22, 2011. JI has been linked to the Al-Khidmat Foundation, a charity organization.

110. "2008: Extremist Recruitment," *Dawn*, May 22, 2011.

111. Abou Zahab, "Salafism in Pakistan," 133, 137.

112. International Crisis Group, *Pakistan: Karachi's Madrasas and Violent Extremism.*

113. Abou Zahab, "Salafism in Pakistan," 132.

114. Abou Zahab, "Salafism in Pakistan," 132–33.

115. International Crisis Group, *Pakistan: Madrasas, Extremism and the Military*, 11.

116. It is worth noting that Ahle Hadith madrasas are one of the only sources of education available for indigent children in Khyber Pakhtunkhwa. Haqqani, "Ideologies of South Asian Jihadi Groups," 24.

117. Al-Rasheed, *Kingdom without Borders*, 189.

118. Through the hawala system, money is not transferred physically or electronically. Rather, moneychangers "receive cash in one country and their counterparts in another country dispense an identical amount to a recipient or to a bank account. It is estimated that $2 billion to $5 billion move through the hawala system annually in Pakistan." International Crisis Group, *Pakistan: Madrasas, Extremism and the Military*, 15. See also Jolly, "Wahhabi Invasion."

119. Abou Zahab, "Salafism in Pakistan," 133.

120. Burki, "Creeping Wahhabization Pukhtunkhwa," 165.

121. Roy, *Globalised Islam*, 236; Sareen, *Jihad Factory*, 282.

122. Alexiev, "Pakistani Time Bomb," 49.

123. Thomas L. Friedman, "In Pakistan, It's Jihad 101," *New York Times*, November 13, 2001.

124. Siddique, *Red Mosque Operation*, 8.

125. Issam Ahmed, "Do School Texts Fuel Bias?," *Christian Science Monitor*, January 21, 2009, https://www.csmonitor.com/World/Asia-South -Central/2009/0121/p04s03-wosc.html/%28page%29/2.

126. Hussain, Salim, and Naveed, *Connecting the Dots*, 10, 52.

127. King Faisal bin Abdul-Aziz provided more than $120 million for the mosques' construction in 1986. Al-Rasheed, *Kingdom without Borders*, 189.

128. "History of IIUI," International Islamic University, https://www.iiu.edu.pk/?page_id=30.

129. Hoodbhoy, "Pakistan's Westward Drift."

130. Ashraf, "Islamization of Pakistan's Educational System."

131. Islam was also used as a "leveling force to tie Sindhi, the Pathan and the Baloch tribes, and initially the Bengals, together with the overarch regional and ethnic loyalties." Imtiaz Alam, "Of Punjabi and Punjabiyat," *News International* (Pakistan), April 20, 2001. See also Saigol, "Boundaries of Consciousness," 41-76.

132. Aly, "Education in Pakistan."

133. Hussain, Salim, and Naveed, *Connecting the Dots*, 42.

134. Hoodbhoy, "How Education Fuels Terrorism in Pakistan."

135. There were some education reforms in 2006 that slightly improved public textbooks by reducing sectarian biases, religious exclusions, and historical inaccuracies. However, these changes were marginal. Hussain, Salim, and Naveed, *Connecting the Dots*, 22.

136. Bubalo, Phillips, and Yasmeen, *Talib or Taliban?*, 20.

137. Joscelyn, "Al Qaeda Cell Targeted."

138. Hassan was sent back to Sudan despite JTF-GTMO's assessment that he posed very "high" risks to the United States and its allies. Joscelyn, "Al Qaeda Cell Targeted."

139. Saudi Arabia and Iran are fueling the fire by financing and arming Sunni and Shia extremist groups, respectively. David Montero, "Shiite-Sunni Conflict Rises in Pakistan," *Christian Science Monitor*, February 2, 2007, https://www.csmonitor.com/2007/0202/p01s02-wosc.html.

140. The spread of Islamism in Pakistan has also notably led to violence outside of Pakistan. The rise of the Taliban in Afghanistan during the 1990s was supported and facilitated by Islamist institutions within Pakistan.

141. Saudi investments in Pakistan make it unlikely for Pakistan to push back against Islamist/Wahhabi influences. Joseph Hincks, "Saudi Arabia Is Investing $20 Billion in Pakistan: Here's What It's Getting in Return," *Time*, February 19, 2019, https://time.com/5531724/saudi-arabia-pakistan-mbs-imran-khan/.

5. ISLAMISM IN BRITAIN

Chris Hucke provided research assistance for this chapter.

1. Pargeter, *New Frontiers of Jihad*, ix.

2. E. Brown, "After the Ramadan Affair," 9.

3. Sudarsan Raghavan and Joby Warrick, "How a 91-Year-Old Imam Came to Symbolize the Feud between Qatar and Its Neighbors," *Washington Post*, June 27, 2017, https://www.washingtonpost.com/world/middle _east/how-a-91-year-old-imam-came-to-symbolize-feud-between -qatar-and-its-neighbors/2017/06/26/601d41b4-5157-11e7-91eb -9611861a988f_story.html?utm_term=.e33ce98c2ed6; E. Brown, "After the Ramadan Affair," 9.

4. "History of Islam in the UK," BBC, last updated September 7, 2009, http://www.bbc.co.uk/religion/religions/islam/history/uk_1.shtml.

5. "History of Islam in the UK," BBC.

6. Gilliat-Ray, *Muslims in Britain*, 46; House of Commons, Home Affairs Committee, *Implications for the Justice and Home Affairs Area of the Accession of Turkey to the European Union*.

7. Gilliat-Ray, *Muslims in Britain*, 46.

8. Al-Rasheed, "Saudi Religious Transnationalism in London," 152.

9. Gilliat-Ray, *Muslims in Britain*, 50.

10. Whine, "Penetration of Islamist Ideology in Britain."

11. "Religion in England and Wales 2011," Office for National Statistics, https://www.ons.gov.uk/ons/rel/census/2011-census/key-statistics-for -local-authorities-in-england-and-wales/rpt-religion.html.

12. Ansari, *Muslims in Britain*.

13. As the Office for National Statistics notes, there are many factors driving changes in religious affiliation, including natural growth (a younger demographic profile), migration, changes in willingness to report, and awareness of the question. See "Religion in England and Wales 2011," Office of National Statistics.

14. S. Ali, "Second and Third Generation Muslims in Britain," 2008, 4, https://www.linkedin.com/pulse/second-third-generation-muslims -britain-socially-excluded-ralph-davis.

15. Brice, "Minority within a Minority," 11.

16. Bowen, *Medina in Birmingham, Najaf in Brent*.

17. Ansari, *Muslims in Britain*, 6.

18. Ansari, *Muslims in Britain*, 6.

19. "Our Affiliates," Muslim Council of Britain, https://mcb.org.uk/about/.

20. Al-Rasheed, "Saudi Religious Transnationalism in London," 156.

21. Phillips, *Londonistan*, 10.

22. "Britain," in Sfeir, *Columbia World Dictionary of Islamism*, 95.

23. Phillips, *Londonistan*, 10.

24. Kepel, *Allah in the West*, 83–84.

25. Kepel, *Allah in the West*, 4–5.

26. Kepel, *Allah in the West*, 135, 189 (quote). See also Al-Rasheed, "Introduction," 5.

27. Phillips, *Londonistan*, 12.

28. Jorgen S. Nielsen, "Obituary: Kalim Siddiqui," *The Independent* (UK), April 20, 1996, https://www.independent.co.uk/news/people/obituary-kalim-siddiqui-1305799.html.

29. Al-Rasheed, "Saudi Religious Transnationalism in London," 161.

30. Phillips, *Londonistan*, 6.

31. Phillips, *Londonistan*, 13.

32. Abedin, "Al-Muhajiroun in the UK."

33. Muslim World League London Office, http://www.mwllo.org.uk/about/.

34. *Dispatches*, episode "Undercover Mosque," aired January 15, 2007, on Channel 4.

35. MacEoin, "Hijacking of British Islam," 6 (quote), 26.

36. Al-Rasheed, "Saudi Religious Transnationalism in London," 155.

37. Al-Rasheed, "Saudi Religious Transnationalism in London," 153.

38. Center for Religious Freedom, *Saudi Publications on Hate*, 3.

39. Saleem, "History of Mosques in Britain."

40. Al-Rasheed, "Saudi Religious Transnationalism in London," 155.

41. Al-Rasheed, "Saudi Religious Transnationalism in London," 154, 155.

42. Pew Research Center, *Muslim Networks and Movements in Western Europe*, 23.

43. Abedin, "How to Deal with Britain's Muslim Extremists?"

44. Pew Research Center, *Muslim Networks and Movements in Western Europe*, 21.

45. Whine, "Penetration of Islamist Ideology in Britain."

46. Gilliat-Ray, *Muslims in Britain*, 76.

47. Quoted in Jamie Doward, "British Muslim Leader Urged to Quit over Gaza," *The Guardian*, March 7, 2009, https://www.theguardian.com/world/2009/mar/08/daud-abdullah-gaza-middle-east.

48. Pew Research Center, *Muslim Networks and Movements in Western Europe*, 23.

49. Whine, "Penetration of Islamist Ideology in Britain."

50. Pew Research Center, *Muslim Networks and Movements in Western Europe*, 22; "The Islamic Right—Key Tendencies," Awaaz–South Asia Watch, June 2006, http://web.archive.org/web/20070928033832/http://www.awaazsaw.org/awaaz_pia4.pdf.

51. Husain, *The Islamist*, 167, 207.

52. Husain, *The Islamist*, 24–25.

53. "Islamic Right—Key Tendencies," 3.

54. "Islamic Right—Key Tendencies," 3.

55. Hamid, "Development of British Salafism," 10.

56. Quoted in Johann Hari, "Renouncing Islamism: To the Brink and Back Again," *The Independent* (UK), November 16, 2009, https://www.independent.co.uk/voices/commentators/johann-hari/renouncing-islamism-to-the-brink-and-back-again-1821215.html.

57. Hari, "Renouncing Islamism."

58. Ansari, *Muslims in Britain*, 81.

59. Briggs and Birdwell, "Radicalisation among Muslims in the UK," 21.

60. Phillips, *Londonistan*, 7.

61. *Dispatches*, episode "Undercover Mosque—The Return," aired September 1, 2008, on Channel 4, https://vimeo.com/97538433; MacEoin, *Hijacking of British Islam*, 108.

62. Jamie Doward and Gaby Hinsliff, "PM Shelves Islamic Group Ban," *The Guardian*, December 24, 2006, https://www.theguardian.com/world/2006/dec/24/religion.uk.

63. Editorial, *Daily Times* (Pakistan), July 14, 2005.

64. Abedin, "Al-Muhajiroun in the UK."

65. Quoted in Abedin, "Al-Muhajiroun in the UK."

66. Abedin, "Al-Muhajiroun in the UK."

67. Ulph, "Londonistan."

68. Quoted in Abedin, "Al-Muhajiroun in the UK."

69. Quoted in Hari, "Renouncing Islamism."

70. Quoted in Hari, "Renouncing Islamism."

71. Ansari, *Muslims in Britain*, 80; Hamid, "Islamic Political Radicalism in Britain," 156.

72 All quoted in Abedin, "Al-Muhajiroun in the UK."

73. Ulph, "Londonistan."

74. "Islamic Right—Key Tendencies."

75. Vikram Dodd, "'I Still Have Influence,' Says Preacher Who Claims He Schooled Woolwich Suspect," *The Guardian*, May 24, 2013, http://www.guardian.co.uk/uk/2013/may/24/woolwich-murder-influence-preacher-suspect-adebolajo.

76. Raymond, *Al Muhajiroun and Islam4UK*, 8.

77. Wiktorowicz, *Radical Islam Rising*, 121; Raymond, *Al Muhajiroun and Islam4UK*, 12–13 (quote).

78. Dodd, "'I Still Have Influence,' Says Preacher Who Claims He Schooled Woolwich Suspect."

79. Tom Whitehead, "Woolwich Attack: Al Muhajiroun Linked to One in Five Terrorist Convictions," *The Telegraph*, May 24, 2013, https://www.telegraph.co.uk/news/uknews/terrorism-in-the-uk/10079827/Woolwich-attack-Al-Muhajiroun-linked-to-one-in-five-terrorist-convictions.html.

80. Pew Research Center, *Muslim Networks and Movements in Western Europe*, 46, 48 (quote).

81. Quoted in Susan Sachs, "A Muslim Missionary Group Draws New Scrutiny in the US," *New York Times*, July 14, 2003, https://www.nytimes.com/2003/07/14/us/a-muslim-missionary-group-draws-new-scrutiny-in-us.html?pagewanted=all&src=pm.

82. Quoted in Sachs, "Muslim Missionary Group Draws New Scrutiny in the US."

83. Pew Research Center, *Muslim Networks and Movements in Western Europe*, 46; Phillips, *Londonistan*, 8.

84. Pew Research Center, *Muslim Networks and Movements in Western Europe*, 48.

85. Jerome Taylor and Alex Ward, "Rejected: The Mosque Plan That Grew So Big It Attracted the Wrong Sort of Crowd," *The Independent* (UK), December 5, 2012, https://www.independent.co.uk/news/uk/home-news/rejected-the-mosque-plan-that-grew-so-big-it-attracted-the-wrong-sort-of-crowd-8386158.html.

86. Ulph, "Londonistan"; Michael Radu, "Preaching Jihad on Welfare: The Story of Abu Qatada," Foreign Policy Research Institute, July 16, 2008, https://theromangate.wordpress.com/2008/07/16/preaching-jihad-on-welfare-the-story-of-abu-qatada/.

87. O'Neill and McGrory, *Suicide Factory*, 134.

88. "Britain Finally Deports Qatada to Jordan after Decade Long Saga," *The Telegraph*, July 7, 2013, https://www.telegraph.co.uk/news/uknews/10164915/Britain-finally-deports-Abu-Qatada-to-Jordan-after-decade-long-saga.html.

89. O'Neill and McGrory, *Suicide Factory*, 14, 32–33.

90. O'Neill and McGrory, *Suicide Factory*, 106.

91. Mahan Abedin, "The Dangers of Silencing Saudi Dissent," *Asia Times*, January 21, 2005.

92. John Sweeney, "Bin Laden Connected to London Dissident," BBC News, March 10, 2002, http://news.bbc.co.uk/2/hi/uk_news/1862579.stm.

93. Paul Peachey and David Connett, "British Dissident Investigated over Colonel Gaddafi Plot to Assassinate Saudi King," *The Independent* (UK), March 25, 2016, https://www.independent.co.uk/news/uk/crime/british -dissident-investigated-over-colonel-gaddafi-plot-to-assassinate-saudi -king-a6952756.html.

94. Whine, "Penetration of Islamist Ideology in Britain."

95. Saleem, "History of Mosques in Britain."

96. Neumann and Rogers, *Recruitment and Mobilisation for the Islamist Militant Movement in Europe*.

97. Dyke, *Mosques Made in Britain*, 39.

98. Dyke, *Mosques Made in Britain*, 8.

99. Quoted in Dyke, *Mosques Made in Britain*, 12.

100. Dyke, *Mosques Made in Britain*, 17.

101. Al-Rasheed, "Saudi Religious Transnationalism in London," 157.

102. Al-Rasheed, "Saudi Religious Transnationalism in London," 156.

103. Sara Hassan, "Preachers of Separatism at Work inside Britain's Mosques," *The Telegraph*, August 31, 2008, https://www.telegraph.co .uk/news/uknews/2653266/Preachers-of-separatism-at-work-inside -Britains-mosques.html.

104. *Dispatches*, episode "Undercover Mosque," aired January 15, 2007.

105. *Dispatches*, episode "Undercover Mosque—The Return," aired September 1, 2008.

106. Dyke, *Mosques Made in Britain*, 39.

107. Al-Rasheed, "Saudi Religious Transnationalism in London," 157 (quote), 158.

108. *Dispatches*, episode "Undercover Mosque—The Return," aired September 1, 2008.

109. East London Mosque, http://www.eastlondonmosque.org.uk.

110. Husain, *The Islamist*, 24–25.

111. Husain, *The Islamist*, 29.

112. Husain, *The Islamist*, 280.

113. *Dispatches*, episode "Britain's Islamic Republic," aired March 1, 2010, on Channel 4, reporter's transcript available at https://andrewgilliganblog .wordpress.com/2010/10/22/britains-islamic-republic-full-transcript -of-channel-4-dispatches-programme-on-lutfur-rahman-the-ife-and -tower-hamlets-the-full-transcript/.

114. *Dispatches*, episode "Undercover Mosque," aired January 15, 2007; UK Islamic Mission, http://www.ukim.org.

115. Dyke, *Mosques Made in Britain*, 39–40, 42.

116. Pargeter, *New Frontiers of Jihad*, 180.

117. Sue Clough and John Steele, "Cleric Who Poisoned the Young Drip by Drip," *The Telegraph*, February 25, 2003, http://www.telegraph.co.uk/news /uknews/1423022/Cleric-who-poisoned-the-young-drip-by-drip.html.

118. Paul Kelso, "Terror Recruits Warning: Young Muslims 'Fall Prey to Extremists,'" *The Guardian*, December 26, 2001, http://www.guardian .co.uk/uk/2001/dec/27/september11.usa; Helen Gibson, "Looking for Trouble," *Time*, January 21, 2002, http://content.time.com/time /magazine/article/0,9171,193661,00.html.

119. O'Neill and McGrory, *Suicide Factory*, 40.

120. Neville Dean and Nick Allen, "Finsbury Park Mosque's Terror- ist Roll Call," *The Independent* (UK), February 7, 2006, https://www .independent.co.uk/incoming/finsbury-park-mosques-terrorist-roll-call -6109711.html.

121. O'Neill and McGrory, *Suicide Factory*, 43.

122. Chris Cook, "Saudis Donate Most to UK Universities," *Financial Times*, September 27, 2012, https://www.ft.com/intl/cms/s/0/b276dcc0-0893 -11e2-b37e-00144feabdc0.html#axzz2marbtJf8.

123. All-Party Parliamentary Group on Homeland Security, "Keeping Britain Safe: An Assessment of UK Homeland Security Strategy," April 2011, 36, https://henryjacksonsociety.org/publications/keeping-britain-safe-an -assessment-of-uk-homeland-security-strategy/.

124. Birt, "Wahhabism in the United Kingdom," 170.

125. Paul Vallely, "Wahhabism: A Deadly Scripture," *The Independent* (UK), November 1, 2007, https://www.independent.co.uk/news/uk/home -news/wahhabism-a-deadly-scripture-398516.html.

126. Malise Ruthven, "How the Saudis Used Oil Money to Export a Hardline Ideology That Fuels Islamist Terror," *The Independent* (Ireland), October 30, 2007, http://www.independent.ie/lifestyle/travel/how-the-saudis -used-oil-money-to-export-a-hardline-ideology-that-fuels-islamist -terror-26439342.html.

127. "Saudi School Lessons in UK Concern Government," bbc, November 21, 2010, https://www.bbc.co.uk/news/uk-11799713.

128. *Dispatches*, episode "Undercover Mosque—The Return," aired Septem- ber 1, 2008.

129. MacEoin, *Hijacking of British Islam*, 51–58.

130. *Dispatches*, episode "Undercover Mosque—The Return," aired Septem- ber 1, 2008.

131. T. Abbas, *Islamic Political Radicalism*, 5.

132. All-Party Parliamentary Group on Homeland Security, "Keeping Britain Safe."

133. Choudhury and Fenwick, *Impact of Counter-Terrorism Measures on Muslim Communities*, 68.

134. Center for Social Cohesion, *Radical Islam on UK Campuses*, 1, 12.

135. Center for Social Cohesion, *Radical Islam on UK Campuses*, 32, 33–35.

136. Pargeter, *New Frontiers of Jihad*, 143.

137. Hamid, "Islamic Political Radicalism in Britain," 149.

138. Tom Whitehead, "Extremists Attend More Than 200 University Events," *The Telegraph*, January 12, 2013, https://www.telegraph.co.uk/news /uknews/law-and-order/9796681/Extremists-attend-more-than-200 -university-events.html.

139. Quoted in Whitehead, "Extremists Attend More Than 200 University Events."

140. Mahsood, *British Muslims*, 50.

141. Mahsood, *British Muslims*, 50.

142. Mahsood, *British Muslims*, 50, 51.

143. Phillips, *Londonistan*, 2.

144. O'Neill and McGrory, *Suicide Factory*, 107, 112–13.

145. Vallely, "Wahhabism."

146. *Dispatches*, episode "Undercover Mosque—The Return," aired September 1, 2008.

147. Mahsood, *British Muslims*, 51.

148. Raymond, *Al Muhajiroun and Islam4UK*, 14.

149. Ruthven, "How the Saudis Used Oil Money."

150. Salafi Publications, https://twitter.com/SalafiPubs; Salafi Radio, http:// www.radiosalafi.com.

151. Ruthven, "How the Saudis Used Oil Money."

152. Quoted in Ruthven, "How the Saudis Used Oil Money."

153. Hamid, *Sufis, Salafis and Islamists*, 124.

154. Brandon and Murray, *Hate on the State*, 32.

155. Birt, "Wahhabism in the United Kingdom," 174.

156. "Islamic Right—Key Tendencies."

157. Husain, *The Islamist*, 283.

158. "Islamic Right—Key Tendencies," 5.

159. Al-Rasheed, "Saudi Religious Transnationalism in London," 164.

160. "Islamic Right—Key Tendencies," 5.

161. Husain, *The Islamist*, 279.

6. ISLAMISM IN THE UNITED STATES

1. Khaled Abou El Fadl, an Islamic scholar, has repeatedly criticized many U.S. Muslim leaders for their Wahhabi-influenced interpretation of Islam. El Fadl has argued that Islamic jurisprudence encourages intellectual debate, yet the influx of "Wahhabi puritanism" among U.S. Muslims has stifled Islamic dialogue. See El Fadl, *Great Theft*, 5–6, 16; and El Fadl, *And God Knows the Soldiers*, 20.

   Daniel Pipes, president and founder of the Middle East Forum (MEF), is a controversial figure who has discussed the growing Wahhabi influence in the United States and its implications with regard to radicalization. See Pipes, "Saudis' Covert P.R. Campaign," *New York Sun*, August 10, 2004; Pipes, "Scandal of U.S.-Saudi Relations"; and Pipes, "Why Islamism and the Left Hate Daniel Pipes," July 30, 2004, http://www .sullivan-county.com/id2/index2.htm.

   Charles Schumer (D-NY) led a 2003 congressional investigation to determine the extent of Islamic radicalization in U.S. prisons and the military. Schumer argued that Wahhabism was being imported to the United States and that it was infiltrating American society. Devlin Barrett, "Little Backlash When Schumer Led Probe of U.S. Muslims," *Wall Street Journal*, March 16, 2011.

   Stephen Schwartz, senior fellow of the Foundation for the Defense of Democracies, testified before a Senate panel detailing the growing influence of Wahhabism in the United States: "Shia and other non-Wahhabi Muslim community leaders estimate that 80 percent of American mosques—out of a total ranging between an official estimate of 1,200 and an unofficial figure of 4[000]–6,000—are under Wahhabi control." *Terrorism: Growing Wahhabi Influence in the United States: Hearing before the Subcommittee on Terrorism, Technology and Homeland Security of the Senate Committee on the Judiciary*, 108th Cong., 1st sess., June 26, 2003, 17, http://www.gpo.gov/fdsys/pkg/CHRG-108shrg91326/pdf/CHRG -108shrg91326.pdf.

   Zuhdi Jasser, founder and president of the American Islamic Forum for Democracy, an American Muslim advocacy organization, has repeated the discredited claim that 80 percent of mosques are run by extremists. Michelle Boorstein, "Anxiety on All Sides of Upcoming House Hearing on Radicalization of U.S. Muslims," *Washington Post*, February 27, 2011, http://www.washingtonpost.com/wp-dyn/content /article/2011/02/26/AR2011022600330.html.

2. According to a Pew Research Center report on American Muslims, American Muslim youth "are more likely than older Muslim Americans to express a strong sense of Muslim identity and are more likely to say that suicide bombing in the defense of Islam can be at least sometimes justified." The report also indicated that American Muslim youth are more religiously observant and attend services at mosques more than older American Muslims. They are also more accepting of Islamic extremism (15 percent believe suicide is allowed in defense of Islam). Rosentiel, *Muslim Americans*, 1, 7.

3. Institute of International Education, *Open Doors*.

4. GhaneaBassiri, *History of Islam in America*, 264.

5. This does not necessarily suggest that all these students were militants for these pan-Islamic organizations, such as the Muslim Brotherhood or JI. GhaneaBassiri, *History of Islam in America*, 273.

6. GhaneaBassiri, *History of Islam in America*, 275.

7. GhaneaBassiri, *History of Islam in America*, 275–89.

8. The Nation of Islam (NOI) was founded by Elijah Muhammad (formerly known as Marcus Garvey) in 1930 as an Islamic movement primarily for African Americans. The Moorish Science Temple of America was founded by Noble Drew Ali in the 1930s as a way to help African Americans develop a sense of national identity. Much of the scripture from *The Holy Koran of the Moorish Science Temple of America* completely deviated from the teachings of the Quran. The sole focus of the doctrine was on black salvation and a return to Africa. Smith, *Islam in America*, 80–81; Horgan and Braddock, *Terrorism Studies*, 472. African Americans constitute 20 percent of U.S. Muslims overall. Also, more than half of native-born Muslims are African American. Rosentiel, *Muslim Americans*.

9. Horgan and Braddock, *Terrorism Studies*, 470–72.

10. According to James Piscatori, when U.S. troops were dispatched to Saudi Arabia during the Gulf War, the majority of Muslims throughout the world condemned both the United States and Saudi Arabia. The former was accused of "violating the integrity of Muslim territory" and the latter, of agreeing to have their country occupied by the "enemies of Islam." Piscatori, "Religion and Realpolitik," 3–7.

11. Piscatori, "Religion and Realpolitik," 3–11.

12 "A Statement on the Recent Conflict in the Middle East," *Islamic Horizons*, July–August 1990, 8–9, https://issuu.com/isnacreative/docs.

13. Haddad, "Arab Muslims and Islamic Institutions in America," 70; Poston, *Islamic Da'wah in the West*, 102; Gold, *Hatred's Kingdom*, 147; Ahmed, "Muslim Organizations in the United States," 14.

14. Ahmed, "Muslim Organizations in the United States," 14–15.

15. GhaneaBassiri, *History of Islam in America*, 267.

16. The MWL was established as a counter to secular Arab nationalists. Its primary goal is da'wa, and it has historically financed other Wahhabi-leaning Islamists, which included JI members and the Muslim Brotherhood. DeCaro, *On the Side of My People*, 255–57; Curtis, "Islamism and Its African American Muslim Critics," 695; Pew Research Center, *Muslim Networks and Movements in Europe*, appendix 1.

17. GhaneaBassiri, *History of Islam in America*, 266–67.

18. Chris Hawley, "New York Police Department Monitored Muslim Students All over the Northeast," *Christian Science Monitor*, February 20, 2012, https://www.csmonitor.com/USA/Latest-News-Wires/2012 /0220/New-York-Police-Department-monitored-Muslim-students-all -over-the-Northeast.

19. Ba-Yunus and Kone, *Muslims in the United States*, 49–51.

20. Neil MacFarquhar, "For Muslim Students, a Debate on Inclusion," *New York Times*, February 1, 2008, https://www.nytimes.com/2008/02/21 /education/21muslim.html?pagewanted=1&_r=0&mtrref=undefined &gwh=5BF9A9425CCCCFD2565035A23AC9CA26&gwt=pay& assetType=REGIWALL.

21. Ba-Yunus and Kone, *Muslims in the United States*, 49–51.

22. MacFarquhar, "For Muslim Students, a Debate on Inclusion."

23. Cesari, *Encyclopedia of Islam in the United States*, 454.

24. The author has witnessed this directly among MSAs at UC Berkeley, UCLA, and UC Santa Barbara.

25. Abdo, *Mecca and Main Street*, 194–98.

26. Cesari, *Encyclopedia of Islam in the United States*, 454.

27. Lindsay Jordan, "Fast A Thon Enlightens People about Islam," *The Collegian* (Penn State University), September 24, 2013, https://www .collegian.psu.edu/news/campus/article_2c496398-2485-11e3-a341 -001a4bcf6878.html; "Fast-a-Thon Seeks to Raise Awareness for HIV/ AIDS, Ebola," *Penn State News*, December 3, 2014, https://news.psu .edu/story/336993/2014/12/03/campus-life/fast-thon-seeks-raise -awareness-hivaids-ebola.

28. GhaneaBassiri, *History of Islam in America*, 269.

29. Yigal Schleifer, "FBI Memo Illustrates How Hamas Raised Millions through Texas Charity," *Jerusalem Report*, December 31, 2001.

30. Emerson, *American Jihad*, 185.

31. Muzammil Siddique, ISNA's president from 1996 to 2000, received his master's degree from the Islamic University of Madinah. Previously, in the 1970s, he had worked for the Muslim World League's office at the United Nations. Mohammad Nur Abdullah, another former ISNA president, received his higher education from Umm al-Qura University in Mecca in the early 1980s. "Muzammil Siddiqi," ISNA, http://www.isna .net/muzammil-siddiqi/.

32. GhaneaBassiri, *History of Islam in America*, 336; Piscatori, "Religion and Realpolitik," 3–11; "Statement on the Recent Conflict in the Middle East," 8–9; Emerson, *American Jihad*, 184 (quote).

33 Steven Emerson has accused former ISNA leaders of endorsing anti-Israel, anti-American, and antisemitic sentiments, in addition to voicing support for Islamic fundamentalism in Sudan, Algeria, and Turkey. Emerson, *American Jihad*, 218.

34. Statement of J. Michael Waller, *Terrorist Recruitment and Infiltration in the United States: Prisons and Military as an Operational Base; Hearing before the Subcommittee on Terrorism, Technology, and Homeland Security of the Senate Committee on the Judiciary*, 108th Cong., 1st sess., October 14, 2003, http://web.archive.org/web/20080212073904/http:// judiciary.senate.gov/testimony.cfm?id=960&wit_id=2719.

35. Stephen Schwartz, "Wahhabism & Islam in the U.S.," *National Review*, June 30, 2003.

36. Islamic Society of North America, http://www.isna.net/azhar-azeez/.

37. Alexiev, "Wages of Extremism," 68, 75, 116.

38. "North American Islamic Trust (NAIT)," Clarion Project, February 11, 2013, https://clarionproject.org/north-american-islamic-trust-nait/.

39. In 1992 the institute formally began offering a bachelor's degree, the equivalent to what would be received at IBSIU. Heffelfinger, *Radical Islam in America*, 82.

40. Heffelfinger, *Radical Islam in America*, 81; Jerry Markon and Susan Schmidt, "Islamic Institute Raided in Fairfax," *Washington Post*, July 2, 2004, https://www.washingtonpost.com/wp-dyn/articles/A22243 -2004Jul1.html.

41. Heffelfinger, *Radical Islam in America*, 82.

42. Elmasry, "Salafis in America," 222.

43. Quoted in Mark Townsend, "Stockholm Bomber's Mosque Website Carries Links to Extremist Preacher," *The Guardian*, December 18, 2010, http://www.theguardian.com/world/2010/dec/19/abdaly-luton -mosque-stockholm-bomber. Philips is a Jamaican-born imam who has Canadian citizenship.

44. Gerard McManus, "John Howard Bans Islamic Leader," *Herald Sun* (Melbourne), April 4, 2007, available at https://www .couriermail.com.au/news/national/john-howard-bans-islamic -leader/news-story/9e5cd196b0377e12354da6ce93e61ecd?sv= 7bcabbadef8fc5e5282cd3e2eca1c0ef.

45. Andrew Gilligan, "Hizb ut Tahrir Is Not a Gateway to Terrorism, Claims Whitehall Report," *The Telegraph*, July 25, 2010, http://www.telegraph .co.uk/journalists/andrew-gilligan/7908262/Hizb-ut-Tahrir-is-not-a -gateway-to-terrorism-claims-Whitehall-report.html.

46. Dan Bilefsky and Jan Richter, "Muslim Leaders Denounce Police over Raids in Czech Capital." *New York Times*, April 28, 2014, http://www .nytimes.com/2014/04/29/world/europe/muslim-leaders-denounce -police-over-raids-in-czech-capital.html?_r=1.

47. Stewart Bell, "Controversial Canadian Muslim Preacher Accused of Inciting Terrorism and Arrested in Philippines," *National Post* (Toronto), September 10, 2014, https://nationalpost.com/news/canadian-muslim -preacher-accused-of-inciting-terrorism-arrested-in-philippines#_ _federated=1.

48. Elmasry, "Salafis in America," 222; Felix Allen, "Islamic Preacher Who Called Jews 'Filth' to Speak at London University," *Evening Standard* (UK), February 25, 2010, https://www.standard.co.uk/news/islamic-preacher -who-called-jews-filth-to-speak-at-london-university-6713828.html.

49. Quick later refuted the accusations made against him by stating in his blog, "The implicit—and obvious understanding for anyone who heard my lecture—was that I was asking God to heal the spiritual corruption that afflicts some members of religious groups which in turn leads to injustice against innocent people." Abdullah Hakim Quick, "How I Am Still Being Digitally Transformed into a Hate Cleric," HakimQuick.com, http://hakimquick.com/2014/01/. See also Sheri Shefa, "U of T Urged to Cancel Seminar by Islamic Scholar," *Canadian Jewish News*, November 2, 2011, https://www.cjnews.com/featured/jewish-learning/u-t-urged -cancel-seminar-islamic-scholar.

50. Heffelfinger, *Radical Islam in America*, 95.

51. Silber and Bhatt, *Radicalization in the West*, 60; Heffelfinger, *Radical Islam in America*, 97.

52. Jerry Markon, "Muslim Lecturer Sentenced to Life," *Washington Post*, July 14, 2005, https://www.washingtonpost.com/wp-dyn/content /article/2005/07/13/AR2005071302169.html.

53. Heffelfinger, *Radical Islam in America*, 98.

54. Masoud Khan was a Pakistani American who spent part of his childhood in Pakistan and Saudi Arabia. He came back to the United States at seventeen and attended Gaithersburg High School. After completing his GED, Khan enrolled in online courses at American Open University, which was founded by Jafar Idris in 1995. Khan then earned a scholarship to study at Riyadh University in Saudi Arabia. Upon graduating, Khan returned to Washington DC. Stephen Baxter, "Hanover a Stop in Jihadist's Travels," *York (PA) Daily Record*, November 21, 2004, 17.

55. Heffelfinger, *Radical Islam in America*, 92; Markon, "Muslim Lecturer Sentenced to Life."

56. Carlyle Murphy, "For Conservative Muslims, Goal of Isolation a Challenge," *Washington Post*, September 5, 2006, http://www.washingtonpost .com/wp-dyn/content/article/2006/09/04/AR2006090401107.html.

57. Markon and Schmidt, "Islamic Institute Raided in Fairfax."

58. Elmasry, "Salafis in America," 222.

59. Murphy, "For Conservative Muslims, Goal of Isolation a Challenge."

60. Heffelfinger, *Radical Islam in America*, 83; Murphy, "For Conservative Muslims, Goal of Isolation a Challenge." The raid was a joint effort by the United States and the Saudi monarchy. No one affiliated with the institute was charged with a terrorism-related crime.

61. Quoted in Markon and Schmidt, "Islamic Institute Raided in Fairfax."

62. Heffelfinger, *Radical Islam in America*, 86.

63. Barrett, *American Islam*, 225; Susan Schmidt, "Spreading Saudi Fundamentalism in the US," *Washington Post*, October 2, 2003, https://www .washingtonpost.com/archive/politics/2003/10/02/spreading-saudi -fundamentalism-in-us/771dbe9e-20e3-4d0e-95cd-3e531a93e5c9/.

64. Quoted in Heffelfinger, *Radical Islam in America*, 86.

65. Heffelfinger, *Radical Islam in America*, 87; "Magazine Writers Moved on to Islamist Groups," *Pittsburgh Tribune-Review*, August 4, 2002, https:// archive.triblive.com/news/magazine-writers-moved-on-to-islamist -groups/#axzz2pGt3YGM9 (quotes).

66. Barrett, *American Islam*, 226, 228.

67. Heffelfinger, *Radical Islam in America*, 53.

68. Gold, *Hatred's Kingdom*, 152, 153.
69. *Charitable and Humanitarian Organizations in the Network of International Financing: Testimony of Matthew Levitt before the Subcommittee on International Trade and Finance, Senate Committee on Banking, Housing, and Urban Affairs*, 107th Cong., 2nd sess., August 1, 2002; Gold, *Hatred's Kingdom*, 152.
70. "Data & Graphics: Population of the Communications Management Units," National Public Radio, March 3, 2011, https://www.npr.org/2011/03/08/134227726/data-graphics-population-of-the-communications-management-units.
71. "Former Muslim Charity Leader Keeps Citizenship, Trial Pending," Muslim Legal Fund of America, September 14, 2015, https://mlfa.org/news/former-muslim-charity-leader-keeps-citizenship-trial-pending/; Heffelfinger, *Radical Islam in America*, 75.
72. Perouz Sedaghaty was also known as Pete Seda. Bryan Denson, "Ashland Islamic Charity Seeks Removal from U.N. List of Entities Associated with al-Qaida," *The Oregonian*, August 30, 2013, https://www.oregonlive.com/pacific-northwest-news/2013/08/ashland_charity_seeks_removal.html.
73. "Former U.S. Head of Al-Haramain Islamic Foundation Sentenced to 33 Months in Federal Prison," Federal Bureau of Investigation, September 27, 2011, https://archives.fbi.gov/archives/portland/press-releases/2011/former-u.s.-head-of-al-haramain-islamic-foundation-sentenced-to-33-months-in-federal-prison.
74. Schwartz, "Wahhabism & Islam in the U.S." The funds were used to purchase land in Washington DC and to construct a headquarters facility.
75. Pipes and Chadha, "CAIR: Islamists Fooling the Establishment."
76. Neil MacFarquhar, "Scrutiny Increases for a Group Advocating for Muslims in U.S." *New York Times*, March 14, 2007, http://www.nytimes.com/2007/03/14/washington/14cair.html?_r=3&pagewanted=all&oref=slogin&oref=slogin&.
77. Jon Sawyer and Tim Townsend, "Randall 'Ismail' Royer's Letters from Prison," *St. Louis Post-Dispatch*, December 6, 2005, accessed at Pulitzer Center on Crisis Reporting, https://pulitzercenter.org/reporting/randall-ismail-royers-letters-prison.
78. Gretel Kovach, "Five Convicted in Terrorism Financing Trial," *New York Times*, November 24, 2008, http://www.nytimes.com/2008/11/25/us/25charity.html?_r=0.

79. "Threats and Response: Deportation; Man Sent Home to Lebanon Joins Relatives," *New York Times*, July 17, 2003, http://www.nytimes.com /2003/07/17/us/threats-and-responses-deportation-man-sent-home -to-lebanon-joins-relatives-there.html.

80. "Dispelling Rumors about CAIR," Council on American Islamic Relations, updated October 2017, https://www.cair.com/about_cair /dispelling-rumors-about-cair/.

81. Schwartz, *Two Faces of Islam*, 256. Schwartz refers to testimony by Sheikh Hisham Kabbini, president of the Islamic Supreme Council of America (ISCA), before a Senate committee in 1999. Kabbini, however, provided no evidence for his claims.

82. Testimony of Stephen Schwartz, *Hearing on Terrorism: Growing Wahhabi Influence in the United States, Subcommittee on Terrorism and Homeland Security, Senate Committee on the Judiciary*, 108th Cong., 1st sess., June 26, 2003, https://www.judiciary.senate.gov/imo/media/doc/Schwartz %20Testimony%20062603.pdf.

83. Shea, introduction to *Saudi Publications on Hate Ideology Invade American Mosques*, 2–3.

84. Blaine Harden, "Saudis Seek US Muslims for Their Sect," *New York Times*, October 20, 2001, https://www.nytimes.com/2001/10/20/us/a -nation-challenged-american-muslims-saudis-seek-to-add-us-muslims -to-their-sect.html.

85. Quoted in David Ottaway, "U.S. Eyes Money Trails of Saudi-Backed Charities," *Washington Post*, August 19, 2004, https://www .washingtonpost.com/wp-dyn/articles/A13266-2004Aug18.html.

86. As of 1994, there has been a 74 percent increase in the number of mosques throughout the United States. New York has the most mosques, with California coming in second. Bagby, *American Mosque 2011*, 4–5.

87. Heffelfinger, *Radical Islam in America*, 80.

88. Americans for Peace and Tolerance, *Case against the Islamic Society of Boston*.

89. Charles Radin and Stephen Kurkjian, "Saudi Bank's Role in Mosque Is Questioned," *Boston Globe*, January 10, 2007, http://www.boston.com /news/local/articles/2007/01/10/saudi_banks_role_in_mosque_is _questioned/; Jeff Jacoby, "The Boston Mosque's Saudi Connection," *Boston Globe*, January 10, 2007, http://www.boston.com/news/globe /editorial_opinion/oped/articles/2007/01/10/the_boston_mosques _saudi_connection/?page=full (quote).

90. Jerry Markon, "Muslim Activist Sentenced to 23 Years for Libya Contacts," *Washington Post*, October 16, 2004, https://www.washingtonpost.com/wp-dyn/articles/A36718-2004Oct15.html.

91. Siddique had married Khalid Sheik Mohammad's nephew, Ammar Al-Baluchi. Scroggins, *Wanted Women*, 246.

92. Oren Dorell, "Mosque That Boston Suspects Attended Has Radical Ties," *USA Today*, April 25, 2013, https://www.usatoday.com/story/news/nation/2013/04/23/boston-mosque-radicals/2101411/.

93. For a list of all ISB-affiliated people tied to terrorism, see Americans for Peace and Tolerance, *Case against the Islamic Society of Boston*.

94. Alexiev, "Wages of Extremism," 76–77; Patrick McDonnell, "Saudi Envoy in L.A. Is Deported," *Los Angeles Times*, May 10, 2003, https://articles.latimes.com/2003/may/10/local/me-deport10.

95. "Services," King Fahad Mosque, http://kingfahadmosque.org/services/.

96. "About," American Moslem Society, http://amsdearborn.org/history/.

97. Yemeni immigrants also stealthily began incorporating and emulating the deeply rigid and conservative cultural practices common in Yemen. Abdo, *Mecca and Main Street*, 50–53.

98. Abdo, *Mecca and Main Street*, 49; Khalil Al Hajal, "State's Oldest Mosque Celebrating 70 Years," *Arab American News*, May 2, 2009, https://www.arabamericannews.com/2009/05/02/States-oldest-mosque-celebrating-70-years/.

99. Abdo, *Mecca and Main Street*, 38. While the local government banned the *adhan* in other American cities, Dearborn was a rare exception because a significant proportion of residents are Muslims.

100. Abdo, *Mecca and Main Street*, 50.

101. In the 2000 census Arab Americans made up 40 percent of Dearborn's population. The city has the largest proportion of Arab Americans of any municipality in the United States. G. Patricia de la Cruz and Angela Brittingham, "The Arab Population: 2000," Census Bureau, December 2003, 7–8, https://www.census.gov/prod/2003pubs/c2kbr-23.pdf.

102. Mark Hicks, "Dearborn Mosque Hosts Open House after Threat," *Detroit News*, February 25, 2017, https://www.detroitnews.com/story/news/local/wayne-county/2017/02/25/dearborn-mosque-hosts-open-house-threat/98392612/.

103. Raphaeli, "Financing of Terrorism," 68.

104. Glenn Simpson, "Terror Investigators Followed Funds to a Saudi Businessman," *Wall Street Journal*, November 26, 2002, https://www.wsj.com/articles/SB1038261957100299628.

105. Raphaeli, "Financing of Terrorism," 68.

106. Raphaeli, "Financing of Terrorism," 26, 66 (quote).

107. Angel Jennings and Teresa Watanabe, "Mosque-Building Rises as Muslim American Clout Grows," *Los Angeles Times*, June 23, 2013, http://articles.latimes.com/2013/jun/23/local/la-me-ln-mosque-building-booms-as-muslim-american-clout-grows-20130623.

108. Some sources suggest that there are 350,000 Muslim inmates within the U.S. prison system. Islam is the fastest growing religion in U.S. prisons, where more than thirty thousand to forty thousand conversions take place annually. Ammar and Weaver, "Crime, Punishment, and Justice among Muslim Inmates," 66; Testimony of Michael Waller, *Terrorism: Radical Islamic Influence of Chaplaincy of the U.S. Military and Prisons, Hearing before the Subcommittee on Terrorism, Technology, and Homeland Security of the Committee on the Judiciary, United States Senate*, 108th Cong., 1st sess., October 14, 2003, 1, https://www.govinfo.gov/content/pkg/CHRG-108shrg93254/html/CHRG-108shrg93254.htm; "Facts and Fictions about Islam in Prison: Assessing Prisoner Radicalization in Post-9/11 America," Institute for Social Policy and Understanding, January 4, 2013, 9, https://www.ispu.org/facts-and-fictions-about-islam-in-prisons-assessing-prisoner-radicalization-in-post-911-america/.

109. "Dr. [Michael] Waller's Senate Testimony on Terrorist Infiltration," Center for Security Policy, October 14, 2003, https://www.centerforsecuritypolicy.org/2003/10/14/waller-testimony-on-terrorist-infiltration-2/.

110. Quoted in Hamm, *Spectacular Few*, 159.

111. "The Enemy Within: Gaffney Warns of Islamist Influence Operation in the U.S.," Center for Security Policy, December 9, 2003, https://www.centerforsecuritypolicy.org/2003/12/09/the-enemy-within-gaffney-warns-of-islamist-influence-operation-in-the-u-s-2/.

112. "A Review of the Bureau of Prisons' Selection of Muslim Religious Services Providers," U.S. Department of Justice Office of the Inspector General, April 2004, 8, https://oig.justice.gov/special/0404/index.htm.

113. "Facts and Fictions about Islam in Prison," 6.

114. Hamm, "Prisoner Radicalization," 18.

115. Prison Islam is being practiced when inmates "take certain parts of the overall Islamic tradition, such as adopting names and certain idioms, and graft them onto a gang lifestyle and other ideologies." "Facts and Fictions about Islam in Prison," 21. See also Malik, *Black America, Prisons and Radical Islam*; Hamm, *Terrorist Recruitment in American Correctional*

Institutions; John S. Pistole, Statement for the Record, *Terrorism: Radical Islamic Influence of Chaplaincy of the U.S. Military and Prisons, Hearing before the Subcommittee on Terrorism, Technology, and Homeland Security of the Committee on the Judiciary, United States Senate*, 108th Cong., 1st sess., October 14, 2003, 65, https://www.govinfo.gov/content/pkg /CHRG-108shrg93254/html/CHRG-108shrg93254.htm.

116. Center for Religious Freedom, *Saudi Publications on Hate Ideology Invade American Mosques.*

117. Doumato, "Saudi Arabian Expansion in the United States," 310.

118. Despite the differences in outcomes, ascribing too much causal weight to the exceptionalism of American Muslims is problematic. McCauley and Scheckter, "What's Special about U.S. Muslims?"

119. Ba-Yunus and Kone, *Muslims in the United States*, 27.

120. El Fadl, *Great Theft*, 170.

121. The United States reportedly has between three million and six million Muslims, although no official study of the census data has been conducted. GhaneaBassiri, *History of Islam in America*, 437; Ba-Yunus and Kone, *Muslims in the United States*, 24.

122. Pew Research Center, *World's Muslims.*

123. Quoted in Harden, "Saudis Seek US Muslims for Their Sect."

124. Ba-Yunus and Kone, *Muslims in the United States*, 26.

125. Muslim Public Affairs Council, https://www.mpac.org/; Heffelfinger, *Radical Islam in America*, 37. There are numerous Muslim advocacy organizations. According to its website, https://aicongress.org/, the American Islamic Congress is a 501(c)(3) entity committed to promoting responsible leadership and "two-way" interfaith understanding. The organization has "been involved in sensitivity training for law enforcement professionals and members of the armed forces, run workshops on non-violence, and lectured at universities and civic organizations." The American Islamic Forum for Democracy (https://aifdemocracy.org/) is an "online forum dedicated to promote [*sic*] an understanding of Islam in line with the separation of church and state and the principles of free market capitalism through providing news resources and commentary." The American Society for Muslim Advancement (https://www.asmasociety.org/) is "dedicated to building bridges between Muslims and the American Public." The Free Muslims Coalition (https://www.freemuslims.org/) works with Muslims in the United States and abroad to address the concerning trend of recourse to violence by some Muslims. The Islamic Information Center (https://islamicinformationcenter.org/) provides outreach on political,

media, and interfaith fronts. Muslim Advocates (https://muslimadvocates .org/) is "an organization committed to providing sophisticated and constructive legal and policy expertise to leaders in government and the Muslim American community." The Muslim Public Affairs Council (MPAC, https://www.mpac.org/) is "working to promote the civil rights of Muslims, the integration of Islam into American pluralism, and a positive, constructive relationship between American Muslims."

126. Pew Research Center, *World's Muslims*.

127. In the early part of the twenty-first century most American Muslims are first-generation immigrants (foreign born). It is estimated that by 2030 more than 40 percent of U.S. Muslims will be native born. In 2009 Pakistan and Bangladesh ranked as the top countries of origin for Muslim immigrants, and that is expected to be true in 2030. Among U.S. Muslims overall, the breakdown is 34 percent South Asian, 26 percent Arab, and 20 percent African American. Pew Research Center, *Future of the Global Muslim Population*; Rosentiel, *Muslim Americans*.

128. El Fadl has also argued that there is a "schism in Islam between Muslim moderates and what I will call the Muslim puritans. Both . . . claim to represent the true and authentic Islam. Both believe that they represent the Divine message as God intended it to be, and both believe that their convictions are thoroughly rooted in the Holy Book, the Qur'an, and in authentic traditions of the Prophet Muhammad, who was God's final prophet and messenger to humanity. Puritans, however, accuse the moderates of having changed and reformed Islam to the point of diluting and corrupting it." El Fadl, *Great Theft*, 5. He further elaborates, "Moderates constitute the silent majority of Muslims in the world, but puritans have an impact upon the religion that is wildly disproportionate to their numbers" (6). He refers to both hard-line Sunnis and Shias as puritans (16). See also El Fadl, *And God Knows the Soldiers*, 20.

129. El Fadl characterizes puritans as absolutist and uncompromising in their beliefs. Puritans are intolerant of competing views and consider pluralist realities to be a form of contamination of the unadulterated truth. The distinction that he makes is that this group is not always extremist (even though it is prone to radical rhetoric), but it is always puritanical. El Fadl, *Wrestling Islam from the Extremists*, 18–19.

130. "Hamza Yusuf: Follow a Madhab or Follow a Wahhabi/Salafi?," YouTube, October 10, 2013, https://www.youtube.com/watch?v=S -01WsNKNAE.

131. Cesari, *Encyclopedia of Islam in the United States*, 26. Keller is a Muslim convert who is a specialist in Islamic law and a sheikh (Islamic scholar) in the Shadhili Tariqa order, a Sufi order of Sunni Islam. Abu Zahra Foundation, 2018, http://www.abuzahra.org/teachers/sheikh-nuh-ha-mim-keller/. Wahhabis and Salafis do not accept two traditional Sunni schools of theology to which the majority of Sunnis have adhered for more than a millennium. One of these schools is the Ashari, named after Abu al-hasan al-Ashari (d. 935). The second is the Maturidis, named after Abu Mansour al-Maturidi (d. 944). The Ashari and Maturidi schools evolved out of the Sunni debates with the Mutazilites, who engaged in *kalam* (speech or debates) about Quranic interpretation. Salafis and Wahhabis consider kalam to be *bida'ah* (innovation) and thus heretical. Cesari, *Encyclopedia of Islam in the United States*, 20–23. Shakir is a Muslim American scholar, public speaker, author, and the co-founder of Zaytuna College in Berkeley, California. "American Learning Institute for Muslims," 2018, https://www.alimprogram.org/.

132. GhaneaBassiri, *History of Islam in America*, 264, 361.

133. "Safe Spaces Initiative," Muslim Public Affairs Council, https://www.mpac.org/safespaces/.

134. Barrett, *American Islam*, 12.

135. Rosentiel, *Muslim Americans*.

136. "Prominent Saudi Journalist: Extremism, Takfir, Are Everywhere in Saudi Arabia and the Authorities Are Doing Little to Stop This," Special Dispatch No. 6243, MEMRI TV, December 23, 2015, https://www.memri.org/reports/prominent-saudi-journalist-extremism-takfir-are-everywhere-saudi-arabia-and-authorities-are.

137. Hermansen, "How to Put the Genie Back in the Bottle?," 310.

138. Barrett, *American Islam*, 13.

139. Heffelfinger, *Radical Islam in America*, 79.

140. El Fadl, *Great Theft*, 168–69, 170.

141. Mark Potok, "FBI Reports Dramatic Spike in Anti-Muslim Hate Violence," *HuffPost*, November 14, 2011, https://www.huffpost.com/entry/fbi-reports-dramatic-spik_b_1092996.

142. "First Generation Muslim-Americans Navigate Challenges of Faith and Country," WNYC, October 16. 2013, https://www.wnyc.org/story/muslim-americans/.

143. Barrett, *American Islam*, 278.

7. COUNTERING AN IDEOLOGY

1. For a comprehensive account of Islamist activity around the world, see any of the yearly publications of the American Foreign Policy Council's *World Almanac of Islamism*.
2. Murawiec, *Princes of Darkness*, 49–50; Rabasa and Larrabee, *Rise of Political Islam in Turkey*; Baran, *Torn Country*; Eligür, *Mobilization of Political Islam in Turkey*; Ozgur, *Islamic Schools in Modern Turkey*; Delibas, *Rise of Political Islam in Turkey*.
3. Carlotta Gall, "How Kosovo Was Turned into Fertile Ground for ISIS," *New York Times*, May 21, 2016. This article offers a chronicle of the Wahhabification of Kosovo.
4. Bojan Pancevski, "Saudis Fund Balkan Muslims Spreading Hate of the West," *The Times* (UK), May 28, 2010; Ehrenfeld, "Their Oil Is Thicker Than Our Blood," 132.
5. Dan Bilefsky, "Islamic Revival Tests Bosnia's Secular Cast," *New York Times*, December 26, 2008; Choksy and Choksy, "Saudi Connection"; Valentine, *Force and Fanaticism*, 255–56; "CIA Report on NGOs with Terror Links," https://en.wikisource.org/wiki/CIA_Report_on_NGOs_With_Terror_Links.
6. Bala, "Financing of Islamist Groups in Albania," 186–92.
7. "Albania," in Sfeir, *Columbia World Dictionary of Islam*, 29.
8. Panovski, "Spread of Islamic Extremism in the Republic of Macedonia."
9. Speckhard and Akhmedova, "New Chechen Jihad," 106; Henkin, "From Tactical Terrorism to Holy War," 194–95.
10. Henkin, "From Tactical Terrorism to Holy War," 196.
11. Sharon LaFraniere, "How Jihad Made Its Way to Chechnya," *Washington Post*, April 26, 2003.
12. Speckhard and Akhmedova, "New Chechen Jihad," 111.
13. Napoleoni, *Terror Incorporated*, 123.
14. The article by LaFraniere, "How Jihad Made Its Way to Chechnya," claims al-Haramain sent $1 million and five hundred weapons to Chechen rebels in 1999. See also Henkin, "From Tactical Terrorism to Holy War," 199.
15. Henkin, "From Tactical Terrorism to Holy War," 197–99; Speckhard and Akhmedova, "New Chechen Jihad."
16. McCormack, *African Vortex*, 2; Solomon, *Terrorism and Counter-Terrorism in Africa*, 21, 29.
17. McCormack, *African Vortex*, 2.

18. McCormack, *African Vortex*, 6, 13.

19. McCormack, *African Vortex*, 7.

20. Solomon, *Terrorism and Counter-Terrorism in Africa*, 31.

21. McCormack, *African Vortex*, 7, 8–12; Loimeier, *Islamic Reform and Political Change in Northern Nigeria*; Valentine, *Force and Fanaticism*, 250.

22. McCormack, *African Vortex*, 6, 7.

23. Solomon, *Terrorism and Counter-Terrorism in Africa*, 30; International Crisis Group, *Countering Terrorism in a Failed State*, 13.

24. McCormack, *African Vortex*, 8.

25. "Saudi Government Paper: Billions Spent by Saudi Royal Family to Spread Islam to Every Corner of the Earth," Special Dispatch No. 360, MEMRI TV, March 27, 2002, https://www.memri.org/reports/saudi -government-paper-billions-spent-saudi-royal-family-spread-islam -every-corner-earth.

26. "Koran Study," *The Economist*, April 21, 2012, 66; Alexiev, "Wages of Extremism," 46–64; "German Ban on Islamist Group True Religion Confirmed as Complaints Dropped," Reuters, December 19, 2017, https://www.reuters.com/article/us-germany-security/german-ban -on-islamist-group-true-religion-confirmed-as-complaints-dropped -idUSKBN1ED1RC.

27. De Graaf, "Nexus between Salafism and Jihadism in the Netherlands," 22. The author also notes that the Hofstad Group was likely radicalized before attending the al-Fourqaan Mosque.

28. Schanzer and Miller, *Facebook Fatwa*, vi, 57.

29. Meleagrou-Hitchens and Kaderbhai, *Research Perspectives on Online Radicalisation*, 35.

30. Meleagrou-Hitchens and Kaderbhai, *Research Perspectives on Online Radicalisation*, 19, 31.

31. Kurlantzick, "Rise of Islamist Groups in Malaysia and Indonesia."

32. Gall, "How Kosovo Was Turned into Fertile Ground for ISIS."

33. De Graaf, "Nexus between Salafism and Jihadism in the Netherlands," 21; Schanzer and Miller, *Facebook Fatwa*, 16.

34. Bjørgo and Horgan, *Leaving Terrorism Behind*; Fink and Hearne, *Beyond Terrorism*; Stern, "Mind over Martyr"; Katherine Zoepf, "Deprogramming Jihadists," *New York Times Magazine*, November 23, 2008; Katharina Lestari, "Indonesia's Deradicalization Program under Fire," UCA News (Union of Catholic Asia), November 24, 2016, https://www .ucanews.com/news/indonesias-deradicalization-program-under-fire /77698; S. Khan, "Deradicalization Programming in Pakistan."

35. Huq, "Community-Led Counterterrorism."

36. "The Slow Backlash," *The Economist*, September 6, 2014.

37. Vermeulen, "Suspect Communities," 295.

38. Spalek and Weeks, "Role of Communities in Counterterrorism," 2017; U. Hasan, *Balance of Islam*; Vermeulen, "Suspect Communities," 299, 301; Dalgaard-Nielsen and Schack, "Community Resilience to Militant Islam," 314–19.

39. Jeff Jacoby, "Indonesia's Anti-Extremist," *Boston Globe*, January 22, 2006.

40. Khudi Pakistan, Twitter profile, https://twitter.com/khudipk; Ron Nixon, "U.S. Quietly Backs Nigerian TV Channel to Counter Terror Group," *New York Times*, June 6, 2014; Nicholas Kristof, "The Terrorists the Saudis Cultivate in Peaceful Countries," *New York Times*, July 2, 2016; Gall, "How Kosovo Was Turned into Fertile Ground for ISIS."

41. Aly, Taylor, and Karnovsky, "Moral Disengagement and Building Resilience to Violent Extremism," 369.

42. Husain, *Global Venture to Counter Violent Extremism*; Mohamed, "Saudi Arabia's Global Center for Combating Extremist Ideology."

43. "Quilliam Foundation Exposed by New Report as Having No Support amongst UK Muslims," *Engage*, June 15, 2009.

44. A. Ali, *Challenge of Dawa*, 16, 53.

45. For an example of how this could be done in Pakistan, see A. Khan, *Pakistan and the Narratives of Extremism*.

46. Kimiko de Freytas-Tamura, "Great Britain Appeals to Anti-Extremist Imams in Effort to Uproot Seeds of Radicalization," *New York Times*, August 24, 2014.

47. Simmons, "Making Enemies, Part Two," 42.

48. Nixon, "U.S. Quietly Backs Nigerian TV Channel to Counter Terror Group."

49. Popper discusses the paradox of tolerance in *Open Society and Its Enemies*.

50. A. Ali, *Challenge of Dawa*, 19, 21, 58.

51. McCormack, *African Vortex*, 3, 13.

52. "Manipulating the Minarets," *The Economist*, August 2, 2014; Wolf, "Radicalization of Tunisia's Mosques"; Singh, *Talibanization of Southeast Asia*, 137; A. Ali, *Challenge of Dawa*, 56.

53. For example, the prime minister of Kosovo tried to pass a law banning extremist religious sects but failed because freedom of religion is a civil right. Gall, "How Kosovo Was Turned into Fertile Ground for ISIS."

54. "Going by the Book," *The Economist*, June 26, 2014.

55. Rajab, *Re-Programming British Muslims*; Vikram Dodd, "List Sent to Terror Chief Aligns Peaceful Muslim Groups with Terrorist Ideology," *The Guardian*, August 4, 2010; Schanzer and Miller, *Facebook Fatwa*, 17 (quote).

56. See "The Levi Guidelines, 1976," in chapter 2 of *The Federal Bureau of Investigation's Compliance with the Attorney General's Investigative Guidelines (Redacted)*, Special Report, Office of the Inspector General, September 2005, https://oig.justice.gov/special/0509/.

57. Schwartz, *Two Faces of Islam*, 276; Prados and Blanchard, *Saudi Arabia*; U.S. Department of the Treasury Press Release, "Treasury Designates Al-Haramain Islamic Foundation," June 19, 2008, https://www.treasury.gov/press-center/press-releases/Pages/hp1043.aspx; United Nations Security Council, "Security Council Committee Pursuant to Resolutions 1267 (1999) 1989 (2011) and 2253 (2015) concerning Islamic State in Iraq and the Levant (Da'esh), Al-Qaida and Associated Individuals, Groups, Undertakings and Entities," https://www.un.org/securitycouncil/sanctions/1267.

58. Haynes, "Islamic Militancy in East Africa," 1324.

59. Gall, "How Kosovo Was Turned into Fertile Ground for ISIS."

60. Levitt, "Charitable Organizations and Terrorist Financing."

61. For a list of Islamic charities and their ties to terrorism, see Gold, *Hatred's Kingdom*, 229.

62. ACLU, *Blocking Faith, Freezing Charity*; Financial Action Task Force, *Anti-Money Laundering and Combating the Financing of Terrorism*; Byman, "U.S.-Saudi Arabia Counterterrorism Relationship."

63. Wahid, *Illusion of an Islamic State*, 19; Gall, "How Kosovo Was Turned into Fertile Ground for ISIS."

64. The picture might not be so rosy, however, if domestic consumption cuts into exports or if the price of oil drops. Both could lower revenues gained from oil exports. Daniel Tencer, "Saudi Arabia Oil Reserves: CitiGroup Notes Says Country May Be Oil Importer by 2030," *Huffington Post Canada*, updated November 12, 2012, https://www.huffingtonpost.ca/2012/09/06/saudi-arabia-oil-reserves_n_1862018.html.

65. For more on the economics of Saudi oil, see Luciani, "From Price Taker to Price Maker?"

66. Gold, *Hatred's Kingdom*, 245–48; Schwartz, *Two Faces of Islam*, 307; Ed Husain, "Saudis Must Stop Exporting Extremism," *New York Times*, August 22, 2014.

67. Mohammad Javad Zarif, "Let Us Rid the World of Wahhabism," *New York Times* (opinion), September 14, 2016.

68. Taddonio, "Saudi Official Makes Rare Reflection"; Hardy, "Ambivalent Ally," 109.

69. Saudi citizens are far from monolithic in their support for the Wahhabis. For more on the internal liberal critics of the Saudi regime, see Bradley, *Saudi Arabia Exposed*.

70. Al-Rasheed, *Kingdom without Borders*; Al-Rasheed, *Contesting the Saudi State*.

71. Al-Rasheed, *Muted Modernists*, 5.

72. Al-Rasheed, *Muted Modernists*, 2, 3; "Crown Prince Says Saudis Want Return to Moderate Islam," *BBC News*, October 25, 2017, https://www .bbc.com/news/world-middle-east-41747476.

73. Kamel Daoud, "If Saudi Arabia Reforms, What Happens to Islamists Elsewhere?," *New York Times*, November 16, 2017.

74. Bunzel, "Kingdom and the Caliphate," 20–25; Sageman, *Understanding Terror Networks*, 53, 182; Burr and Collins, *Alms for Jihad*, 48; "Saudi Arabia to Send 70 Imams to 35 Countries to Lead Taraweeh and to Teach against Extremism," *Milli Chronicle*, April 24, 2019, https:// millichronicle.com/2019/04/saudi-arabia-to-send-70-imams-to-35 -countries-to-lead-taraweeh-and-teach-moderate-islam/; Prados and Blanchard, *Saudi Arabia*; "U.S. Religious Freedom Body Urges Saudi to Prioritize Textbook Reform," Reuters, March 25, 2018, https://www .reuters.com/article/us-saudi-education/u-s-religious-freedom-body -urges-saudi-to-prioritize-textbook-reform-idUSKBN1H10NW.

75. Bunzel, "Kingdom and the Caliphate," 21. See also Hardy, "Ambivalent Ally," 107.

76. Voltaire, *Treatise on Tolerance*, 13.

77. Harvey, introduction to *Treatise on Tolerance*, by Voltaire, ix.

Bibliography

Abbas, Hassan. *Pakistan's Drift to Extremism: Allah, the Army, and America's War on Terror*. New York: M. E. Sharpe, 2005.

Abbas, Tahrir, ed. *Islamic Political Radicalism: A European Perspective*. Edinburgh: Edinburgh University Press, 2007.

Abdo, Geneive. *Mecca and Main Street: Muslim Life in America after 9/11*. Oxford: Oxford University Press, 2007.

Abedin, Mahan. "Al-Muhajiroun in the UK: An Interview with Sheikh Omar Bakri Mohammed." *Spotlight on Terror* 2, no. 5 (2004). https://jamestown.org/interview/al-muhajiroun-in-the-uk-an-interview-with-sheikh-omar-bakri-mohammed/.

———. "How to Deal with Britain's Muslim Extremists? An Interview with Kemal Helbawy." *Spotlight on Terror* 3, no. 7 (2005). https://jamestown.org/interview/how-to-deal-with-britains-muslim-extremists-an-interview-with-kamal-helbawy/.

Abou Zahab, Mariam. "Salafism in Pakistan: The Ahl-e Hadith Movement." In Meijer, *Global Salafism*, 126–42.

Abou Zahab, Mariam, and Oliver Roy. *Islamist Networks: The Afghan-Pakistan Connection*. New York: Columbia University Press, 2004.

Abrahamian, Ervand. *Khomeinism: Essays on the Islamic Republic*. Berkeley: University of California Press, 1993.

AbuKhalil, As'ad. "Determinants and Characteristics of the Saudi Role in Lebanon: The Post-Civil War Years." In Al-Rasheed, *Kingdom without Borders*, 81–100.

Abuza, Zachary. "Funding Terrorism in Southeast Asia: The Financial Net-
work of Al Qaeda and Jemaah Islamiyah." NBR Analysis 14, no. 5 (2003).
——. "Muslims, Politics, and Violence in Indonesia: An Emerging Jihadist-
Islamist Nexus?" NBR Analysis 15, no. 3 (2004).
Addelton, Johnathan S. "The Impact of the Gulf on Migration and Remit-
tances in Asia and the Middle East." International Migration 29, no. 4
(1991): 509–26.
Ahmed, Gutbi Mahdi. "Muslim Organizations in the United States." In The
Muslims of America, edited by Yvonne Yazbeck Haddad, 11–24. Oxford:
Oxford University Press, 1991.
Al-Rasheed, Madawi. Contesting the Saudi State: Islamic Voices from a New Gen-
eration. Cambridge: Cambridge University Press, 2007.
——. "Introduction: An Assessment of Saudi Political, Religious and Media
Expansion." In Al-Rasheed, Kingdom without Borders, 1–38.
——, ed. Kingdom without Borders: Saudi Political, Religious and Media Fron-
tiers. New York: Columbia University Press, 2008.
——. "The Minaret and the Palace: Obedience at Home and Rebellion
Abroad." In Al-Rasheed, Kingdom without Borders, 199–219.
——. Muted Modernists. Oxford: Oxford University Press, 2016.
——. "Saudi Religious Transnationalism in London." In Al-Rasheed, Trans-
national Connections and the Arab Gulf, 149–67.
——, ed. Transnational Connections and the Arab Gulf. London: Routledge,
2005.
Alexiev, Alex. "The Pakistani Time Bomb." Commentary 115, no. 3 (March
2003). https://www.commentarymagazine.com/articles/alex-alexiev/the
-pakistani-time-bomb/.
——. "Saudi Arabia: Exporting Radicalism." In Confronting Terrorism Financ-
ing, edited by the American Foreign Policy Council, 37–43. Lanham MD:
University Press of America, 2005.
Alexiev, Alexander R. "The Wages of Extremism: Radical Islam's Threat to
the West and the Muslim World." Hudson Institute Report, March 2011.
Ali, Ayaan Hirsi. The Challenge of Dawa: Political Islam as Ideology and Move-
ment and How to Counter It. Stanford CA: Hoover Institution Press, 2017.
Ali, Bizaa Zeynab. "The Religious and Political Dynamics of Jamiat Ahle-
Hadith in Pakistan." Course paper, Columbia University Academic Com-
mons, 2010.
Ali, Sundas. "Second and Third Generation Muslims in Britain: A Socially
Excluded Group?" October 23, 2015. https://www.linkedin.com/pulse
/second-third-generation-muslims-britain-socially-excluded-ralph-davis.

Ali, Tariq. *Clash of Fundamentalisms: Crusades, Jihads and Modernity*. London: Verso, 2002.

Allen, Charles. *God's Terrorists: The Wahhabi Cult and the Hidden Roots of Modern Jihad*. Cambridge MA: Perseus Books, 2006.

Aly, Anne, Elisabeth Taylor, and Saul Karnovsky. "Moral Disengagement and Building Resilience to Violent Extremism: An Education Intervention." *Studies in Conflict and Terrorism* 37, no. 4 (2014): 369–85.

Aly, Javed Hasan. "Education in Pakistan: Document to Debate and Finalize the National Education Policy." National Education Policy Review Team, February 2007.

American Civil Liberties Union. *Blocking Faith, Freezing Charity: Chilling Muslim Charitable Giving in the "War on Terrorism Financing."* New York: American Civil Liberties Union, June 2009.

American Foreign Policy Council. *World Almanac of Islamism: 2014*. New York: Rowman and Littlefield, 2014.

Americans for Peace and Tolerance. *The Case against the Islamic Society of Boston*. Boston: Americans for Peace and Tolerance, 2016. http://www.peaceandtolerance.org/wp-content/uploads/sites/4/2016/05/v2-final-June-2016.pdf.

Ammar, Nawal H., and Robert R. Weaver. "Crime, Punishment, and Justice among Muslim Inmates: The Meaning of Crime and Punishment to Muslim Inmates and Its Policy Implications." *African Journal of Criminology and Justice Studies* 2, no. 2 (2006): 64–100.

Amuzegar, Jahangir. *The Dynamics of the Iranian Revolution: The Pahlavis' Triumph and Tragedy*. Albany: State University of New York Press, 1991.

Ananta, Aris. *The Indonesian Crisis: A Human Development Perspective*. Singapore: Institute of Southeast Asian Studies, 2003.

Ansari, Humayun. *Muslims in Britain*. Report for Minority Rights Group International, August 2002. https://minorityrights.org/wp-content/uploads/old-site-downloads/download-129-Muslims-in-Britain.pdf.

Ashraf, Nasim. "The Islamization of Pakistan's Educational System: 1979–1989." In *The Islamization of Pakistan, 1979–2009*, 25–27. Publication no. 16. Washington DC: Middle East Institute, July 2009.

Aslan, Reza. *No God but God: The Origins, Evolution, and Future of Islam*. New York: Random House, 2005.

Ayoob, Mohammed. "The Many Faces of Political Islam." Working paper, Institute for Defence and Strategic Studies, December 29, 2006.

Bagby, Ihsan. *The American Mosque 2011: Basic Characteristics of the American Mosque Attitudes of Mosque Leaders*. Report No. 1 from the U.S. Mosque

Study 2011, January 2012. Accessed at Islamic Circle of North America, http://www.icna.org/wp-content/uploads/2012/02/The-American-Mosque-2011-web.pdf.

Bala, Eduart. "The Financing of Islamist Groups in Albania." In *Financing Terrorism: Case Studies*, edited by Michael Freeman, 183–96. Farnham, UK: Ashgate, 2012.

Bale, Jeffrey. "Islamism and Totalitarianism." *Totalitarian Movements and Political Religions* 10, no. 2 (2009): 73–96. https://doi.org/10.1080/14690760903371313.

Baran, Zeyno. *Torn Country: Turkey between Secularism and Islam*. Stanford CA: Hoover Institution Press, 2010.

Barrett, Paul. *American Islam: The Struggle for the Soul of a Religion*. New York: Picador, 2007.

Barton, Greg. "The Historical Development of Jihadi Islamist Thought in Indonesia." In *Radical Islamic Ideology in Southeast Asia*, edited by Scott Helfstein, 30–53. West Point NY: Combating Terrorism Center, United States Military Academy, 2009. https://apps.dtic.mil/dtic/tr/fulltext/u2/a502410.pdf.

——. *Indonesia's Struggle: Jemaah Islamiyah and the Soul of Islam*. Sydney: University of New South Wales Press, 2004.

Ba-Yunus, Ilyas, and Kassim Kone. *Muslims in the United States*. Westport CT: Greenwood Press, 2006.

Bergen, Peter. *Holy War, Inc.* New York: Simon and Schuster, 2002.

Bin Ali, Mohamed. *The Roots of Religious Extremism: Understanding the Salafi Doctrine of Al-Wala' wal Bara'*. London: Imperial College Press, 2016.

Birt, Jonathan. "Wahhabism in the United Kingdom: Manifestations and Reactions." In Al-Rasheed, *Transnational Connections and the Arab Gulf*, 168–84.

Bjørgo, Tore, and John Horgan. *Leaving Terrorism Behind: Individual and Collective Disengagement*. New York: Routledge, 2009.

Bokhari, Laila. "Radicalization, Political Violence, and Militancy." In *The Future of Pakistan*, edited by Stephen P. Cohen, 82–90. Washington DC: Brookings Institution Press, 2011.

Bonnefoy, Laurent. "Salafism in Yemen: A 'Saudisation'?" In Al-Rasheed, *Kingdom without Borders*, 245–62.

Borer, Douglas A. *Superpowers Defeated: Vietnam and Afghanistan Compared*. London: Frank Cass, 1999.

Bowen, Innes. *Medina in Birmingham, Najaf in Brent: Inside British Islam*. London: Hurst, 2014.

Bradley, John R. *Saudi Arabia Exposed: Inside a Kingdom in Crisis*. New York: Palgrave Macmillan, 2005.

Bradsher, Henry Saint Amant. *Afghan Communism and Soviet Intervention*. Oxford: Oxford University Press, 1999.

Brandon, James, and Douglas Murray. *Hate on the State: How British Libraries Encourage Islamic Extremism*. London: Centre for Social Cohesion, 2007. http://henryjacksonsociety.org/wp-content/uploads/2013/01/hate-on-the-state.pdf.

Breen, Heidi. *Violent Islamism in Egypt from 1997 to 2002*. Norwegian Defense Research Establishment (FFI), June 3, 2013. https://docs.google.com/viewer?a=v&pid=sites&srcid=ZGVmYXVsdGRvbWFpbnxqaWhhZGlzbXNOdWRpZXNuZXR8Z3g6MTdhNWViZjRjNjcxOWI1Yw.

Brice, Kevin M. A. "A Minority within a Minority: A Report on Converts to Islam in the United Kingdom." Faith-Matters.org, 2011.

Briggs, Rachel, and Jonathan Birdwell. "Radicalisation among Muslims in the UK." MICROCON Policy Working Paper 7, May 2009. https://www.academia.edu/14358639/Radicalisation_among_Muslims_in_the_UK?auto=download.

Brown, Eric. "After the Ramadan Affair: New Trends in Islamism in the West." In *Current Trends in Islamist Ideology*, vol. 2, edited by Hillel Fradkin, Husain Haqqani, and Eric Brown, 7–29. Washington DC: Hudson Institute, 2005.

Brown, Vahid, and Don Rassler. *Fountainhead of Jihad: The Haqqani Nexus, 1973–2012*. Oxford: Oxford University Press, 2013.

Bubalo, Anthony, and Greg Fealy. "Joining the Caravan? The Middle East, Islamism and Indonesia." Lowy Institute for International Policy, Paper 5, 2005.

Bubalo, Anthony, Sarah Phillips, and Samina Yasmeen. *Talib or Taliban? Indonesian Students in Pakistan and Yemen*. Sydney: Lowy Institute for International Policy, 2011.

Bunzel, Cole. "The Kingdom and the Caliphate: Duel of the Islamic States." Carnegie Endowment for International Peace, February 2016. http://carnegieendowment.org/files/cp_265_Bunzel_Islamic_States_Final.pdf.

Burke, Jason. *Al-Qaeda: Casting the Shadow of Terror*. London: I. B. Tauris, 2004.

Burki, Shireen K. "The Creeping Wahhabization in Pukhtunkhwa: The Road to 9/11." *Comparative Strategy* 30, no. 2 (2011): 154–76.

Burr, J. Millard, and Robert O. Collins. *Alms for Jihad: Charity and Terrorism in the Islamic World*. Cambridge: Cambridge University Press, 2006.

Byman, Daniel L. "The U.S. Saudi Arabia Counterterrorism Relationship." Brookings Institution, May 24, 2016. https://www.brookings.edu
/testimonies/the-u-s-saudi-arabia-counterterrorism-relationship/.

Caryl, Christian. "1979: The Great Backlash." *Foreign Policy*, June 21, 2009.
https://foreignpolicy.com/2009/06/21/1979-the-great-backlash/.

Center for Religious Freedom. *Saudi Publications on Hate Ideology
Invade American Mosques*. Washington DC: Freedom House, 2005.
https://freedomhouse.org/sites/default/files/inline_images/Saudi
%20Publications%20on%20Hate%20Ideology%20Invade%20American
%20Mosques.pdf.

Center for Religious Freedom, with the Institute for Gulf Affairs. *Saudi Arabia's Curriculum of Intolerance*. Washington DC: Freedom House, 2006.

Center for Social Cohesion. *Radical Islam on UK Campuses: A Comprehensive List of Extremist Speakers at UK Universities*. London, 2010. http://
henryjacksonsociety.org/wp-content/uploads/2013/01/RADICAL
-ISLAM-ON-CMAPUS.pdf.

Cesari, Jocelyne. *Encyclopedia of Islam in the United States*. London: Greenwood Press, 2007.

Choksy, Carol E. B., and Jamsheed K. Choksy. "The Saudi Connection: Wahhabism and Global Jihad." *World Affairs* 178, no. 1 (2015): 23–24.

Choudhury, Tufyal, and Helen Fenwick. *The Impact of Counter-Terrorism Measures on Muslim Communities*. Durham University, Equality and Human
Rights Commission—Research Report 72, 2011.

Cohen, Stephen Philip. *The Idea of Pakistan*. Washington DC: Brookings Institution Press, 2004.

Commins, David. *The Mission and the Kingdom: Wahhabi Power behind the
Saudi Throne*. Rev. ed. London: I. B. Tauris, 2016.

———. *The Wahhabi Mission and Saudi Arabia*. New York: I. B. Tauris, 2006.

Crile, George. *Charlie Wilson's War: The Extraordinary Story of the Largest
Covert Operation in History*. London: Atlantic Books, 2002.

Cronin, Audrey Kurth. "Behind the Curve." *International Security* 27, no. 3
(2002–3): 30–58.

———. "Sources of Contemporary Terrorism." In Cronin and Ludes, *Attacking
Terrorism*, 19–45.

Cronin, Audrey Kurth, and James M. Ludes, eds. *Attacking Terrorism: Elements
of a Grand Strategy*. Washington DC: Georgetown University Press, 2004.

Curtis, Edward E., IV. "Islamism and Its African American Muslim Critics:
Black Muslims in the Era of the Arab Cold War." *American Quarterly* 59, no.
3 (2007): 683–709.

Dalgaard-Nielsen, Anja, and Patrick Schack. "Community Resilience to Militant Islam: Who and What? An Explorative Study of Resilience in Three Danish Communities." *Democracy and Security* 12, no. 4 (2016): 309–27.

Davis, Paul K., and Kim Cragin, eds. *Social Sciences for Counterterrorism: Putting the Pieces Together*. Santa Monica CA: RAND, 2009.

DeCaro, Louis, Jr. *On the Side of My People: A Religious Life of Malcolm X*. New York: New York University Press, 1997.

de Graaf, Beatrice. "The Nexus between Salafism and Jihadism in the Netherlands." *CTC Sentinel* 3, no. 3 (2010): 17–22.

Delibas, Kayhan. *The Rise of Political Islam in Turkey: Urban Poverty, Grassroots Activism and Islamic Fundamentalism*. New York: I. B. Tauris, 2015.

Denoeux, Guilain. "The Forgotten Swamp: Navigating Political Islam." *Middle East Policy* 9, no. 2 (2002): 56–81. https://doi.org/10.1111/1475-4967 .00057.

Doumato, Eleanor Abdella. "Saudi Arabian Expansion in the United States: Half-Hearted Missionary Work Meets Rock-Solid Resistance." In Al-Rasheed, *Kingdom without Borders*, 301–21.

Dreyfuss, Robert. *Devil's Game: How the United States Helped Unleash Fundamentalist Islam*. New York: Owl Books, 2005.

Dyke, Anya Hart. *Mosques Made in Britain*. London: Quilliam Foundation, 2009. https://www.quilliaminternational.com/shop/printed-publications /mosques-made-in-britain/.

Ehrenfield, Rachel. "Their Oil Is Thicker Than Our Blood." In *Saudi Arabia and the Global Islamic Terrorist Network*, edited by Sarah H. Stern, 123–52. New York: Palgrave Macmillan, 2011.

El Fadl, Khaled Abou. *And God Knows the Soldiers: The Authoritative and the Authoritarian in Islamic Discourses*. Lanham MD: University Press of America, 2001.

———. *The Great Theft: Wrestling Islam from the Extremists*. New York: Harper-Collins, 2005.

Eligür, Banu. *The Mobilization of Political Islam in Turkey*. New York: Cambridge University Press, 2010.

Elmasry, Shadee. "The Salafis in America: The Rise, Decline and Prospects for a Sunni Muslim Movement among African-Americans." *Journal of Muslim Minority Affairs* 3, no. 2 (2010): 217–36.

Emerson, Steven. *American Jihad: The Terrorists Living among Us*. New York: Free Press, 2002.

Fair, C. Christine. *The Madrassah Challenge: Militancy and Religious Education in Pakistan*. Washington DC: United States Institute of Peace, 2008.

Fair, C. Christine, Neil Malhotra, and Jacob N. Shapiro. "Islam, Militancy, and Politics in Pakistan: Insights from a National Sample." *Terrorism and Political Violence* 22, no.4 (2010): 495–521.

Fealy, Greg, and Aldo Borgu. *Local Jihad: Radical Islam and Terrorism in Indonesia.* Barton: Australian Strategic Policy Institute, 2005.

Financial Action Task Force. *Anti-Money Laundering and Combating the Financing of Terrorism: Kingdom of Saudi Arabia.* Mutual Evaluation Report, June 25, 2010. http://www.fatf-gafi.org/media/fatf/documents/reports/mer/mer%20ksa%20full.pdf.

Fink, Naureen Chowdhury, with Ellie B. Hearne. *Beyond Terrorism: Deradicalization and Disengagement from Violent Extremism.* New York: International Peace Institute, October 2008.

Frum, David, and Richard Perle. *An End to Evil: How to Win the War on Terror.* New York: Random House, 2003.

Galeotti, Mark. *Afghanistan: The Soviet Union's Last War.* London: Frank Cass, 1995.

Gerges, Fawaz. *The Far Enemy: Why Jihad Went Global.* Cambridge: Cambridge University Press, 2005.

GhaneaBassiri, Kambiz. *A History of Islam in America: From the New World to the New World Order.* New York: Cambridge University Press, 2010.

Gilliat-Ray, Sophie. *Muslims in Britain: An Introduction.* Cambridge: Cambridge University Press, 2010.

Gold, Dore. *Hatred's Kingdom: How Saudi Arabia Supports the New Global Terrorism.* Washington DC: Regnery, 2003.

Goodson, Larry P. *Afghanistan's Endless War: State Failure, Regional Politics, and the Rise of the Taliban.* Seattle: University of Washington Press, 2001.

Haddad, Yvonne Y. "Arab Muslims and Islamic Institutions in America: Adaptation and Reform." In *Arabs in the New World,* edited by Sameer Y. Abraham and Nabeel Abraham. Detroit: Wayne State University Center for Urban Studies, 1983.

Haider, Ziad. "Ideologically Adrift." In Lodhi, *Pakistan.*

———. "Islam and the Early History of Pakistan." *Defining Ideas: A Hoover Institution Journal,* May 3, 2011. https://www.hoover.org/research/islam-and-early-history-pakistan.

Hamid, Sadek. "The Development of British Salafism." *ISIM Review* 21 (Spring 2008): 10–11.

———. "Islamic Political Radicalism in Britain: The Case of Hizb-ut-Tahrir." In Abbas, *Islamic Political Radicalism,* 145–59.

———. *Sufis, Salafis and Islamists: The Contested Ground of British Islamic Activism*. London: I. B. Tauris, 2016.

Hamm, Mark S. "Prisoner Radicalization: Assessing the Threat in U.S. Correctional Institutions." *National Institute of Justice Journal*, no. 261 (October 2008): 14–19. https://www.ncjrs.gov/pdffiles1/nij/224085.pdf.

———. *The Spectacular Few: Prisoner Radicalization and the Evolving Terrorist Threat*. New York: New York University Press, 2013.

———. *Terrorist Recruitment in American Correctional Institutions: An Exploratory Study of Non-Traditional Faith Groups*. Washington DC: National Institute of Justice, 2007.

Haqqani, Hussain. "The Ideologies of South Asian Jihadi Groups." In *Current Trends in Islamist Ideology*, vol. 1, edited by Hillel Fradkin, Husain Haqqani, and Eric Brown, 12–26. Washington DC: Hudson Institute, 2005.

Hardy, Roger. "Ambivalent Ally: Saudi Arabia and the 'War on Terror.'" In Al-Rasheed, *Kingdom without Borders*, 99–112.

Harvey, Simon. Introduction to *Treatise on Tolerance and Other Writings*, by Voltaire, vi–xix. Cambridge: Cambridge University Press, 2000.

Hasan, Noorhaidi. *Laskar Jihad: Islam, Militancy, and the Quest for Identity in Post-New Order Indonesia*. Ithaca NY: Cornell Southeast Asia Program, 2006.

———. "The Salafi Madrasas of Indonesia." In Noor, Sikand, and van Bruinessen, *Madrasa in Asia*, 247–74.

———. "The Salafi Movement in Indonesia: Transnational Dynamics and Local Development." *Comparative Studies of South Asia, Africa and the Middle East* 27, no. 1 (2007): 83–94.

———. "Saudi Expansion, the Salafi Campaign and Arabised Islam in Indonesia." In Al-Rasheed, *Kingdom without Borders*, 263–81.

Hasan, Usama. *The Balance of Islam in Challenging Extremism*. London: Quilliam Foundation, 2012.

Hassan, Muhammad Haniff. "The Danger of Takfir (Excommunication): Exposing IS' Takfiri Ideology." *Counter Terrorist Trends and Analyses* 9, no. 4 (2017): 3–12.

Haykel, Bernard. "On the Nature of Salafi Thought and Action." In Meijer, *Global Salafism*, 33–57.

Haykel, Bernard, Thomas Hegghammer, and Stéphane Lacroix, eds. *Saudi Arabia in Transition: Insights on Social, Political, Economic and Religious Change*. New York: Cambridge University Press, 2015.

Haynes, Jeffrey. "Islamic Militancy in East Africa." *Third World Quarterly* 26, no. 8 (2005): 1321–40.

Heffelfinger, Chris. *Radical Islam in America: Salafism's Journey from Arabia to the West*. Washington DC: Potomac Books, 2011.

Hegghammer, Thomas. *Jihad in Saudi Arabia: Violence and Pan-Islamism since 1979*. Cambridge: Cambridge University Press, 2010.

——. "The Rise of Muslim Foreign Fighters: Islam and the Globalization of Jihad." *International Security* 35, no. 3 (2010–11): 53–94.

Henkin, Yagil. "From Tactical Terrorism to Holy War: The Evolution of Chechen Terrorism, 1995–2004." *Central Asian Survey* 25, nos. 1–2 (2006): 193–203.

Hermansen, Marcia. "How to Put the Genie Back in the Bottle? 'Identity' Islam and Muslim Youth Cultures in America." In *Progressive Muslim: On Justice, Gender and Pluralism*, edited by Omid Safi, 306–19. Oxford: One World Publication, 2003.

House of Commons. Home Affairs Committee. *Implications for the Justice and Home Affairs Area of the Accession of Turkey to the European Union*. Tenth Report of Session 2010–12. London: House of Commons, August 2011. http://www.statewatch.org/news/2011/aug/eu-hasc-turkey-jha-report.pdf.

Hoodbhoy, Pervez. "How Education Fuels Terrorism in the Islamic Republic of Pakistan." Presentation at the Democracy Forum, London, June 22, 2012. http://www.scribd.com/doc/98851124/How-Education-Fuels -Terrorism-In-Pakistan-Dr-Pervez-Hoodbhoy-s-Presentation.

——. "Pakistan: The Threat from Within." Pakistan Security Research Unit, Brief no. 13, May 23, 2007. https://www.dur.ac.uk/resources/psru/briefings /archive/Brief13finalised.pdf.

——. "Pakistan's Westward Drift." *HIMAL South Asian*, September 2008. Available at https://www.countercurrents.org/hoodhoy080908.htm.

Horgan, John, and Kurt Braddock, eds. *Terrorism Studies: A Reader*. New York: Routledge, 2011.

Hosen, Nadirsyah. "Religion and the Indonesian Constitution: A Recent Debate." *Journal of Southeast Asian Studies* 36, no. 3 (2005): 419–40.

Huntington, Samuel. *The Clash of Civilizations and the Remaking of World Order*. New York: Simon and Schuster, 1996.

Huq, Aziz. "Community-Led Counterterrorism." *Studies in Conflict and Terrorism* 40, no. 12 (2017): 1038–53.

Husain, Ed. *A Global Venture to Counter Violent Extremism*. Policy Innovation Memorandum No. 37. New York: Council on Foreign Relations, September 2013.

——. *The Islamist*. London: Penguin Books, 2007.

Hussain, Azhar, Ahmad Salīm, and Arif Naveed. *Connecting the Dots: Education and Religious Discrimination in Pakistan*. Washington DC: U.S. Commission on International Religious Freedom, 2011.

Hussain, Zahid. *Frontline Pakistan: The Struggle with Militant Islam*. New York: Columbia University Press, 2007.

Ingram, Haroro J. "An Analysis of *Inspire* and *Dabiq*: Lessons from AQAP and Islamic State's Propaganda War." *Studies in Conflict and Terrorism* 40, no. 5 (2017): 357–75.

Institute of International Education. *Open Doors: Report on International Education Exchange, 1948–2004*. New York: Institute of International Education, 2005.

International Crisis Group. "Al-Qaeda in Southeast Asia: The Case of the Ngruki Network in Indonesia." Indonesia Briefing, Jakarta/Brussels, August 8, 2002. https://www.crisisgroup.org/asia/south-east-asia /indonesia/al-qaeda-southeast-asia-case-ngruki-network-indonesia.

———. *Countering Terrorism in a Failed State*. Africa Report No. 45. Nairobi/ Brussels, 2003.

———. *How Indonesian Extremists Regroup*. Asia Report No. 228, July 16, 2012. https://www.crisisgroup.org/asia/south-east-asia/indonesia/how -indonesian-extremists-regroup.

———. *Indonesia Backgrounder: Why Salafism and Terrorism Mostly Don't Mix*. Asia Report No. 83. Southeast Asia/Brussels, September 13, 2004.

———. "Indonesia: Implications of the Ahmadiyah Decree." Asia Briefing No. 78. July 13, 2008. https://www.crisisgroup.org/asia/south-east-asia /indonesia/indonesia-implications-ahmadiyah-decree.

———. "Indonesia: Jemaah Islamiyah's Current Status." Asia Briefing No. 63. Jakarta/Brussels, May 3, 2007.

———. *Indonesia: Jemaah Islamiyah's Publishing Industry*. Asia Report No. 147. February 28, 2008.

———. "Indonesia: Radicalization of the 'Palembang Group.'" Asia Briefing No. 92. Jakarta/Brussels, May 20, 2009.

———. "Indonesia: The Dark Side of Jema'ah Ansharut Tauhid (JAT)." Asia Briefing No. 107. Jakarta/Brussels, July 6, 2010.

———. *Indonesia: Violence and Radical Muslims*. Indonesia Briefing Report. Jakarta/Brussels, October 10, 2001. https://www.crisisgroup.org/asia /south-east-asia/indonesia/indonesia-violence-and-radical-muslims

———. *Jemaah Islamiyah in Southeast Asia: Damaged but Still Dangerous*. Asia Report No. 63. Jakarta/Brussels, August 26, 2003.

———. *Pakistan: Karachi's Madrasas and Violent Extremism*. Asia Report. No. 130. March 29, 2007.

———. *Pakistan: Madrasas, Extremism and the Military*. Asia Report No. 36. Islamabad/Brussels, July 29, 2002.

———. *Recycling Militants in Indonesia: Darul Islam and the Australian Embassy Bombing*. Asia Report No. 92, February 22, 2005.

———. *Terrorism in Indonesia: Noordin's Networks*. Asia Report No. 114. Jakarta/Brussels, May 5, 2006.

Joscelyn, Thomas. "Al Qaeda Cell Targeted by Treasury Department Tied to Multiple Terror Groups." FDD's *Long War Journal*, August 23, 2011. http://www.longwarjournal.org/archives/2011/08/the_treasury_departm.php.

Juergensmeyer, Mark. *Terror in the Mind of God: The Global Rise of Religious Violence*. 3rd ed. Berkeley: University of California Press, 2003.

Katzman, Kenneth. *Al Qaeda: Profile and Threat Assessment*. Congressional Research Service Report, August 17, 2005. https://fas.org/sgp/crs/terror/RL33038.pdf.

Keddie, Nikki. *Roots of Revolution: An Interpretive History of Modern Iran*. New Haven CT: Yale University Press, 1981.

Kepel, Gilles. *Allah in the West: Islamic Movements in America and Europe*. Stanford CA: Stanford University Press, 1997.

———. *Jihad: The Trail of Political Islam*. Cambridge MA: Harvard University Press, 2002.

Kfir, Isaac. "Islam in Post-9/11 Pakistan: The Role of Education in Heightening or Diminishing Pakistan's Security Dilemma." *Middle East Review of International Affairs* 16, no. 1 (2012): 59–73.

Khan, Amil. *Pakistan and the Narratives of Extremism*. Unites States Institute of Peace, Special Report 327, March 2013.

Khan, Hamid. *Constitutional and Political History of Pakistan*. Karachi: Oxford University Press, 2001.

Khan, Selina Adam. "Deradicalization Programming in Pakistan." United States Institute of Peace, September 14, 2015. https://www.usip.org/publications/2015/09/deradicalization-programming-pakistan.

Khuri, Richard K. *Freedom, Modernity, and Islam: Toward a Creative Synthesis*. Syracuse NY: Syracuse University Press, 1998.

Kurlantzick, Joshua. "The Rise of Islamist Groups in Malaysia and Indonesia." Council on Foreign Relations, February 27, 2018. https://www.cfr.org/expert-brief/rise-islamist-groups-malaysia-and-indonesia.

Lacroix, Stéphane. "Understanding Stability and Dissent in the Kingdom." In Haykel, Hegghammer, and Lacroix, *Saudi Arabia in Transition*, 167–80.

Lauzière, Henri. *The Making of Salafism: Islamic Reform in the Twentieth Century*. New York: Columbia University Press, 2016.

Lesch, David W. *1979: The Year That Shaped the Modern Middle East*. Boulder CO: Westview Press, 2001.

Lewis, Bernard. *The Crisis of Islam: Holy War and Unholy Terror*. New York: Random House, 2003.

Levitt, Matthew. "Charitable Organizations and Terrorist Financing: A War on Terror Status-Check." Paper presented at the Dimensions of Terrorist Financing workshop, University of Pittsburgh, March 19, 2004. http://www.washingtoninstitute.org/policy-analysis/view/charitable-organizations-and-terrorist-financing-a-war-on-terror-status-che.

Lodhi, Maleeha, ed. *Pakistan: Beyond the Crisis State*. New York: Oxford University Press, 2011.

Loimeier, Roman. *Islamic Reform and Political Change in Northern Nigeria*. Evanston IL: Northwestern University Press, 1997.

Luciani, Giacomo. "From Price Taker to Price Maker? Saudi Arabia and the World Oil Market." In Haykel, Hegghammer, and Lacroix, *Saudi Arabia in Transition*, 71–96.

Lynch, Thomas F., III. *Sunni and Shi'a Terrorism: Differences That Matter*. West Point NY: Combating Terrorism Center, December 29, 2008. https://gsmcneal.com/wp-content/uploads/2008/12/sunni-and-shia-terrorism-differences-that-matter.pdf.

Mabon, Simon. *Saudi Arabia and Iran: Power and Rivalry in the Middle East*. London: I. B. Tauris, 2016.

Magouirk, Justin. "Connecting a Thousand Points of Hatred." *Studies in Conflict and Terrorism* 31, no. 4 (2008): 327–49.

Magouirk, Justin, Scott Atran, and Marc Sageman. "Connecting Terrorist Networks." *Studies in Conflict and Terrorism* 31, no. 1 (2008): 1–16.

Maitra, Ramtanu. "Benazir Bhutto Visit Removes Saudi Doubts." *Executive Intelligence Review* 16, no. 6 (February 3, 1989): 52–53.

Mamdani, Mahmood. *Good Muslim, Bad Muslim*. New York: Doubleday, 2004.

MacEoin, Denis. *The Hijacking of British Islam: How Extremist Literature Is Subverting Mosques in the UK*. London: Policy Exchange, 2007.

Malik, Imaad. *Black America, Prisons and Radical Islam: A Report*. Washington DC: Center for Islamic Pluralism, 2008.

Masood, Ehsan. *British Muslims: Media Guide*. London: British Council, 2006.

McAdam, Doug, Sidney Tarrow, and Charles Tilly. *Dynamics of Contention*. Cambridge: Cambridge University Press, 2001.

McCauley, Clark, and Sarah Scheckter. "What's Special about U.S. Muslims? The War of Terrorism as Seen by Muslims in the United States, Morocco, Egypt, Pakistan, and Indonesia." *Studies in Conflict and Terrorism* 31, no. 11 (2008): 1024–31.

McCormack, David. *An African Vortex: Islamism in Sub-Saharan Africa*. Occasional Paper Series, No. 4. Washington DC: Center for Security Policy, January 2005.

Means, Gordon P. *Political Islam in Southeast Asia*. Boulder CO: Lynne Rienner, 2009.

Meijer, Roel, ed. *Global Salafism: Islam's New Religious Movement*. New York: Columbia University Press, 2009.

Meleagrou-Hitchens, Alexander, and Nick Kaderbhai. *Research Perspectives on Online Radicalisation: A Literature Review, 2006–2016*. London: International Centre for the Study of Radicalisation, King's College, 2017.

Mir, Amir. *The Fluttering Flag of Jehad*. Lahore: Mashal Books, 2008.

Mohamed, A. Z. "Saudi Arabia's Global Center for Combating Extremist Ideology: An Exercise in Futility?" Gatestone Institute, June 6, 2017. https://www.gatestoneinstitute.org/10484/saudi-arabia-extremist-ideology.

Mousseau, Michael. "Market Civilization and Its Clash with Terror." *International Security* 27, no. 3 (2002–3): 5–29.

Murawiec, Laurent. *Princes of Darkness: The Saudi Assault on the West*. Lanham MD: Rowman and Littlefield, 2003.

Napoleoni, Loretta. *Terror Incorporated: Tracing the Dollars behind the Terror Networks*. New York: Seven Stories Press, 2005.

Nasr, S. V. R. "Islam, the State, and the Rise of Sectarian Militancy in Pakistan." In *Pakistan: Nationalism without a Nation*, edited by Christophe Jaffrelot, 85–114. London: Zed Books, 2002.

Nasr, Vali. *International Relations of an Islamist Movement: The Case of the Jama'at-i Islami of Pakistan*. New York: Council on Foreign Relations, 2000.

———. *The Shia Revival: How Conflicts within Islam Will Shape the Future*. New York: New York: Norton, 2006.

Nawaz, Shuja. *Crossed Swords: Pakistan, Its Army, and the Wars Within*. New York: Oxford University Press, 2008.

Neumann, Peter R., and Brooke Rogers. *Recruitment and Mobilisation for the Islamist Militant Movement in Europe*. London: King's College, December 2007. https://ec.europa.eu/home-affairs/sites/homeaffairs/files/doc_centre/terrorism/docs/ec_radicalisation_study_on_mobilisation_tactics_en.pdf.

Noor, Farish A. "Ngruki Revisited: Modernity and Its Discontents at the Pondok Pesantren al-Mukmin of Ngruki, Surakarta." Working paper, Nanyang Technological University, Singapore, October 1, 2007.

Noor, Farish A., Yoginder Sikand, and Martin van Bruinessen, eds. *The Madrasa in Asia: Political Activism and Transnational Linkages*. Amsterdam: Amsterdam University Press, 2008.

O'Neill, Sean, and Daniel McGrory. *The Suicide Factory: Abu Hamza and the Finsbury Park Mosque*. London: Harper Perennial, 2006.

Osman, Mohamed Nawab Mohamed. "Reviving the Caliphate in the *Nusantara*: Hizbut Tahrir Indonesia's Mobilization Strategy and Its Impact in Indonesia." *Terrorism and Political Violence* 22, no. 4 (2010): 601–22.

Ozgur, Iren. *Islamic Schools in Modern Turkey: Faith, Politics, and Education*. New York: Cambridge University Press, 2012.

Panovski, Atanas. "The Spread of Islamic Extremism in the Republic of Macedonia." Thesis, Naval Postgraduate School, December 2011. http://www .dtic.mil/dtic/tr/fulltext/u2/a556492.pdf.

Pape, Robert A. *Dying to Win: The Strategic Logic of Suicide Terrorism*. New York: Random House, 2005.

Pargeter, Alison. *The New Frontiers of Jihad: Radical Islam in Europe*. London: I. B. Tauris, 2008.

Pew Research Center. *The Future of the Global Muslim Population*. Pew Forum on Religion and Public Life, January 27, 2011. http://www.pewforum.org /The-Future-of-the-Global-Muslim-Population.aspx.

———. *Muslim Networks and Movements in Western Europe*. Pew Forum on Religion and Public Life Report, September 15, 2010. https://www.pewforum .org/2010/09/15/muslim-networks-and-movements-in-western-europe/.

———. *The World's Muslims: Religion, Politics and Society*. Pew Forum on Religion and Public Life, April 30, 2013. http://www.pewforum.org/Muslim /the-worlds-muslims-religion-politics-society-exec.aspx.

Phillips, Melanie. *Londonistan*. New York: Encounter Books, 2007.

Pipes, Daniel. "The Scandal of U.S.-Saudi Relations." *National Interest*, no. 70 (Winter 2002–3): 66–78. http://www.danielpipes.org/995/the-scandal-of -us-saudi-relations.

Pipes, Daniel, and Sharon Chadha. "CAIR: Islamists Fooling the Establishment." *Middle East Quarterly* 13, no. 2 (2006): 3–20. https://www.meforum .org/articles/2006/cair-islamists-fooling-the-establishment.

Piscatori, James. "Religion and Realpolitik: Islamic Response to the Gulf War." In *Islamic Fundamentalism and the Gulf Crisis*, edited by James Piscatori. Chicago: Fundamentalism Project, American Academy of Arts and Sciences, 1991.

Popper, Karl. *The Open Society and Its Enemies*. London: Routledge, 1945.

Poston, Larry. *Islamic Da'wah in the West: Muslim Missionary Activity and the Dynamics of Conversion to Islam*. New York: Oxford University Press, 1992.

Prados, Alfred, and Christopher Blanchard. *Saudi Arabia: Terrorist Financing Issues*. Congressional Research Service Report, February 8, 2006.

Rabasa, Angel, and F. Stephen Larrabee. *The Rise of Political Islam in Turkey*. Santa Monica CA: RAND, 2008.

Rajab, Talal. *Re-Programming British Muslims: A Study of the Islam Channel*. London: Quilliam Foundation, 2010.

Rānā, Muhammad Āmir. *A to Z of Jehadi Organizations in Pakistan*. Lahore, Pakistan: Mashal Books, 2004.

Raphaeli, Nimrod. "Financing of Terrorism: Sources, Methods, and Channels." *Terrorism and Political Violence* 15, no. 4 (2003): 59–82.

Rapoport, David C. "The Four Waves of Modern Terrorism." In Cronin and Ludes, *Attacking Terrorism*, 46–74.

———. "It Is Waves, Not Strains." *Terrorism and Political Violence* 28, no. 2 (2016): 217–24.

Raymond, Catherine Zara. *Al Muhajiroun and Islam4UK: The Group behind the Ban*. King's College London: International Centre for the Study of Radicalisation and Political Violence, May 2010. https://icsr.info/wp-content /uploads/2010/06/ICSR-Feature-Al-Muhajiroun-and-Islam4UK-The -group-behind-the-ban.pdf.

Redissi, Hamadi. "The Refutation of Wahhabism in Arabic Sources, 1745–1932." In Al-Rasheed, *Kingdom without Borders*, 157–81.

Riaz, Ali. "Global Jihad, Sectarianism and the Madrassahs in Pakistan." Working paper, Institute of Defense and Strategic Studies, Singapore, 2005.

Robinson, Glenn E. "Hamas as Social Movement." In Wiktorowicz, *Islamic Activism*, 112–40.

Rosentiel, Tom. *Muslim Americans: Middle Class and Mostly Mainstream*. Pew Research Center, May 22, 2007. http://www.pewresearch.org/2007/05/22 /muslim-americans-middle-class-and-mostly-mainstream/.

Roy, Oliver. *Globalised Islam: The Search for a New Ummah*. London: Hurst, 2004.

Sageman, Marc. *Leaderless Jihad: Terror Networks in the Twenty-First Century*. Philadelphia: University of Pennsylvania Press, 2008.

———. *Understanding Terror Networks*. Philadelphia: University of Pennsylvania Press, 2004.

Sahni, Ajai. "Pakistan." In *Guide to Islamist Movements*, vol. 2, edited by Barry Rubin, 347–60. Armonk NY: M. E. Sharp, 2010.

Saigol, Rubina. "Boundaries of Consciousness: Interface between the Curriculum, Gender and Nationalism." In *Locating the Self: Reflections on Women and Multiple Identities*, edited by Rubina Saigol and Nigat Said Khan. Lahore: ASR Publications, 1994.

Saleem, Shahed. "A History of Mosques in Britain." *Architects' Journal*, April 19, 2012. https://www.architectsjournal.co.uk/buildings/a-history-of-mosques-in-britain/8629263.article.

Sareen, Sushant. *The Jihad Factory: Pakistan's Islamic Revolution in the Making*. New Delhi: Har-Anand Publications, 2005.

Schanzer, Jonathan, and Steven Miller. *Facebook Fatwa: Saudi Clerics, Wahhabi Islam, and Social Media*. Washington DC: FDD Press, 2012.

Schmidt, John R. *The Unraveling: Pakistan in the Age of Jihad*. New York: Farrar, Straus, and Giroux, 2011.

Schwartz, Stephen. *The Two Faces of Islam*. New York: Anchor Books, 2003.

Scroggins, Deborah. *Wanted Women: Faith, Lies, and the War on Terror; The Lives of Ayaan Hirsi Ali and Aafia Siddiqui*. New York: Harper Perennial, 2013.

Sfeir, Antoine, ed. *The Columbia World Dictionary of Islamism*. Translated by John King. New York: Columbia University Press, 2007.

Shea, Nina. Introduction to *Saudi Publications on Hate Ideology Invade American Mosques*. Washington DC: Freedom House, 2005. https://freedomhouse.org/sites/default/files/inline_images/Saudi%20Publications%20on%20Hate%20Ideology%20Invade%20American%20Mosques.pdf.

Shehabi, Saeed. "The Role of Religious Ideology in the Expansionist Policies of Saudi Arabia." In Al-Rasheed, *Kingdom without Borders*, 183–97.

Sick, Gary. *All Fall Down: America's Tragic Encounter with Iran*. New York: Random House, 1985.

Siddique, Qandeel. *The Red Mosque Operation and Its Impact on the Growth of the Pakistani Taliban*. NOREF-FFI Report No. 2008/01915. Norwegian Defense Research Establishment, October 8, 2008.

Silber, Mitchell D., and Arvin Bhatt. *Radicalization in the West: The Homegrown Threat*. New York: New York Police Department, 2007.

Simmons, Anna. "Making Enemies, Part Two." *American Interest* 11, no. 1 (2006): 35–45.

Singh, Bilveer. *The Talibanization of Southeast Asia: Losing the War on Terror to Islamist Extremists*. Westport CT: Praeger Security International, 2007.

Smith, Jane I. *Islam in America*. New York: Columbia University Press, 2010.

Solomon, Hussein. *Terrorism and Counter-Terrorism in Africa: Fighting Insurgency from Al Shabaab, Ansar Dine and Boko Haram.* New York: Palgrave Macmillan, 2015.

Spalek, Basia, and Douglas Weeks. "The Role of Communities in Counterterrorism: Analyzing Policy and Exploring Psychotherapeutic Approaches within Community Settings." *Studies in Conflict and Terrorism* 40, no. 12 (2017): 991–1003.

Speckhard, Anne, and Khapta Akhmedova. "The New Chechen Jihad: Militant Wahhabism as a Radical Movement and a Source of Suicide Terrorism in Post-War Chechen Society." *Democracy and Security* 2, no. 1 (2006): 103–55.

Stern, Jessica. "Mind over Martyr: How to Deradicalize Islamic Extremists." *Foreign Affairs* 89, no. 1 (2010): 95–108.

———. *Terror in the Name of God.* New York: HarperCollins, 2003.

Taddonio, Patrice. "Saudi Official Makes Rare Reflection on Kingdom's Role in Rise of Extremism." *Frontline*, PBS, February 20, 2018. https://www.pbs.org/wgbh/frontline/article/saudi-official-makes-rare-reflection-on-kingdoms-role-in-rise-of-extremism/.

Talbot, Ian. *Pakistan: A Modern History.* New York: St. Martin's Press, 1998.

Tellis, Ashley J. "The Menace That Is Lashkar-e-Taiba." Carnegie Endowment for International Peace, March 2012. https://carnegieendowment.org/2012/03/13/menace-that-is-lashkar-e-taiba-pub-47512.

Trofimov, Yaroslav. *The Siege of Mecca: The 1979 Uprising at Islam's Holiest Shrine.* New York: Random House, 2007.

Ulph, Stephen. "Londonistan." *Terrorism Monitor* 2, no. 4 (July 7, 2005). https://jamestown.org/program/londonistan/.

U.S. Institute of Peace. *The Jihadi Threat: ISIS, al-Qaeda, and Beyond.* Washington DC: U.S. Institute of Peace, December 2016–January 2017.

Valentine, Simon Ross. *Force and Fanaticism: Wahhabism in Saudi Arabia and Beyond.* London: Hurst, 2015.

van Bruinessen, Martin. "Genealogies of Islamic Radicalism in Post-Suharto Indonesia." *South East Asia Research* 10, no. 2 (2002): 117–54.

———. "*Ghazwul Fikri* or Arabization? Indonesian Muslim Responses to Globalization." Paper presented at the JICA workshop Islam and Development in Southeast Asia, Singapore, November 21–22, 2009.

———. "Indonesian Muslims and Their Place in the Larger World of Islam." Paper presented at the Twenty-Ninth Indonesia Update conference, Australian National University, Canberra, September 30–October 2, 2011.

https://www.academia.edu/3168028/Indonesian_Muslims_and_their
_place_in_the_larger_world_of_Islam.

———. "Traditionalist and Islamist Pesantrens in Contemporary Indonesia."
In Noor, Sikand, and van Bruinessen, *Madrasa in Asia*, 217–46.

———. "Wahhabi Influences in Indonesia, Real and Imagined." Paper presented at the Journée d'Etudes du CEIFR et MSH sur le Wahhabisme, Paris,
June 10, 2002.

———. "What Happened to the Smiling Face of Indonesian Islam? Muslim
Intellectualism and the Conservative Turn in Post-Suharto Indonesia."
Working paper, S. Rajaratnam School of International Studies, January 6,
2011.

Vermeulen, Floris. "Suspect Communities—Targeting Violent Extremism at
the Local Level: Policies of Engagement in Amsterdam, Berlin, and London." *Terrorism and Political Violence* 26, no. 2 (2014): 286–306.

Voltaire. *Treatise on Tolerance and Other Writings*. Edited by Simon Harvey.
Translated by Brian Masters. Cambridge: Cambridge University Press, 2000.

Wahid, Abdurrahman, ed. *The Illusion of an Islamic State: Expansion of Transnational Islamic Movements in Indonesia*. Jakarta: LibForAll Foundation, 2011.

Wanandi, Jusuf. "Islam in Indonesia: Its History, Development and Future
Challenges." *Asia-Pacific Review* 9, no. 2 (2002): 104–12.

Wehr, Hans. *Dictionary of Modern Written Arabic*. Edited by J. M. Cowan. 3rd
ed. Ithaca NY: Spoken Language Services, 1976.

Whine, Michael. "The Penetration of Islamist Ideology in Britain." In *Current
Trends in Islamist Ideology*, vol. 1, edited by Hillel Fradkin, Husain Haqqani,
and Eric Brown, 50–58. Washington DC: Hudson Institute, 2005. https://
www.hudson.org/research/9886-the-penetration-of-islamist-ideology-in
-britain.

Wiktorowicz, Quintan. "Anatomy of the Salafi Movement." *Studies in Conflict and Terrorism*, no. 29 (2006): 207–39. https://doi.org/10.1080
/10576100500497004.

———, ed. *Islamic Activism: A Social Movement Theory Approach*. Bloomington:
Indiana University Press, 2004.

———. *Radical Islam Rising: Muslim Extremism in the West*. Lanham MD: Rowman and Littlefield, 2005.

Windsor, Jennifer L. "Promoting Democracy Can Combat Terrorism." *Washington Quarterly* 26, no. 3 (2003): 43–58.

Wolf, Anne. "The Radicalization of Tunisia's Mosques." *CTC Sentinel* 7, no. 6
(June 30, 2014): 17–20.

Woodward, Mark, Ali Amin, Inaya Rohmaniyah, and Chris Lundry. *A New Cultural Path for Indonesia's Islamist PKS?* Consortium for Strategic Communication Report 1102, Arizona State University, 2011. http://csc.asu.edu/wp-content/uploads/pdf/127.pdf.

Woodward, Mark, and Inayah Rohmaniyah. "Contesting New Media, Indonesia vs. the Muslim World League." Arizona State University Center for Strategic Communications, December 19, 2011. http://csc.asu.edu/2011/12/19/contesting-new-media-indonesia-vs-the-muslim-world-league/.

Woolsey, R. James. Foreword to *Saudi Publications on Hate Ideology Invade American Mosques*, by Center for Religious Freedom, 7–9. Washington DC: Freedom House, 2005.

Wright, Lawrence. *The Looming Tower: Al-Qaeda and the Road to 9/11*. New York: Knopf, 2006.

Yusuf, Huma. *Sectarian Violence: Pakistan's Greatest Security Threat?* NOREF Report, July 2012.

Zaidi, Manzar. *Insights on Security in Pakistan*. Lahore: Shirkat, 2012.

Index

Page numbers in italic indicate illustrations.

9 781640 123700